STUDIES IN CONTEMPORARY HISTORY

Series Editors: T. G. Fraser and J. O. Springhall

PUBLISHED

THE ARAB-ISRAELI CONFLICT
T. G. Fraser

THE ULSTER QUESTION SINCE 1945
James Loughlin

THE RISE AND FALL OF THE SOVIET EMPIRE
Raymond Pearson

THE CIVIL RIGHTS MOVEMENT: Struggle and Resistance
William T. Martin Riches

THE UNITED NATIONS AND INTERNATIONAL POLITICS
Stephen Ryan

JAPAN SINCE 1945
Dennis B. Smith

DECOLONIZATION SINCE 1945: THE COLLAPSE OF
EUROPEAN OVERSEAS EMPIRES
John Springhall

Studies in Contemporary History
Series Standing Order
ISBN 978-0-333-71706-6 hardcover
ISBN 978-0-333-69351-3 paperback
(*outside North America only*)

You can receive future titles in this series as they are published by placing a standing order. Please contact your bookseller or, in the case of difficulty, write to us at the address below with your name and address, the title of the series and the ISBN quoted above.

Customer Services Department, Macmillan Distribution Ltd
Houndmills, Basingstoke, Hampshire RG21 6XS, England

DECOLONIZATION SINCE 1945

THE COLLAPSE OF EUROPEAN OVERSEAS EMPIRES

JOHN SPRINGHALL

palgrave

First published 2001 by
PALGRAVE
Houndmills, Basingstoke, Hampshire RG21 6XS and
175 Fifth Avenue, New York, N. Y. 10010
Companies and representatives throughout the world

PALGRAVE is the new global academic imprint of St. Martin's
Press LLC Scholarly and Reference Division and Palgrave
Publishers Ltd (formerly Macmillan Press Ltd).

ISBN 978-0-333-74599-1 hardback
ISBN 978-0-333-74600-4   ISBN 978-1-137-10614-8 (eBook)
DOI 10.1007/978-1-137-10614-8

This book is printed on paper suitable for recycling and
made from fully managed and sustained forest sources.

A catalogue record for this book is available
from the British Library.

Library of Congress Cataloging-in-Publication Data
Springhall, John.
    Decolonization since 1945: the collapse of European overseas
    empires / John Springhall.
        p. cm. — (Studies in contemporary history)
    Includes bibliographical references and index.
    ISBN 978-0-333-74599-1-ISBN 978-0-333-74600-4 (pbk.)
    1. Decolonization.   2. Europe—Colonies—History—20th
century.   I. Title.   II. Studies in contemporary history
(New York, N. Y.)

JV151 .D67 2000
325′.3′09409045—dc21   00–034486

10   9   8   7   6   5   4   3   2   1
10 09 08 07 06 05 04 03 02 01

CONTENTS

Contents

Contents

Contents

SERIES EDITORS' PREFACE

There are those, politicians among them, who feel that historians should not teach or write about contemporary events and people – many of whom are still living – because of the difficulty of treating such matters with historical perspective, that it is right to draw some distinction between the study of history and the study of current affairs. Proponents of this view seem to be unaware of the concept of contemporary history to which this series is devoted, that the history of the recent past can and should be written with a degree of objectivity. As memories of the Second World War recede, it is surely time to place in perspective the postwar history that has shaped all our lives, whether we were born in the 1940s or the 1970s.

Many countries – Britain, the United States and Germany among them – allow access to their public records under a thirty-year rule, opening up much of the postwar period to archival research. For more recent events, diaries, memoirs, and the investigations of newspapers and television, confirm the view of the famous historian Sir Lewis Namier that all secrets are in print provided you know where to look for them. Contemporary historians also have the opportunity, denied to historians of earlier periods, of interviewing participants in the events they are analysing. The problem facing the contemporary historian is, if anything, the embarrassment of riches.

In any case, the nature and extent of world changes since the late 1980s have clearly signalled the need for concise discussion of major themes in post-1945 history. For many of us the difficult thing to grasp is how dramatically the world has changed over recent years: the end of the Cold War and of Soviet hegemony over eastern Europe; the collapse of the Soviet Union and Russian communism; the unification of Germany; the pace of integration in the European Union; the disintegration of Yugoslavia; political and economic turbulence in South East Asia; communist China's reconciliation with consumer capitalism; the faltering economic progress of Japan. Writing in a structured and cogent way about these seismic changes is what makes contemporary history so challenging and we hope that the end result will convey some of this excitement and interest to our readers.

The general objective of this series, written by members of the School of History, Philosophy and Politics of the University of Ulster, is to offer concise and up-to-date treatments of postwar themes considered of historical and political significance and to stimulate critical thought about the theoretical assumptions and conceptual apparatus underlying interpretation of the topics under discussion. The series should bring some of the central themes and problems confronting students and teachers of recent history, politics, and international affairs, into sharper focus than the textbook writer alone could provide. The blend required to write contemporary history which is both readable and easily understood but also accurate and scholarly is not easy to achieve, but we hope that this series will prove worthwhile for both students and teachers interested in world affairs since 1945.

University of Ulster at Coleraine   T. G. FRASER
J. O. SPRINGHALL

ACKNOWLEDGEMENTS

Grateful thanks to my coeditor, Tom Fraser, and colleagues Dennis Smith, Keith Jeffery, Ray Pearson and Bill Hart in the School of History, Philosophy and Politics of the University of Ulster, together with the publisher's reader, for carrying out one of the essential penances of academic life by offering their careful comments and suggestions on chapters in draft form. I am also grateful to Joanne Taggart for tidying up chapters on disc and to Gillian Coward for work on the maps. This book is dedicated to Richmond Young Liberal stalwart Bob Gordon-Adams, wherever he is now, who gave me Stuart Easton's *The Rise and Fall of Western Colonialism* (1964) on my 21st birthday – *exitus acta probat*.

JOHN SPRINGHALL

Portstewart
Northern Ireland

CHRONOLOGY OF EUROPEAN DECOLONIZATION

Year of independence of post-1945 decolonized states, using their post-colonial modern names.

Jordan, the Philippines	1946
India, Pakistan	1947
Ceylon (after 1972 Sri Lanka), Burma (now Myanmar)	1948
Israel (former Palestine)	1948
Indonesia (former Netherlands East Indies)	1949
Libya	1951
Eritrea (united with Ethiopia)	1952
Laos, Cambodia	1953
North and South Vietnam, Pondicherry (India)	1954
Sudan, (French) Morocco, Tunisia	1956
Ghana, Malaya (after 1963 Malaysia)	1957
Cyprus, Nigeria, Somalia, Senegal, Congo (1971–97 Zaire)	1960
Gabon, Ivory Coast, Mali, Mauritania	1960
Chad, Cameroon, Niger, Togo, Upper Volta	1960
Central African Republic, Dahomey	1960
Malagasy Republic, (French) Congo Republic	1960
Sierra Leone, Tanganyika (after 1964 Tanzania), Goa	1961
Algeria, Western Samoa, Jamaica	1962
Trinidad & Tobago, Rwanda, Burundi, Uganda	1962
Zanzibar, Kenya,	1963

Sabah, Sarawak (as part of Federation of Malaysia)	1963
State of Singapore (1965 leaves Malaysia)	1963
West Irian (former Dutch New Guinea)	
joins Indonesia	1963
Malawi, Malta, Zambia	1964
The Gambia, Maldives	1965
Guyana, Botswana, Lesotho, Barbados	1966
Aden (now South Yemen)	1967
Mauritius, Swaziland, Nauru, Equatorial Guinea	1968
Tonga, Fiji	1970
Bahamas	1973
Grenada, Guinea-Bissau	
(formerly Portuguese Guinea)	1974
Papua New Guinea, East Timor,	
São Tomé e Principe, Surinam	1975
Angola, Mozambique, Cape Verde Islands	1975
Seychelles	1976
Dominica, Solomon Islands, Tuvalu	1978
St Vincent & the Grenadines, St Lucia, Kiribati	1979
Zimbabwe, Vanuatu (formerly New Hebrides)	1980
Belize, Antigua & Barbuda	1981
St Kitts (former St Christopher) & Nevis	1983
Brunei	1984
Namibia (formerly South West Africa)	1994
Hong Kong	1997
Macao	1999

LIST OF ABBREVIATIONS

ABAKO	Alliance des Bakongo (Congo)
AEF	Afrique Equatoriale Française
AFO	Anti-Fascist Organisation (Burma)
AFPFL	Anti-Fascist People's Freedom League (Burma)
AKEL	Cypriot Communist Party
ALN	Armée de Libération Nationale (Algeria)
ANC	African National Congress (acc. to context)
ANC	African National Council (Southern Rhodesia)
AOF	Afrique Occidentale Française
ARC	Alliance Révolutionnaire Caraïbe (Caribbean)
BMA	British Military Administration
CAF	Central African Federation
CCP	Chinese Communist Party
CIA	Central Intelligence Agency (United States)
CONAKAT	Confédération des Associations Ethniques du Katanga
CPP	Convention People's Party (Gold Coast)
DOM-TOM	Départements et Territoires D'Outre Mer
DP	Displaced Person (Jewish refugees)
DRV	Democratic Republic of Vietnam
EEC	European Economic Community
ENOSIS	Union with Greece (Cyprus)
EOKA	Ethniki Organosis Kyprion Aghoniston (National Organization of Cypriot Fighters)

FLN	Front de Libération Nationale (Algeria)
FLNKS	Front de Libération Nationale Kanake et Socialiste (New Caledonia)
FLOSY	Front for the Liberation of South Yemen
FNLA	Frente Nacional de Libertação de Angola
FRELIMO	Frente de Libertação de Moçambique
HNP	Reunited Nationalist Party (South Africa)
ICP	Indochina Communist Party
IFP	Inkatha Freedom Party (South Africa)
IOM	Overseas Independents' Group (Africa)
IZL	Irgun Zvai Leumi (Palestine)
KADU	Kenya African Democratic Union
KANU	Kenya African National Union
KAU	Kenya African Union
KCA	Kikuyu Central Association (Kenya)
KISA	Kenya Independent Schools Association
KNIL	Royal Netherlands Indies Army
MCP	Malayan Communist Party
MFA	Movement of the Armed Forces (Portugal)
MLP	Malta Labour Party
MNC	Mouvement National Congolais
MPAJA	Malayan People's Anti-Japanese Army
MPLA	Movimento Popular de Libertação de Angola
NAC	Nyasaland African Congress
NATO	North Atlantic Treaty Organisation
NCNC	National Council of Nigeria and the Cameroons
NDP	National Democratic Party (Southern Rhodesia)
NEI	Netherlands East Indies (Indonesia)
NLD	National League for Democracy (Burma)
NLF	National Liberation Front (Aden)
NPC	Northern Peoples' Congress (Nigeria)
OAS	Organisation de L'Armée Secrète (Algeria)
OAU	Organization of African Unity

List of Abbreviations

OCAJA	Overseas Chinese Anti-Japanese Army (Malaya)
OSS	Office of Strategic Services (United States)
OTs	Overseas Territories (Britain)
PAC	Pan-Africanist Congress (South Africa)
PAIGC	Partido Africano da Indepéndencia da Guiné e Cabo Verde (Guinea-Bissau and Cape Verde Islands)
PAP	People's Action Party (Singapore)
PCF	Parti Communist Français
PDCI	Parti Démocratique de la Côte d'Ivoire (Ivory Coast)
PDG	Parti Démocratique de Guinée (French Guinea)
PF	Patriotic Front (Southern Rhodesia)
PKI	Partai Komunis Indonesia (Indonesian CP)
PNI	Perserikatan Nasional Indonesia
PPA	Parti du Peuple Algérien
PSA	Parti Solidaire Africain (Congo)
RDA	Rassemblement Démocratique Africain
RENAMO	Resistência Nacional Moçambicana (Mozambique)
RPCR	Rassemblement pour la Calédonie dans la République (New Caledonia)
SEAC	South East Asia Command
SFTU	Singapore Federation of Trade Unions
SLORC	State Law and Order Restoration Council (Burma)
TANU	Tanganyika African National Union
UC	Union Calédonienne (New Caledonia)
UDF	United Democratic Front (South Africa)
UDI	Unilateral Declaration of Independence (Rhodesia)
UGCC	United Gold Coast Convention
UMNO	United Malays National Organization
UN[O]	United Nations [Organization]

UNIP	United National Independence Party (Zambia)
UNITA	União Nacional de Indepéndencia Total de Angola
UNP	United National Party (Ceylon)
UNSCOP	United Nations Special Committee on Palestine
UP	United Party (Southern Rhodesia)
UPC	Union des Populations du Cameroun
UPLG	Union Populaire pour la Libération de Guadeloupe
VIETMINH	Vietnam Independence League
VNQDD	Vietnamese Nationalist Party
VP	Vanua'aku Party (New Hebrides)
ZANC	Zambian African National Congress
ZANU	Zimbabwe African National Union
ZAPU	Zimbabwe African People's Party

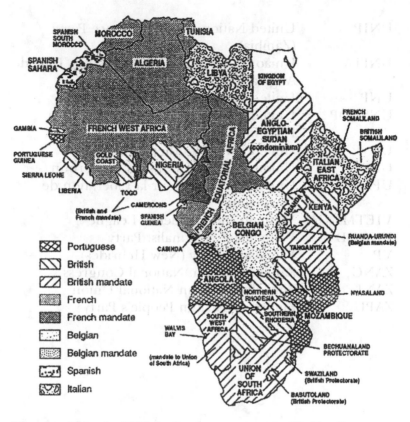

Map 1 Africa in 1939, indicating areas controlled by European powers

Source: Henry S. Wilson, *African Decolonization* (Arnold, 1994)

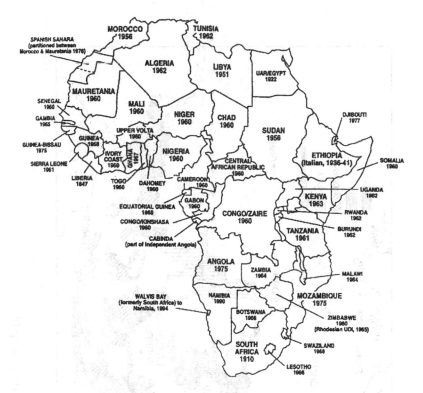

Map 2 The chronology of independence
Source: Henry S. Wilson, *African Decolonization* (Arnold, 1994)

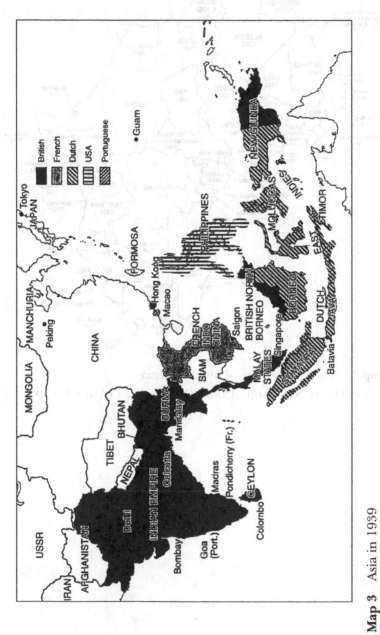

Map 3 Asia in 1939

Source: based on *The Hamlyn Historical Atlas*, 1981, map 86.

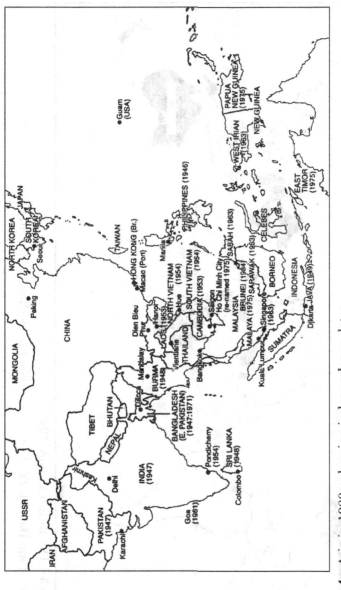

Map 4 Asia in 1980s, showing independence dates
Source: as for Map 3.

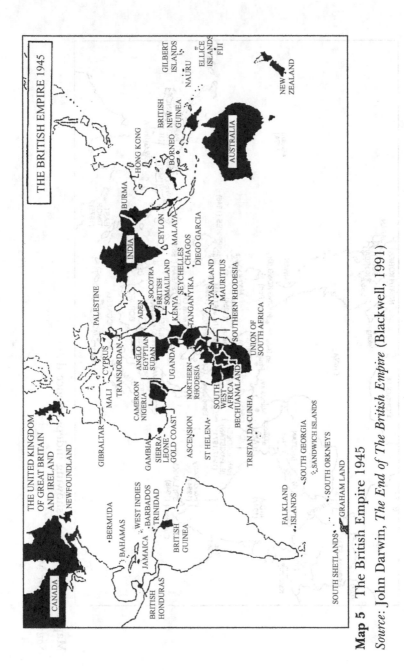

Map 5 The British Empire 1945

Source: John Darwin, *The End of The British Empire* (Blackwell, 1991)

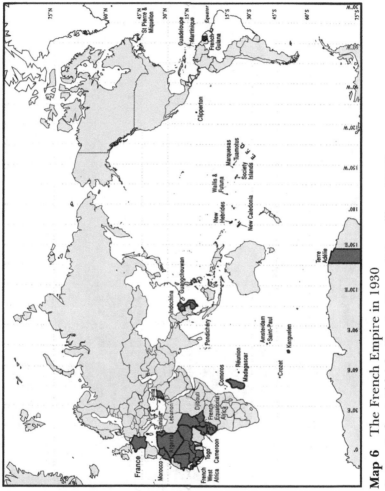

Map 6 The French Empire in 1930

Source: Robert Aldrich, *Greater France* (Macmillan, 1996).

1

INTRODUCTION: DEFINITIONS AND EXPLANATIONS

One of the most momentous changes to take place in the post-1945 world has been the dismemberment and almost complete removal of the European colonial or maritime empires set up in Africa, Asia, the Middle East, the Pacific, the Mediterranean and the Caribbean. When the Second World War broke out in 1939, roughly a third of the world's entire population lived under imperial or colonial rule; today less than 0.1 per cent of the global population lives in dependent territories. The idea that a developed nation should physically occupy and colonize another territory overseas simply because it had the power and resources to do so gradually became unacceptable to international opinion – even before the advent of total war against Germany, its European allies and, subsequently, Japan.

On the other hand, the removal of colonial occupation did not gather pace until after 1945, representing a drawn-out historical process rather than a sudden event. This book sets out to explain why and how the European empires that were so prominent before the Second World War had all but disappeared only 30 years after that war ended in victory for the major Western colonial powers.

Particular attention will be given to the various mechanisms of European departure around the world, with each major colony receiving separate, extensive and consecutive treatment, rather than being subject to chronological or thematic subdivision.

The primary aim of what follows is to enable readers to understand the seismic adjustment whereby vast tracts of the world achieved freedom from European occupation or colonial rule. The central theme of most chapters will be the consensual view that imperial disengagement can only be understood within the international political context of the postwar world, the legitimization of nationalist movements as against imperial ascendancy, and the colonial policies of the metropolitan powers. No one strand alone can portray the experience of decolonization – it is the linkages between them which provide the crucial element.

The author also hopes to convey some of the sheer excitement of this sprawling topic: the pressure of events on harassed colonial officials; the problematic interventions of the two superpowers; and the harsh choices facing nationalist leaders often unable to defeat far superior European armies. This introductory chapter starts by looking at definitions of 'decolonization', then summarizes various explanations for European withdrawal from empire that have been put forward by historians over recent years, broadly speaking: (1) nationalist or colonial; (2) international or global; (3) metropolitan or domestic.

The Meaning of Decolonization

'Decolonization' signifies here the surrender of external political sovereignty, largely Western European, over colonized non-European peoples, plus the emergence of independent territories where once the West had ruled, or the transfer of power from empire to nation-state. The historical process that this overarching term draws our attention to has not yet acquired an agreed definition among historians, but 'decolonization' usually means the taking of measures by indigenous peoples and/or their white overlords intended eventually to end external control over *overseas* colonial territories and the attempt to replace formal political rule by some new kind of relationship. The 'decolonizing' of Soviet Russia's post-1945 *continental* empire in east central Europe and the Balkans from 1985–90 will hence be excluded from the chapters that follow, although others have recently considered it part of the same general historical experience (Pearson, 1998; Chamberlain, 1999).

Citizens of the new nation-states, and their admirers, often prefer to speak of 'national liberation' rather than use the term 'decolonization' generally favoured by Western scholars. In itself, this reflects different views ('push out' versus 'pull out') of what actually took place. 'Decolonialism' would, perhaps, be a more neutral academic term. The rather forbidding term 'decolonization', used here because of its overall convenience and familiarity, appears to have been coined in 1932 by an expatriate German scholar, Moritz Julius Bonn, for his section on 'Imperialism' in the *Encyclopaedia of the Social Sciences*. It took 20 years to pass into more general currency and first featured in a book title when Henri Labouret, a liberal French administrator, interpreted it in *Colonisation, Colonialisme, Décolonisation* (1952) as a natural climax of imperial rule whose arrival was being unwisely hastened by contemporary pressures (Hargreaves, 1976, 1988).

'Decolonization' will be used here both in the *general* sense, as a historical movement which tended to encourage the removal of non-indigenous rule, and in relation to an ongoing historical process in *particular* colonial situations. Chapters will focus on how European powers after 1945 attempted to disengage from or were driven out of formal political occupation of their overseas possessions and also how, in some cases, they tried to reassert colonial supremacy. For those colonial rulers who lost or conceded

3

sovereignty, decolonization invariably meant the attempt to replace imperialist control by some new kind of commercial or strategic relationship. On the surface, post-1945 decolonization effectively demolished the old international system – economic, geographic, and cultural – by which the developed or urban-industrial Western nations had once dominated the rest of the world.

If these nations continued to dominate, it was no longer through various forms of *political* incorporation into their colonial empires but (in the absence of the coercive powers of the colonial state) by exercising commercial and financial hegemony over their former possessions, a relationship sometimes known as *neocolonialism*. The fragmentation of economic area that decolonized West Africa underwent, for example, has been interpreted as creating an irresistible pressure for the maintenance of colonial structures and 'development' policies which in turn, no less overwhelmingly, produced foreign domination and underdevelopment (Amin, 1973).

Explanations of Decolonization

One of the problems in writing about decolonization is that we know the end of the story. Whether self-government is seen as either the result of deliberate preparation/abrupt withdrawal by a colonial state ('decolonization') or as a triumph wrested from the colonizers by nationalist movements ('liberation struggle'), the story allows itself to be read backwards in order to privilege the process of ending colonial rule over anything else that was happening in the postwar years. Firstly, those favouring a *nationalist* or – to use Eurocentric terminology – 'peripheral' explanation (Easton, 1964; Grimal, 1978; Low, 1993), emphasize that indigenous upheavals invariably set the pace for decolonization, while the disappearance of collaborative elites also made continued European colonial rule unworkable (see Chapter 8).

4

Secondly, those historians who favour the *international* explanation of imperial disengagement (McIntyre, 1977; Lapping, 1985) point out that, in the new bipolar world after 1945, both the United States and the Soviet Union were hostile to old-style imperialism, although for different ideological reasons. Newly independent Third World states like India and Ceylon (Sri Lanka since 1972) also exerted international pressure through the United Nations (UN) to accelerate the process of decolonization. Thirdly, a focus on the domestic consequences of international relations, the *metropolitan* or domestic constraints approach (Kahler, 1984; Holland, 1985), illuminates how empire was fast becoming too burdensome and served no strategic or economic purpose for the mother country. From this perspective, loss of the 'will to rule' led to a belief that it was not worth expending men and money to preserve what were perceived as colonial liabilities by the middle-class taxpayer.

(1) Nationalist Explanations

It 'now seems scarcely tenable', argues an eminent historian who stresses indigenous resistance, 'that international pressures and domestic constraints were at least as important as colonial [nationalist] pressures in propelling the west's former imperial powers to decolonise' (Low, 1993: 262). The explanation that anti-colonial nationalism was the *primary* factor in inducing an imperial power to disengage from formal control of a colonial territory is linked to the 'peripheral' or colony-based explanation of decolonization. 'The winning of independence by the former colonies has therefore been in very large measure the work of the nationalists in the colonies themselves', concluded the American author of an ambitious early synthesis on the rise and fall of Western colonialism, writing at the height of African decolonization:

Their 'positive action' and agitation, including in some instances armed insurrection, have gradually made it clear to the colonial powers that, in the existing state of world opinion, it was not worth their while to attempt to hold the colony by force and that it was better to retreat with the best face possible, salvaging what they could and trying to retain as much good will as possible for the post-independence era. (Easton, 1964: 370)

Decades later, there are grounds for doubting whether nationalism, however powerful and decisive it may have been in certain cases, really was the crucial determining factor in accelerating imperial retreat generally. Some historians attribute equal importance to loss of the allegiance of collaborative elites – in part an outcome of the spread of nationalism – on whom the European colonial rulers so heavily depended.

The advocates of nationalism as a deciding element argue that decolonization in nearly all cases required first the growth of anti-colonial nationalist sentiments and nationalist forces within a colonial territory itself. But this growth alone was never the whole story. Assuming that international pressures were not always of great significance, 'what was then of prime importance were the particularities of the imperial [or metropolitan] response, which to a major degree determined the nature of the confrontation which then ensued – though hardly ever the eventual outcome' (Low, 1993: xii). Whether the occupying power responded by force or negotiation to nationalist demands was obviously crucial in determining the outcome of decolonization. Those historians emphasizing nationalism none the less argue that international persuasion or economic self-interest did not provoke Europe's accelerated decolonization in Africa after 1959, more nationalist pressures forcing countries like Britain and France to confront and resolve contradictions in their colonial position.

Nationalist leaders themselves combined cloudy anti-colonial rhetoric with the search for grass-roots support – such as Jomo Kenyatta discovered in the land-hungry Kikuyu squatters kept out of the British white-settler 'Highlands' in Kenya and Indonesian nationalist Ahmed Sukarno in Javanese peasant fear of the return of prewar Dutch taxes and compulsory demand for export crops. Kwame Nkrumah built a popular base in West Africa's Gold Coast after 1949 by mobilizing trade unions, farmers, traders, 'verandah boys' and various other interest groups. What charismatic, Western-educated nationalist leaders offered such relatively deprived sections of the community was the future possibility of a mass political movement capable of representing remote districts in a provincial or colonial capital far more effectively than purely local, tribal or sectional pressure groups. Nationalist politicians accumulated power and influence only by representing a political machine that spoke for cocoa farmers, coffee growers, chiefs, cultivators, urban traders and lorry owners. 'Where they lacked such a machine, the colonial state crushed them like flies' (Darwin, 1991: 89).

Anti-colonial risings incited by nationalist politicians could exert a terrible price and result in more immediate death and destruction to the nationalists' own countrymen, sometimes instituted by the guerilla fighters themselves, than to their well-armed European rulers. Over the period 1954–56 the Muslim FLN leadership in Algeria raised political passions by calculated acts of violence, directed as often against those who refused to cooperate with them as against Frenchmen. For every European murdered by the FLN it is estimated that they killed eight of their own people. Indigenous peoples who found employment as police or military under European colonial rule, such as the Arab auxiliaries in Algeria known as *harkis*, could expect no quarter if those rulers were compelled to depart by armed force. Equally, while fighting the British in Malaya after 1948, the communists used violence to eliminate their

Chinese Kuomintang guerilla opponents, to disrupt economic life, to dissuade peasants from aiding the British and
to persuade Malayans to provide them with food, money
and supplies. Vietminh intimidation of non-communist
peasants during the struggle against the French in Indochina, and their removal of VNQDD supporters in the
north, is also often disregarded (see Chapter 3). Events
between 1952 and 1956 in British Kenya, during which
time Mau Mau resistance was broken, saw African security
force casualties of around 500. On the other hand, African
civilian victims of the Mau Mau numbered 1817 – adding
weight to the argument that the Emergency was a civil war
between militants on the one hand and loyalist Kikuyu on
the other, as well as a Mau Mau campaign against white
settlement (see Chapter 6).

If we dismiss exaggerated contemporary fears that communist or Soviet conspiracies were behind various nationalist movements beyond South East Asia in the 1950s and
1960s, then a more persuasive explanation for the increase
in nationalist resistance to imperialism concerns the
mutually reinforcing 'contagion effects' of British and
French decolonizations, in Africa in particular, acting as
both stimulus and model to nationalists in their own colonies and elsewhere. For example, after Britain's Gold Coast
achieved independence as Ghana in 1957, the demands for
autonomy from French West and Equatorial Africa became
difficult to resist (see Chapter 5). The contagion explanation does not really address, on the other hand, the basic
question as to why the colonial populations were suscept-
ible to 'contagion' in the first place. One long-term explanation for nationalist potency is that, in the post-1945 period,
by increasing the productive capacity of their colonies, the
European powers created the very conditions which
encouraged the colonized peoples to challenge imperial
rule: rapid urbanization, plus social and political mobilization behind the ideology of anti-colonial nationalism. Economic development of the colonies and the postwar

8

acceleration in world economic growth created the structural conditions throughout the colonial world in which indigenous nationalism could flourish. Political and economic pressures on European decision-makers hence combined to reinforce existing international pressures for retreat or withdrawal (Sanders, 1990).

Nationalist explanations provide a powerful and attractive theory of colonial 'liberation' and the end of empire. They lend significance to the political movements whose ability to mobilize mass support was so striking a feature of the last decades of colonial rule, especially in Asia and Africa. Nationalist political disturbances clearly had the capacity to promote colonial self-government to the top of the political agenda in various European capitals. Yet are they sufficient to explain the whole complex phenomenon of the breakup of European colonial authority or 'decolonization' without taking into account international and metropolitan pressures to transfer power?

(2) *International Explanations*

To what extent was the breakup of the European colonial empires merely an inevitable outcome of the great transformation in international politics that followed the Second World War? Despite some necessary qualifications, the ensuing postwar decades may easily be characterized as the 'age of the superpowers'. The prewar European Great Powers – Britain, France, Germany and Italy – appear feeble, from this perspective, besides the enormous post-1945 strength and apparent power of the United States and the Soviet Union. In a world of Cold War ideologies and nuclear deterrents, 'colonial empires appeared as quaint survivors of a prewar age, to be quickly dismantled lest they be knocked to pieces in the turbulent wake of the superpowers' (Darwin, 1991: 56). Both the new superpowers were avowedly anti-colonial in outlook, while the ideological struggle against German fascism and Japanese

9

militarism had made the assertion of prewar racist and imperialist attitudes much less in vogue among the victorious Western allies. Furthermore, the 1941 'Atlantic Charter', agreed between Britain and America on common wartime objectives, and the 1945 United Nations Charter enshrined freedom from colonial rule as an ideal.

The emergence of the two superpowers as the arbiters of world affairs and the humiliating defeat of European colonial rulers in South East Asia by the Japanese from 1941–42 seemed to signify the passing of European world primacy and of the 'rickety' colonial structures that formed part of it. In 1945, the Cold War had not yet become the chief influence on the shaping of Western policies and the Soviet Union was not then the most formidable opponent of British, French and Dutch colonialism; at most, she gave ideological support to nationalist movements. It was the United States which most prominently opposed European colonialism. Why, after all, should a dynamic American political economy, bearing the staggering military burden from the North Atlantic Treaty (1949) onwards of defending postwar Western Europe against a supposedly encroaching Soviet Union, be willing to tolerate obsolete spheres of influence or late-nineteenth-century colonial boundaries that reserved markets, oil fields and raw materials to declining European states that were now so dependent upon American economic aid?

Until his death in April 1945, American President Franklin D. Roosevelt's dislike of the European colonial empires (the French one in particular), as the leader of a federated and democratic nation forcibly liberated from British colonial rule in the late-eighteenth-century, chimed with Soviet communist denunciations of capitalist imperialism. Both superpowers tried to discourage middle-ranking European powers, like the Netherlands, from clinging on to Empire to salvage their self-esteem. Bankrupt postwar Britain and a helpless France were also obvious targets of an intermittent attempt by the emerging superpowers to build a non-colonial world order. The formal creation of the United Nations at San Francisco in October 1945 with its stiffer terms for trusteeship, compared with the old League mandates, also reflected a stronger bias in favour of advancing colonial territories to independence. International pressures increased with the admission of newly independent nations such as India, Ceylon and Indonesia to the UN, who skilfully used it as a platform or means of isolating and embarrassing the old colonial powers. In 1960, alongside the entry of many new African states, the UN General Assembly passed the Declaration on the Granting of Independence to Colonial Countries and Peoples which typified colonial rule as a denial of fundamental human rights contrary to the UN Charter.

Conversely, a striking paradox, 'the imperialism of decolonization', has been used to argue that in the immediate postwar period British imperial power was only allowed to recover *with* American support. 'At metropolitan and international levels British imperial power was substantially an Anglo-American revival' (Louis and Robinson, 1994: 469). In March 1946, Prime Minister Attlee speculated that Britain was fast becoming an easterly extension of a strategic arc, the centre of which was the American continent, rather than looking eastwards through the Mediterranean to India and the Far East. By the end of 1947 the Americans were doing a great deal to prop up the British Empire, especially in the eastern Mediterranean and the Middle East. Over the same period, the British government withdrew troops fighting the communists in Greece, had left India, were about to depart from Burma and Ceylon, and not long after to abdicate their mandate in Palestine (see Chapter 4).

Only as the Cold War intensified between 1947 and 1951 did the United States hasten to strengthen Britain and France in defence of Western Europe. Washington relied on the British and French empires to block Sino-Soviet expansion into territories on the rim of southern and western Asia. Hence, with joint policies in Europe and mutual support in Malaya and the Middle East, the British could rely on 'the American shield' against communist intervention. Similarly, after Suez in 1956 ended British aspirations to imperial dominance in the Middle East (see Chapter 4), the British Empire was internationalized then dismantled as part of an Anglo-American coalition. But this was a coalition in which Britain was clearly the junior partner and in which Washington insisted that Britain prioritize the Cold War over its colonial possessions. 'After 1956 the British fell in with the American design for Western alliances [with the ex-colonial powers] with freer trade and free institutions. Such was the imperialism of decolonization' (Louis and Robinson, 1994: 495).

In any event, given such dramatic post-1945 changes in international relations, the contraction of imperial power and the liberation of so many countries from colonial rule can appear, in retrospect, natural and inevitable. This was not how Europe's politicians, diplomats and civil service mandarins necessarily saw their colonial empires developing at the time. British politicians, in looking back, presented the unravelling of empire as an orderly, rational, honourable and deliberate process but the messy reality was much less consistent and unavoidable:

> In short, far from there being a planned withdrawal, a considered transformation from empire to commonwealth, what actually occurred from 1945 until the late 1960s was the unpredictable erosion of position after position, foothold after foothold, followed on each occasion by further efforts to hold together the remnants of world power and influence, by one means or another. (Darwin, 1984: 206)

The orthodox view of British decolonization was that Britain freely abandoned its global imperial status in the 1940s and 1950s, whereas revisonist interpretation suggests a determination to recoup Britain's pre-Second World War role as a world leader, despite living in a new and more hostile postwar environment (Kent, 1993).

(3) Metropolitan (Domestic) Explanations

The home government in the mother country or 'metropole' had to take the ultimate decision about whether or not to transfer power and so an alternative way of explaining imperial retreat has been to see it as a political choice taken by postwar European governments under the pressure of domestic (often economic) constraints and calculations of national interest. In this sense, Europe simply drifted away from her old imperial role; the 'will to rule' gradually slackened and public indifference reinforced the effects of economic decline. The idea that during the 1940s and 1950s there was a sharp change of attitude in Britain towards empire and the burdens of an imperial role, and that this change played a key part in disengagement from colonial responsibilities, has been a recurrent theme in several accounts of the end of the British Empire. Not that the British felt any shame about owning a maritime empire, or had qualms about exploiting it. Rather, it was the case that public opinion at home took little interest in colonial possessions and was, consequently, unwilling to see scarce resources spent on preserving them. It followed that once empire became too much of a nuisance financially, militarily and in international relations, British opinion at home would tolerate getting rid of it as quickly and painlessly as possible (Darwin, 1991).

On the face of it, domestic constraints such as the vicissitudes of the British economy closely paralleled the progressive abandonment of colonial rule with the Commonwealth being used to conceal the realities of declining world power. The economic crisis of the immediate post-Second World War years, when Britain was saved from bankruptcy by American Lend-Lease borrowings and later the Marshall Plan, saw decisions taken to withdraw from India, Burma and Ceylon, and to abandon the Palestine mandate. On the other hand, fears about the prospects for Britain's economic recovery moved politicians in the opposite direction at the same time – for example, towards the greater economic exploitation of colonial East Africa (see Chapter 6) plus tin-and rubber-rich Malaya (see Chapter 3). Structural economic weakness also exposed Britain to pressure from America whose leaders, while not actively hostile to the survival of the British Empire, required conformity with American policy, notably in Palestine. A shift in domestic economic policy under Harold Macmillan's premiership in the late 1950s coincided with accelerating Britain's departure from the dozens of African, Pacific and Caribbean colonial dependencies that still remained (see Chapter 5).

European colonialism, it has been argued, 'became dysfunctional to the operational necessities of the metropole' (Holland, 1985: 205). In other words, an economic shift away from imperial tariffs and trade, as well as the postwar expansion of the welfare state and middle-class devotion to it, helped to pave the way for gradual imperial disengagement. After the Suez watershed, a strategic shift in Britain towards 'interdependence' with the United States and the partnership in nuclear weaponry that followed the 1957 Defence Review, highlighted the contradiction between upholding sterling and funding the counter-insurgency operations needed at times to defend Britain's world role. De Gaulle's shift away from French colonial Africa a few years later can also be explained by the alternative prospect of nuclear greatness. Recognition of the commercial benefits and also job opportunities of the British Empire, 'a gigantic system of out-door relief for the aristocracy of Great Britain' in Victorian radical John Bright's hostile phrase, were also replaced in domestic politics by a sense of its redundancy and burden on the taxpayer.

Economic developments within the European Coal and Steel Community (France, West Germany, Italy, the Netherlands, Belgium and Luxembourg) from 1952 also made previous concerns with unrewarding colonial development policies seem an increasing burden. When de Gaulle returned to power in France in 1958, he had the confidence gained from the setting up a year previously of the European Economic Community (EEC or Common Market) by the Treaty of Rome to scale down French colonial commitments, whereas Britain fell increasingly behind its continental competitors. 'The British Treasury was gripped by a panic-vision of the UK economy not only being bypassed by west European prosperity, but meanwhile being milched by parasitic dependents in Africa and the Caribbean' (Holland, 1985: 207). The British were also preoccupied with the preservation of sterling's role in financing international trade and investment, and with it the earning power of the City of London. By the late 1950s, the restoration of convertibility meant that the City's invisible earnings had more to gain from emerging global opportunities than from remaining confined to the sterling area. 'As the value of the imperial component of the Sterling Area diminished, so did the economic obstacles to decolonisation. Indeed, by moving with the nationalist tide, Britain hoped to benefit from informal ties with the Commonwealth while simultaneously promoting sterling's wider, cosmopolitan role' (Cain and Hopkins, 1993: 266).

Another plausible metropolitan explanation of why colonies were hustled towards independence, with the emergence of a new middle class back home, was to release West European resources for domestic welfare spending. The state was expected to subsidize house purchases, hospital treatment and higher education through tax reliefs and student grants, and any diversion of resources for colonial purposes – such as to defeat Mau Mau insurgents in Kenya or the FLN in French Algeria – became increasingly resented by new and expanding middle-class electorates that benefited disproportionately from increased welfare spending. The survival of British imperial power also appeared to be a matter of electoral apathy in the 1950s and 1960s, quite unlikely to disturb the domestic political scene. Even the emotional appeal to 'kith and kin' at the time of UDI in 1965 by the white minority in Southern Rhodesia attracted only a small backbench group of right-wing Tory MPs (see Chapter 6). The possibility of a decline in public support for the military coercion of terrorist movements, such as those the British encountered after 1945 in Palestine, Malaya, Kenya, Cyprus and Aden, could hence be seen as a further domestic constraint. There was a limit to metropolitan financial resources which could be devoted to colonial repression without pub-lic hostility from ordinary middle-class taxpayers.

Even if domestic politics did not play a decisive role in the removal of British imperial power, they were neither mar-ginal nor of little consequence elsewhere in Europe and contained the power to obstruct or even destroy the efforts of policy makers to respond to external change. The ex-ample of the French Fourth Republic (1946–58) is a remin-der that instability at home could paralyse colonial policy and that colonial issues, such as Indochina and Algeria, could wreck governments and constitutions. It was, after all, the threat of a military coup to shore up French rule in Algeria that cleared the way in 1958 for General de Gaulle and the Fifth Republic. Britain, on the other hand, dis-played striking political stability throughout the years of imperial withdrawal, minimizing the domestic effects of decolonization by *externalizing* the costs of failure. Various areas of troublesome conflict in the 1970s and 1980s – the Middle East, Cyprus, southern Africa, Kashmir, Sri Lanka – were legacies of British decolonization. 'Britain was spared, but the world still lives with the consequences, which are not borne by British society' (Kahler, 1984: 386).

Altogether, these various interpretations of the role of domestic policies, in the case of Britain at least, add up to suggest quite strongly the indifference at best, hostility at worst, of public opinion at home to any over-eager attempts to prevent the dissolution of colonial empire. They suggest

16

that we should see the impulse to decolonize getting stronger as the material concerns of the mass electorate dominated party political calculations in the metropole, as the urgency of domestic social reform increased, and as the electorate came to perceive empire as a drain on scarce resources otherwise available for welfare spending at home. At the same time, international and colonial-nationalist pressures to retreat from empire also became more intense in the 1950s and 1960s and those politicians who favoured a deliberate acceleration of imperial withdrawal enjoyed public tolerance if not enthusiastic support (Darwin, 1991).

Endnote

This book deals both with the eventual dismantling of that British, French, Belgian, Portuguese, Spanish and Netherlands sense of belonging to an imperial nation which ruled large tracts of the world and also with the achievement of a sense of nationhood by newly independent countries that took over the reins of power from the Europeans. That colonial issues remain current, despite the disappearance of empires, is suggested by attention given to the recent decolonizations of Hong Kong (1997) and Macao (1999), plus occasional media coverage of Britain's remaining overseas territories like the Falkland Islands and Gibraltar – claimed respectively by Argentina and Spain – as well as of violent anti-settler outbreaks in the 1980s on New Caledonia, a large island in the South Pacific still under French supervision (see Chapter 7). After consideration of the actual historical processes of disengagement in specific colonies (Chapters 3–6) and a survey of those dependencies remaining (Chapter 7), the various explanatory hypotheses put forward above for decolonization will each be reassessed (Chapter 8). Attention will also be given to the important role of collaborative elites in the context of a 'peripheral' or colony-based interpretation of the end of empire (see Chapter 8).

17

2

EMPIRE AND ITS REJECTION: BEFORE 1945

Younger readers may find the entire concept of empire as a
major fact of political, economic and cultural life difficult to
grasp, but the author grew up in London during the 1950s,
when 'a last generation of schoolchildren was raised on the
moral certainties of imperial rule' (MacKenzie, 1984: 256).
Empire (later Commonwealth) Day was still celebrated at
some public schools on 24 May, Queen Victoria's birthday,
and I attended a church Sunday school whose collections
helped to support British missionaries in Nigeria. I also
recall being taken to the local Odeon cinema as a child to
see the 1951 Royal Command Performance choice, *Where
No Vultures Fly* (aka *Ivory Hunter*, dir. Harry Watt), set in
British Kenya before the Mau Mau Emergency, a semi-
documentary Ealing Studios film about a fair-minded
white game warden (Anthony Steel) dispensing paternalistic advice to grateful Africans threatened by Arab-led ivory
poaching gangs.

While aware of newspaper headlines reporting British
soldiers killed fighting anti-colonial terrorism in Cyprus,
Kenya and Malaya, my reading embraced authors now
labelled 'imperialist' like John Buchan, H. Rider Haggard
and 'Captain' W.E. Johns, plus Henty-style boys' adventure

18

stories set on India's northwest frontier. Stamp collecting also impressed one with the extent of Britain's overseas possessions, as did school geography lessons, *Empire Youth Annuals* and comic papers. Now all that remains of Britain's once-extensive empire, even then under severe threat, are a few remaining overseas (formerly 'dependent') territories: a baker's dozen of islands, military garrisons and uninhabited territories scattered around the world (see Chapter 7).

European Empires

Imperialism embraces a general tendency by one society to acquire, control or exercise power over another and, from 1870 onwards, the organized rule of overseas colonial possessions by representatives from an imperial, predominantly European, metropolitan centre. Late-nineteenth century imperialism hence refers to fundamental shifts in the relationship between 'advanced', industrial Western states and other less developed, non-Western societies. The process of formal political occupation by European colonial powers in Africa, the Middle East, Asia and the Pacific, labelled the 'new imperialism' by historians to distinguish it from previous informal empires of trade or large-scale white settlement, was mostly a product of the last quarter of the nineteenth century. Spain and Portugal could look back on centuries-old contacts (the slavery trade) with Africa but French expansion in sub-Saharan Africa, like that of its colonial rivals Britain and Germany, did not begin in earnest until the 1880s; it then took another 20 years for Africa to be divided.

Because conflict and competition over territorial expansion in West Africa threatened European relations, the German chancellor, Otto von Bismarck, convened the Conference of Berlin in December 1884, initially to control rather than to extend the 'scramble for Africa'. Eighty years later, those colonies over which Britain, France, Germany and Belgium haggled in Berlin had all acquired their independence from external rule. Since the European empires whose collapse is surveyed here nearly all date from only the late-nineteenth century in terms of 'effective occupancy' or formal political rule, their existence, decline and disappearance was encompassed over a relatively brief time span.

In the modern world empire is no longer the norm but denotes one particular historical form in which the inequalities of power that characterized the relationships between Europeans and other, more low-technology, non-white ethnic communities was expressed until its demise from the mid-twentieth century onwards. The United States joined this exclusive imperialist club after its defeat of Spain in 1898, following which the Philippines were sold to the Americans for US $20 million and Cuba, Puerto Rico and Guam were acquired, driving Spain from her New World and Pacific empire after four centuries. The Cuban, Puerto Rican and Filipino patriots who for decades had been fighting against Spain simply exchanged one colonial power for another. For there was a broad agreement during the pre-1914 global world order, encouraged by what are now seen as racist and imperialist ideologies, that the colonial system of government by 'superior' white races of 'inferior' brown, yellow and black ones was perfectly legitimate and even necessary for the progress of 'proper' civilization. The once widely held view that some white peoples possess an innately higher intelligence and hence obligation to occupy and rule others is now denied by the importance of climate, the suitability of local plants and animals for domestication, the exploitation of different technologies and even whether the continent on which you happened to live was on a north–south or an east–west axis, or had a straight or indented coastline. From this perspective, history followed different courses for different peoples because of differences among people's environments, not because of biological differences among people themselves (Diamond, 1996).

European empires were a vast confidence trick, dependent as colonialism must be on the rule of the few over the many, that relied on the docility, cooperation or disunity of the colonized, buttressed by the racial arrogance of their better-armed white governors. Colonial regimes functioned in economic terms for the purposes of extorting production and labour from powerless indigenous peoples and for biasing their commodity markets in favour of metropolitan monopolies. 'Empires were transnational organizations that were created to mobilize the resources of the world' (Hopkins, 1999: 205). Patronizing superiority or benevolent indulgence underlay much colonial government, a belief that 'primitive' peoples were like children who needed firm paternal guidance (a common view in white-settler colonies into the 1960s). That a handful of white administrators, soldiers and policemen, mostly European, held power over vast numbers of the non-white inhabitants of Africa, South and South East Asia, the Middle East, the Caribbean and the Pacific, was regularly eulogized back in the mother country. Less emphasis was placed on the employment of large numbers of local collaborators, under the command of white officers, police chiefs and bureaucrats, who served as the foot soldiers of imperial rule.

The colonial mandarins of Paris, Brussels, Lisbon, The Hague and London, or governors and their secretariats, may have believed that they ruled overseas empires, but district officers, chiefs and sultans were far more important on the ground. The administrative 'man on the spot' embodied the colonial state to most Africans or Asians, not the remote, unknown politicians and civil servants in the European metropolis. Rudyard Kipling, Britain's noted verse writer and story teller, greatly admired the 'doers' of Empire: engineers, railway-builders and administrators, the men who brought peace, order and public works, which he saw as the fruits of imperial rule in India. Kipling's command to the imperialists, as he put it in 'A Song of the English' (1893), was quite simple:

Keep ye the Law – be swift in all obedience –
Clear the land of evil, drive the road and bridge the
  ford...
By the peace among Our peoples let men know we serve
  the Lord!

Britain's colonial Empire in Africa on the eve of the Second World War was greater in size than India and Burma combined and stretched from Swaziland in the south to Gambia in the north west. Yet there were only 1200 British colonial administrators ruling over a total population of some 43 million black Africans spread across nearly two million square miles and backed by only 900 Colonial Service police and military officials (Gardiner, 1997).

A vastly exaggerated concept of the power of the colonial state and its administrators, most colonial states were desperately short of financial resources and manpower, exists to this day in popular understanding. In Nigeria alone in 1938 there were fewer than 400 district officers expected to govern and dispense justice to over 20 million indigenous inhabitants. Not surprisingly, the British in West Africa made a virtue out of necessity and ruled through the resident chieftains, a practice earlier legitimized as 'indirect rule' in Nigeria by imperial proconsul Sir Frederick Lugard. The Sudan Political Service held sway over a million square miles of territory with barely 125 athletic 'Oxbridge'-educated British officials – 'the Land of Blacks ruled by [sports] Blues'. The French colonial Empire was even more ramshackle in parts of French Equatorial Africa: the military territory of Chad was home to only 20 Europeans at the turn of the century, mostly non-commissioned officers. It was their responsibility to administer a territory which measured almost 100 kilometres from north to south and 400 kilometres from east to west. Many Africans never saw a white man despite colonial occupation. In French West Africa between the two world wars, the ratio of European administrators to Africans was 1: 27,000, in the Belgian Congo the ratio was 1: 34,000 but British Nigeria had a ratio of only 1: 54,000, if the secretariat is counted in, because the Islamic northern emirates offered scope to cut British administration to the bone (Wilson, 1994).

The map of Europe itself had been redrawn after Germany's defeat at the end of the First World War, the Paris peace settlement of 1919–20 saw the emergence of a cluster of nation-states in place of lands which were formerly part of the Hapsburg, Romanov and Hohenzollern empires. The Ottoman Empire's defeat and collapse required a separate treaty and then the San Remo Conference (1920) mandated the Middle East along conventional imperialist lines between Britain (Palestine, Mesopotamia [Iraq]) and France (Syria, Lebanon). Yet under American pressure, former German colonies (Tanganyika, South West Africa, Togoland, the Cameroons and various Pacific islands) and Turkish provinces were not handed over as outright colonies to the victorious allies but held as League of Nations mandated territories, whereby 'advanced nations' were to exercise 'tutelage' on behalf of their 'native' peoples (Chamberlain, 1998: 13–14).

Former Turkish Class A mandates were to be brought to self-rule as soon as reasonably possible, whereas Class B and C mandates that embraced former German Africa and various Pacific islands were to remain under the mandatory powers indefinitely. Iraq became independent in 1930 but the other Class A mandates were still under foreign control when the Second World War broke out. The remaining European colonial powers (Britain, France, the Netherlands, Italy, Spain, Portugal and Belgium) did not seriously consider 'granting' self-determination in 1919 to any of their pre-existing African or Asian colonies. Taking its new mandates into account (Palestine, Iraq, Transjordan,

North West Cameroons, Tanganyika and West Togoland), the British Empire was more extensive than ever before in the early 1920s. Following the example of the redistribution of Germany's colonies in 1919, when Italy emerged as a defeated power after the Second World War, having fought on the German side, she was required to surrender her North African colonies (Ethiopia, Eritrea, Italian Somaliland, Libya) which came under British or French administration until the 1950s.

Britain not only resisted dismantling its vast overseas empire but also withdrawal from suzerainty over its close neighbour, Ireland (whether or not Ireland qualified as a colony is a matter of continuing debate among historians). Here, after the 1916 Easter rising in Dublin, popular support for a new Sinn Fein, and the Anglo-Irish War (1919–21), the cause of separatism from a contiguous Britain had become further entrenched. Although the Anglo-Irish Treaty of 1921 that partitioned off the majority Protestant north-east six counties of Ulster stipulated that the leaders of the new Irish Free State in the predominantly Catholic south should take an oath of allegiance to the British crown, the relationship between England and the new dominion was now, in effect, one of constitutional equals. Eamon de Valera and a majority of the Irish Republican Army (IRA) did not see things in this light and took up arms against the Treaty's signatories, among them Michael Collins, killed in the ensuing civil war (1922–23). The Free State government, determined to assert its autonomy, issued its own passports in 1924 and appointed an Irish minister to the United States, the first dominion representative to be accredited to a foreign state. After his Fianna Fail party came to power, de Valera abolished the oath of allegiance in 1932, and his constitution of 1937 reduced the link between the new 'Eire' and the British Commonwealth to the minimal gesture of 'external association'. Neutral in the Second World War, in 1948 Ireland declared itself a Republic (and soon left the Commonwealth altogether in the same year as Burma). Ireland's precocious journey from some kind of colonial relationship, to reluctant dominion status, to fully independent republic, provided a template on which other British subject peoples could model their own decolonization (Martin, 1975).

While the British had the Commonwealth and the availability of dominion status to ease the transition to independence, the French failed to develop any face-saving mechanism before 1960 which might have served as a bridge for the transfer of power to colonial 'subjects'. 'Assimilation', the eventual absorption of colonial subjects as full citizens 'assimilated' to French culture in an enlarged Republic, remained the imperial ideal. The French Union idea, dating from 1946, was federal only in name, the old assimilationist tendency continued, even if a degree of local autonomy was granted. The French National Assembly in Paris still exercised ultimate sovereignty. Psychologically, the French doctrine of 'assimilation', unlike the British concept of 'indirect rule', had the effect of allowing their colonial problem to fester because of the credibility gap between metropolitan democratic theory and colonial practice (Chipman, 1989). 'Assimilation' concealed the realities of Arab nationalism in Algeria from officials in Paris because of the half-hearted pursuit of an equal share for all colonial subjects. The insistence on distinguishing Algeria as an integral part of the French Republic from the rest of *France d'outre-mer* (overseas France), notably West and Equatorial Africa, made any accommodation with Algerian nationalism a difficult choice for French politicians of all persuasions (see Chapter 6).

Pre-1945 Anti-Colonial Revolts

The attempt to overthrow European colonial rule and replace it by some form of indigenous nationalist or communist government was not a phenomenon restricted solely to the post-1945 period. Abd el Krim's Arab warriors from North Africa's wild Rif inflicted a series of humiliating reverses on the Spanish in Morocco from 1921–25 and seriously troubled the French when they invaded French Morocco. This nomadic tribesman was one of the earliest of what became a long line of charismatic twentieth-century leaders of anti-colonial revolt. Spanish Foreign Legion troops in Morocco, commanded by Spain's future military dictator, General Francisco Franco, had a reputation for atrocities committed against the Moorish villages which they attacked. The decapitation of prisoners and the exhibition of severed heads was not uncommon. When the Spanish dictator General Primo de Rivera visited Morocco in 1926, he was appalled to find one battalion of the Legion awaiting inspection with Arab heads stuck on bayonets (Preston, 1995). European claims to moral superiority over those they governed became difficult to sustain once colonial rule was threatened. Anti-French movements led by middle-class Arab Muslim nationalists, like Ferhat Abbas in Algeria, also initiated protests during the interwar years. Nationalist leader Saad Zaghlul's largely middle-class Wafd Party represented an equally sophisticated political response to the persistent British presence in Egypt.

There is also some evidence of anti-colonial resistance in sub-Saharan Africa during and after the First World War but this could often take religious, tribal or cultural forms, rather than 'primary resistance' in the form of armed revolts. In many colonies, as well as in the Union of South Africa, whose white Afrikaner rulers accepted formal decolonization from Britain in 1910, 'the emergence of independent churches, millenarian movements, and new syncretic cults, provided the strongest manifestations of discontent with the new order' (Hargreaves, 1988: 15). Early in 1915, for example, the followers of a charismatic prophet, the Reverend John Chilembwe, attacked Europeans in southern Nyasaland. For many inhabitants of French West Africa, the moment for revolt arrived in

1917 after the imposition of conscription during the world war. In the Congo another evangelical Christian prophet, Simon Kimbangu, so stirred up the Bakongo people in 1921 that he was imprisoned by the Belgians for the remaining 30 years of his life. Yet only after the prophet's death did Kimbanguism really become involved with Congolese nationalism. African political organization was most evident in British Kenya where Nairobi telephone operator Harry Thuku had founded an East Africa Association as early as 1921 (the radical Young Kikuyu Association, later Kikuyu Central Association, started that same year). As a Kikuyu spokesman, Thuku was arrested by the colonial government a year later and deported to enforced residence near the coast. The mines in Northern Rhodesia's copperbelt, whose skilled jobs were reserved for whites, saw serious strikes and violent protests in 1935, at Luanshya police opened fire and killed six African strikers. The deadly new weapon of air-power was used cheaply and effectively, meanwhile, against rebels in Italian Somaliland and British-ruled Sudan.

The overpopulated societies of South and South East Asia, proud of belonging to Muslim, Hindu, and Buddhist civilizations stretching back centuries, were the site of numerous pre-1945 attempts to rise up against external colonial rule, some of which took Ireland as a precedent. In 1930 the British energetically suppressed a peasant rebellion in lower Burma led by Saya San, a Buddhist monk executed in 1937. French Indochina's anti-colonial nationalists (VNQDD) and communists who rebelled from 1930–31 also suffered severe penalties – upwards of 700 Vietnamese were executed and thousands imprisoned by unrelenting French-colonial police. Abortive communist uprisings from 1926–27 in west Java and Sumatra were brutally suppressed by the Dutch. Similarly, in 1933 the emerging Indonesian nationalist movement in Java was all but destroyed, with young engineer and future ruler Ahmed Sukarno exiled to the island of Flores until the

advent of the Japanese in 1942. The British had little difficulty in suppressing Arab risings protesting against Jewish
immigration to Palestine during 1936–39. They were more
shaken by Mahatma ('great-souled') Gandhi's non-violent
passive resistance campaign or *satyagraha* from 1930–31
and 1932–33 in British India. Yet the last was strongly
resisted, with Indian National Congress leaders arrested,
Gandhi imprisoned, Congress outlawed, public meetings
and processions forbidden, until the much-publicized civil
disobedience protest collapsed. The British also took harsh
measures, in Bihar and elsewhere, against the Congress-led
'Quit India' riots in 1942, despite their empire being in the
throes of the Second World War (see Chapter 4).

Disregarding such disturbances on the 'periphery', the
legitimacy of European colonial rule remained the general
world view during the 1920s and 1930s, especially with
American isolationism and an ineffective League of
Nations. Yet Britain's white dominions (self-governing
states within the British Empire) – Australia, New Zealand,
South Africa, Canada and, in particular, the Irish Free State
– had long sought and were granted some definitive proof
of constitutional independence from British rule, ultimately enshrined by the 1931 Statute of Westminster. The
Dominions were accorded full parliamentary autonomy
while remaining under the British monarchy as an emblem
of imperial unity. Between the wars Britain and the Dominions collectively made up the British Commonwealth, as
distinct from the 'dependent empire' (India was a special
case) generally made up of Crown Colonies and Protectorates.

During the Second World War, the Germans overran
much of North Africa in 1941–42 and briefly, until the
tide of battle turned at El Alamein, controlled Tunisia,
Libya and the western part of Egypt. The ability of the
traditional European powers to maintain the old imperial
system was further diminished after the simultaneous Japanese invasions of South East Asian colonial territories, and

many of the Pacific islands which also formed part of colonial empire, met only ineffective European resistance. Following the ignominious surrender of the well-garrisoned but poorly defended island of Singapore to the Japanese in February 1942, referred to in Malay as 'the time the white men ran', the British could no longer claim to be the impregnable protectors of Malaya. The myth of white European invincibility was shattered for ever by the unexpected collapse of colonial Singapore (Chew and Lee, 1996). Even after Japan's surrender in 1945, the French and the Dutch, if not the British, were to experience great difficulty in reasserting imperial rule over their former South East Asian colonial territories (see Chapter 3).

The wartime success of the Japanese in invading most of South East Asia, causing an exodus of European rulers (with the partial exception of the Vichy French in Indochina), acted as a catalyst both to Asian nationalism and the political consciousness of the myriad peoples of the region. 'Is liberty and freedom only for certain favoured peoples of the world?' asked Javanese nationalist Sukarno in October 1945. 'Indonesians will never understand why it is, for instance, wrong for the Germans to rule Holland [under wartime occupation] if it is right for the Dutch to rule Indonesia. In either case the right to rule rests on pure force and not on the sanction of the populations' (McMahon, 1981: 95). If the Dutch proved resistant to this plea, colonial nations like Britain, which had claimed to be fighting a war for democracy and freedom against the Axis powers, found it more difficult after 1945 not to concede the right of self-determination at some time in the future to their own imperial possessions.

Conclusions

Leaders of opposition to colonial rule before 1945 faced formidable obstacles in mobilizing support large enough to frighten their well-armed white rulers, who could show remarkable determination and ruthlessness in putting down often ill-coordinated risings. White supremacy was to prove much more difficult to sustain in a post-1945 world dominated by superpowers America and Russia, as weakened European powers determined to recover prewar colonial authority discovered to their cost before the Cold War intervened. So if the aftermath of the First World War began the process of imperial decline, the Second World War hastened it across Asia by undermining white racial prestige, a long-lasting memento of Japanese occupation. Yet the process of decolonization was not the inevitable result, in some mechanical way, of the 1939–45 world war. Global conflict may have precipitated but did not determine an outcome facilitated rather more by the interlocking of the various general explanations proposed in the preceding chapter.

3

SOUTH EAST ASIA: THE STRUGGLE FOR EUROPEAN 'RECOLONIZATION'

The United States' handover of the Philippine Islands on 4 July 1946 came less than a year after the surrender of the Japanese, with the assurance of an oligarchic, anti-communist government led by Manuel Roxas friendly to America's interests in the Pacific Ocean and safeguards for the maintenance of her naval and military bases. The new constitution demonstrated how a sensible and timely withdrawal could result in imperial economic and strategic interests being preserved intact after 'independence'. Conversely, major European attempts were also made in the years immediately after 1945 to return former South East Asian colonial territories, officially won back from the Japanese, to their prewar white overlords. Military and political campaigns loosely classified here as *recolonization* both precede and overlap with British departure from the subcontinent of India in 1947 (see Chapter 4).

This chapter looks, initially, at the Dutch endeavour, following Japanese surrender and allied military occupation, to reassert colonial rule from 1946–49 over the thousands of islands known as the Netherlands East Indies

31

(NEI), the colonial name for what is now Indonesia. Politicians in The Hague, unable to see forward to a prosperous Dutch future within the EEC, were convinced that their economy could not survive without the riches (oil, rubber, sugar, tobacco, tea and coffee) to be extorted from the outer islands (primarily) of the NEI. Secondly, the focus will be on the attempt to reimpose French authority and thence recover imperial greatness in Indochina, the colonial name for what is now Vietnam, Laos and Cambodia, leading to the Franco-Vietminh struggle (1946–54). 'To think that the people of Indochina would be content to settle for less than Indonesia has gained from the Dutch or India from the British', an American adviser wrote in 1949, 'is to underestimate the power of the forces that are sweeping Asia today' (Jeffrey, 1981: 17).

In most of South and South East Asia, the British were anxious to cut their losses and to withdraw from colonial territories after 1945, to avoid conflict with strong nationalist movements, provided they first secured special political and economic connections. The successful restoration of British colonial rule in the Malayan peninsula, however, meant that its independence came long after India, Burma or Ceylon. The old imperial supremacy in Asia lingered on here, British policy makers showed little hint of any desire to pull out, influenced by Malaya's tin and rubber annually earning Britain more dollars than did all Britain's own exports. Plans drawn up during and immediately after the Second World War revealed instead a determination to extend and strengthen British control of the Malay peninsula. This process of re-establishing British influence was focused after 1948 on the struggle to prevent armed takeover by a communist regime hostile to both British and Western influence. The British were increasingly keen, on the other hand, to distance themselves from the imperial outlook of the French and the Dutch in South East Asia. The different British strategy was designed to eventually lead Malaya to self-government within the Commonwealth.

The British in Java and Sumatra

On 17 August 1945, a few days after Japan's surrender ended the Second World War, a vacillating Ahmed Sukarno, in association with Mohammed Hatta, proclaimed independence from their prewar Dutch rulers in Java – the heartland of 'Indonesian' national consciousness. The political vacuum left by Japanese collapse and withdrawal from nearly all the main towns and cities was rapidly occupied by a functioning Indonesian Nationalist Party (PNI) government determined to oppose the unwelcome return of Dutch rule. Sukarno's republic was thus already well-established, with governors and local revolutionary committees appointed for each of the eight new provinces of 'Indonesia', when allied troops of Vice-Admiral Lord Louis Mountbatten's South East Asia Command (SEAC) arrived in the aftermath of the Japanese capitulation. SEAC took over Java and Sumatra while, at Mountbatten's request to lighten his load, the Australians occupied all of the NEI east of and exclusive of Bali and Lombok. In Java, British-Indian troops had been sent to accept the surrender of and disarm Japanese troops, release Dutch or allied prisoners and maintain order. The Netherlands refused to recognize the new republic but pressure on the Dutch to negotiate with former Japanese-collaborator Sukarno, rather than shoot their way back into power in the former NEI, came from Mountbatten and his Commander-in-Chief for the islands, General Sir Philip Christison.

The British rapidly became eager to escape from the burdens of postwar military occupation by handing over their hard won 'bridgeheads' in Java and Sumatra to Dutch troops; the most significant 'bridgehead' to be handed over in Java ran from Batavia (Jakarta) to Bandung. The ruthless British reoccupation and bombing of Surabaya throughout November 1945 was necessitated by the strategic necessity for a 'bridgehead' in east Java but also by the mysterious shooting of a high-ranking British officer, Brigadier A.W.S. Mallaby, leading to the retreat of the 49th Brigade of the 23rd Indian Division, heavily outnumbered by Japanese-armed republican Indonesians (Springhall, 1996). Thousands of Javanese were killed in the battle for Surabaya, more than in all the Dutch 'police actions' that followed British withdrawal a year later. The NEI's Dutch Lieutenant-Governor Hubertus J. van Mook's grandiose plans for a federal states system under Dutch management foundered, meanwhile, under the combined pressures of nationalist resistance, diehard politicians in Holland, distrust between Dutch and Indonesians and international hostility towards the restoration of any form of colonial rule.

In the absence of a political solution between Dutch and Indonesians, noted Britain's Foreign Secretary Ernest Bevin, the problem was 'very similar to that which we have had to face in India and Burma and in Malaya. It is quite obviously not a problem which under present-day conditions can be solved by force' (PRO). In May 1946, an exasperated Mountbatten, fast losing patience with the ferocious brutality of the Royal Netherlands Indies Army (KNIL) troops under his command (many of them pro-Dutch Ambonese islanders), was called upon by the Chiefs of Staff in London to justify the British position. 'The implementation of my tasks in the NEI has been complicated by the understandably Imperialistic outlook of the local Dutch officials who consider Java theirs by sovereign right', Mountbatten complained. 'This attitude of mind has been imparted to the Dutch troops, with the result that frequent clashes between the Allies and the Indonesians have taken place inside and outside the bridgeheads' (PRO). Chastened by events, the British government privately began to urge the Netherlands to adopt a more flexible policy towards the Indonesian Republic, which the Dutch stubbornly refused to recognize as such. 'If British troops remained too long in Java', reported Bevin's special commissioner for South East Asia, Lord Killearn (former ambassador Sir Miles Lampson), 'our action will be taken to help the Dutch, and if the Indonesians were to protest we might be on an awkward wicket' (PRO).

The military occupation necessitated by the evacuation of Dutch prisoners, allied internees and Japanese troops continued to pose an uncomfortable dilemma for British-Indian forces until, on 12 November 1946, Killearn helped bring about the short-lived Linggadjati Agreement between the nationalists and the Dutch which recognized the Republic as the *de facto* authority in Java, Madura and Sumatra. Both sides also agreed to cooperate in the creation of a federal United States of Indonesia in which the Republic would be but one of the states. The remaining British soldiers were finally withdrawn at the end of November, Mountbatten's SEAC was at last dissolved and responsibility for Java and Sumatra was gratefully handed over to the Dutch. Their troops were substituted for British-Indian troops, as agreed several months before at a secret meeting in London between the Dutch and British premiers.

Could the British simply have left the former NEI to settle its own future in 1945–46, refusing to become involved beyond the simple Red Cross job of shunting Japanese prisoners of war and Dutch internees back to Singapore? The answer must lie in the negative, given British reluctance to withdraw from nearby Malaya, Singapore and Borneo, plus the strong pressure on them as the only allied power with sufficient forces available in the region to restore some sort of order and to avert a rice famine. Britain had to take care not to prejudice its own position and to use influence with the French and the Dutch, said a Foreign Office adviser, 'to ensure that they do not imperil the general position of European powers in the Far East' (Tarling, 1998: 91). A British government less committed to the concept of imperial 'sovereignty' and a Dutch one less intransigent over their former East Indies

35

possessions could, on the other hand, have prevented the years of struggle that followed before outright Indonesian independence was finally achieved.

The Dutch Attempt to Recolonize

Another outsider, the United States, now became more deeply involved in the bitter struggles of Indonesia for complete self-rule, by exerting rather desultory pressure on the Dutch through the United Nations (UN). Fighting between Dutch and local republican youths continued, particularly on Bali and in southwest Sulawesi (Celebes). The latter's resistance was so intense that, early in 1946, the Dutch resorted to employing the notorious Captain Raymond 'Turk' Westerling to 'pacify' the country. He accomplished this by using firing squads, methodically executing hundreds of civilians and republican guerillas. In Minahasa, north Sulawesi, Indonesian soldiers of the KNIL rebelled against the Dutch in February 1946, proclaimed for the Republic, and maintained authority for some weeks. A short period of relative peace occurred during the last few months prior to the withdrawal of British occupation forces and also for several months after the Linggadjati Agreement. Then came the first Dutch 'police action', or armed invasion of the Republic, in July 1947. The United States under President Harry Truman did little to prevent this imperialist act of aggression because of America's need for Dutch anti-communist support in Western Europe, whatever encouragement his predecessor, Roosevelt, might have given to anti-colonial insurgents (McMahon, 1981). Neighbouring Australia reacted by referring the Indonesian question to the UN Security Council which led to the setting up in August of the rather toothless UN Consular Commission and Committee of Good Offices in Indonesia.

The only considerable period of truce between Dutch and Indonesians was that following the agreement reached on board USS *Renville* on 17 January 1948 that the Dutch would not cross the ceasefire line of the previous summer and Sukarno's republic would be allowed to continue on reduced territory with Batavia (Jakarta) as its capital. Plebiscites would eventually be held to allow territories to decide whether they wished to join the new republic or the 'Malino group' of islands (including Bali, Ambon, Sulawesi and Bangka) who in July 1946 had agreed at Malino in south Sulawesi to cooperate in a divisive federal system with the Dutch. The nationalists had their own difficulties, the PNI was split into several groups, and in September 1948 there was a premature attempt at a coup by the Indonesian Communist Party (PKI) at Madiun in east Java, whose violent suppression won American support for the embattled republic. The Renville truce was followed by the second Dutch 'police action' from December 1948 until April 1949, undeterred by the disapproval of the UN and anti-imperialist world opinion. This second invasion of republican territory climaxed in a successful military sweep that brought the arrest of nationalist leaders, including Sukarno and Hatta, at Yogjakarta in south-central Java. Military repression of anti-colonial opposition clearly seemed like a viable option, albeit guerilla resistance in the countryside soon began to weigh down the Dutch military machine.

Thus actual or threatened military action by the well-armed Dutch military was a constant factor in the first four years of the republic's history until, early in 1949, the Americans at last vetoed Dutch re-conquest of what was now recognized as a legitimate anti-communist nationalist regime, threatening to end Marshall Plan aid to the Netherlands if they did not enter into negotiations (the US had already suspended Dutch aid funds intended for Indonesia). So diplomatic or international pressure, as much as republican armed resistance, induced the Dutch to begin yet another round of negotiations. Ultimately, on 7 May 1949, the Rum–Van Roijen Agreement was signed between

President Sukarno and the Dutch, followed by a successful Round Table Conference at The Hague from August to November and the eventual transfer of sovereignty on 27 December 1949 from the NEI to the independent but short-lived Republic of the United States of Indonesia (with the exception of Western New Guinea). The formal unitary constitutional structure of its replacement, the new Republic of Indonesia, capital Jakarta (Batavia), came into being on 17 August 1950.

Indochina from 1940 to 1945

Indochina (Annam, Cochinchina and Tonkin, the three provinces which are now Vietnam, grouped together with Cambodia and Laos) was the 'jewel in the crown' of the French colonial empire. During the Second World War, a general accord in August 1940 between Japan and the Vichy government of unoccupied France provided for the continuation of French sovereignty and administration in Indochina, in return for placing the military facilities and economic resources of the colony at Japan's disposal. This was an unusual arrangement because the Japanese were to destroy European colonialism elsewhere in South East Asia, from 1941–42 driving the British from Malaya, the Dutch from the NEI and the United States from the Philippines. Thereafter the allies, including Chiang Kai-shek's Nationalist China, were engaged in a common struggle against the all-conquering Japanese.

Revolutionary Vietnamese political leader Ho Chi Minh ('He who enlightens', one of numerous aliases), exiled leader of the Indochina Communist Party (ICP), was released early in 1941 from a north Chinese warlord's prison at Chiang's orders to lead the Vietminh (Viet Nam Doc Lap Dong Minh Hoi or Vietnam Independence League) resistance movement against Indochina's discredited French-collaborationist administration run by High Commissioner

Admiral J. Decoux. The ICP leadership of the Vietminh was masked by a nationalist front in order to appeal to a broadly patriotic sentiment. A communist military force was organized under the inexperienced leadership of former history teacher Vo Nguyen Giap, who was to become one of the century's great military leaders. By September 1944 the Vietminh had an army of 5000 and three mountainous provinces in northern Vietnam were under its control. France's wartime Vichy colonial regime eventually succumbed, offering only isolated resistance to its final absorption on 9 March 1945 by Japan, whose own demoralized troops awaited repatriation six months later. Military and other supplies were parachuted in to the Vietminh guerillas fighting the Japanese by, among others, the US Office of Strategic Services (OSS), forerunner of the Central Intelligence Agency (CIA). Pregnant with future irony, an OSS team (the Deer Mission), headquartered in south-west China, also trained Ho Chi Minh's forces in the jungles of northern Indochina (Karnow, 1991).

When Japan surrendered to the allies on 14 August 1945, the Vietminh emerged from their wartime resistance role and elected a National Liberation Committee or provisional government, headed by Ho Chi Minh, to gain independence for the Democratic Republic of Vietnam (DRV) by presenting a nationalist, rather than a communist, programme. On 26 August, after the triumphant Vietminh took over Hanoi, the Japanese puppet emperor, Bao Dai, abdicated in favour of the provisional government, providing the new communist administration with historical legitimacy by handing over his sword and seal as signs of sovereignty (a few years later, the French would bring him back to head a puppet government in the south). On 2 September 1945 a crowd of 500,000 in Hanoi heard Ho Chi Minh proclaim the birth of the DRV, masking evidence of a communist victory (10 out of 15 in the new cabinet were ICP) by quoting from the American Declaration of

Independence, the text of which had helpfully been supplied by an OSS officer.

Meanwhile, the victorious wartime Allies, meeting at Potsdam, a Berlin suburb, in July, had decided not to recognize a future DRV and devised a scheme to disarm the Japanese by asking General Chiang Kai-shek's Nationalist China to occupy Indochina north of the 16th parallel and Britain south of it. The latter responsibility was added to Mountbatten's SEAC, known in American anti-colonial circles as 'Save England's Asian Colonies', whose area already covered Burma, Singapore, Malaya, Borneo, Thailand, Java and Sumatra. Chinese forces arrived in north Indochina in early September, while British-Indian troops of Major-General Douglas Gracey's command flew into Cochinchina's Saigon, for 80 years the southern hub of the French colony, from 12 September 1945 onwards. Mountbatten, Supreme Allied Commander, South East Asia, had ordered Gracey to avoid south Vietnam's internal problems and merely to remove prisoners of war and disarm the surrendered Japanese. 'I was welcomed on arrival by the Viet Minh, who said "Welcome" and all that sort of thing', Gracey recalled unguardedly in 1953, at the height of the French colonial war. 'It was a very unpleasant situation, and I promptly kicked them out. They are obviously Communists' (Duncanson, 1968: 289).

The British in Saigon

When Gracey arrived, Saigon was in chaos, and the discredited French Vichy administration had crumbled, devastated by the defeat of Japan, whose troops awaited repatriation. A Vietminh committee set up to govern was wrangling with de Gaulle's parachuted-in representative Jean Cédile. French residents, afraid to lose their colonial privileges, were bracing for a fight. Meanwhile, private armies or religious cults like the Cao Dai and Hoa Hao, as well as Trotskyites and others, all striving to outbid the Vietminh, had taken to fighting among themselves. Tensions spiralled with the emergence of the Binh Xuyen, a mercenary gang which, until its elimination by Ngo Dinh Diem in 1955, would cheerfully serve the Vietminh and other factions and even police the south for the French in exchange for the franchise to manage brothels, casinos and opium dens. Violence grew in Saigon as rival groups fought each other or clashed with the French (Karnow, 1991).

On 21 September 1945 General Gracey exceeded Mountbatten's instructions by proclaiming martial law, banning public meetings, imposing a curfew and closing down Vietnamese newspapers. With only 1800 British, Indian and Gurkha troops at his disposal, Gracey lacked the muscle to enforce this decree so, encouraged by Cédile, on the following day he released and armed 1400 French army troops, mostly Foreign Legionnaires, who had been imprisoned in Saigon jail by the Japanese. The desperate Vietminh leaders thereupon mobilized a massive protest demonstration deliberately designed to provoke British and French reprisals by causing Vietnamese casualties that would attract world attention. A French orgy of violence preempted them in the early hours of 23 September when, a day after their release, French soldiers went on a rampage, ousting the Vietminh's so-called provisional executive committee and raising the French flag from the rooftops. Their ranks swollen by angry French settlers, the Legionnaires indiscriminately victimized Vietnamese despite pleas for calm by Gracey and Cédile, appalled by the spectacle that they had themselves inspired. 'It was a tragic blunder, grievously compounded by the brutal and hysterical behaviour of the French' (Rosie, 1970: 65).

Responding to the French frenzy, the Vietminh leaders launched a general strike on 24 September 1945, seen by some historians as marking the opening of real hostilities. In a residential suburb, the Cité Hérault, Binh Xuyen bandits led by Vietminh agents slipped past Japanese

41

guards and massacred between 150 and 300 French and Eurasian civilians, sparing neither women nor children. Communist historians predictably omit any mention of this atrocity in accounts of the period. Gracey's inadequate British force was used to suppress the Vietnamese uprising which meant that he had no choice but to make extensive use of the Japanese army, not only in support and auxiliary roles but also as active combat units, often, though not always, under the command of British officers. Lieutenant-Colonel Peter Dewey of the OSS, accidentally killed in a Vietminh ambush near the Saigon golf course on 26 September 1945, was the first of nearly 60,000 Americans later to be killed in Vietnam. The fighting that took place between British-Indian troops, Japanese and nationalists in and around Saigon has been referred to as the First Vietnam War (Dunn, 1985).

The British foreign policy dilemma was that Gracey could not continue to back the French in Indochina without alienating Nationalist China and anti-colonial American opinion. On the other hand, retreat from Saigon would cause consternation among the French and perhaps encourage nationalist revolt in Britain's own colonial possessions in Asia, such as a volatile Burma. So French troops had to be sent to southern Indochina with the utmost dispatch and, after turning it over to them, British troops must be withdrawn as soon as possible. This was, in effect, what took place. The United States, while hesitant to get directly involved in Indochina, raised no objections as the British gave their US military equipment to French units and transported them by ship to Indochina. British military intervention in Cochinchina was mostly over by the end of 1945, subsequently forgotten by the collective memory, and British-Indian combat troops were already on their way to deal with the intractable problem of Dutch re-entry into Indonesia. On 28 January 1946 the British Control Commission in Saigon was wound up and General Gracey departed, leaving the French colonial authorities and the Vietminh to resolve their differences by themselves.

French President Charles de Gaulle selected the arrogant and inflexible former monk Admiral Georges Thierry d'Argenlieu as High Commissioner for Indochina, the equivalent of governor, and as chief military commander chose the devout Catholic aristocrat General Jacques Philippe Leclerc, who had helped liberate Paris in 1944. The first part of Leclerc's expeditionary force arrived in October 1945, first breaking a Vietminh blockade around Saigon, then driving through the Mekong delta, constantly harrassed by enemy guerillas, and up into the highlands. The 9th *Division d'Infanterie Coloniale* (DIC), 17,000 strong and with American equipment, had arrived by the end of the year. There were about 50,000 French troops in the southern zone as the British prepared to withdraw. On the political side, d'Argenlieu created a new administration in Saigon supported by wealthy, collaborative and *évolué* Vietnamese (French-speaking office workers) with an investment in the French presence and encouraged a separate Cochinchina to offset the Vietminh's efforts to reunify Vietnam.

The Vietminh in Hanoi

The situation in the north was different because Ho Chi Minh's influence was greater and his popularity widespread, unlike the ruthless Vietminh leader in the south, Tran Van Giau, who liquidated even communist sympathisers failing to meet his sectarian standards. Under the Potsdam plan, General Chiang Kai-shek's Chinese Nationalists had been delegated to disarm the Japanese in the north and the first of their 200,000 troops, commanded by General Lu Han, arrived in Hanoi like a plague of human locusts in September. Both Ho and the Chinese wanted to prevent the French, soon installed in the south, from regaining the north. But Lu Han sought to promote the Viet Nam Quoc Dan Dang (VNQDD), or Vietnamese Nationalist Party, created in 1927 by Chinese Nationalists and organizer of a failed 1930–31 rising against the French. Another group still active was the Dong Minh Hoi (Nationalist Party), sponsored by China to collect anti-Japanese intelligence during the war in the Tonkin region. By mid-September 1945, Hanoi was divided, with the central and south-eastern suburbs under Vietminh control, while the pro-Chinese nationalists held the north-eastern parts and soon held several provinces (Marr, 1995).

On 11 November 1945, to the surprise of the nationalists, Ho announced the dissolution of the ICP as a gesture of appeasement to Lu Han and offered the VNQDD 70 seats in the upcoming elections to the National Assembly in January 1946. Power was ostensibly shared in a new cabinet composed of the Vietminh, the VNQDD, and others. Then on 8 March 1946, Ho signed a covenant with the French, allowing the presence of 25,000 French troops in Indochina for the next five years, provided that they recognize the DRV as a free state within the French Union – the new name for the old French Empire. Done largely to get free of the hated Chinese Nationalists occupying the north who, after the surrender of the Japanese, had rampaged the countryside in a campaign of loot, plunder and rape, this agreement modifies an heroic view of the Vietminh as dedicated to the uncompromising pursuit of national independence.

Accommodation with the French, provided that they recognize Vietnam's self-rule, seemed preferable to outright war. Ho vigorously defended himself to his critics at a meeting in Hanoi:

> You fools! Don't you realize what it means if the Chinese remain? Don't you remember your history? The last time the Chinese came, they stayed a thousand years. The French are foreigners. They are weak. Colonialism is dying. The white man is finished in Asia. But if the

Chinese stay now, they will never go. As for me, I prefer to sniff French shit for five years than eat Chinese shit for the rest of my life. (Karnow, 1991: 169)

The realities of postwar colonial politics also dictated that the communists had to buy time to look for support far outside of the narrow strata for whom talk of Vietnamese independence would have had any meaning, if they were to compete with the well-established commercial and business pressure groups or 'imperial collaborators' that exercised influence with the French colonial administration. Ho had at least got rid of the Chinese nationalist troops, and with their withdrawal the power of the VNQDD could easily be broken.

The French War in Indochina

The French, meanwhile, tried to strengthen their military and political position. Having no desire to surrender French imperial sovereignty over the former Indochina, the new government of Georges Bidault in Paris hesitated, hedged and finally reneged on most of de Gaulle's assurances. D'Argenlieu declared a Republic of Cochinchina in violation of the March 1946 agreement and Ho, in France seeking to negotiate Vietnam's sovereign independence, suffered humiliation as he was shunted off to Biarritz to isolate him from left-wing sympathizers in the capital. The United States, despite Ho's pleas, had decided to support a strong France. The Soviet Union had neither endorsed his communist regime nor even assigned an observer to Hanoi. On 23 November 1946, the French cruiser *Suffren* bombarded Haiphon, the main northern port in the Gulf of Tonkin, killing over 6000 north Vietnamese in a matter of hours and landing troops who occupied the area. This became a signal for the outbreak of general hostilities between the Vietminh and France.

45

The DRV leadership and its army of 40,000 trained guerilla troops took to the countryside of Tonkin province. The Second Vietnam War (1946–54) had broken out all over Indochina, north and south, and the French had to face dedicated guerilla fighters simultaneously on a number of fronts. Their intention was to drive the Vietminh northward from their major bases in Tonkin, but this was soon frustrated, notably along the line of principal action, Colonial Route 4, which linked Langson to Caobang, on the northernmost border of Indochina with China. In March 1949, having won no decisive battles, the French announced the birth of the Republic of Vietnam as an associated state within the French Union, along with Laos and Cambodia, but this made little difference in practice because the major instruments of power were firmly under French control. The new state was recognized by Great Britain and the United States. The Soviet Union and Mao's Communist China reacted by recognising the DRV, in effect bringing the Cold War to Indochina (Clayton, 1997).

Both sides in the eight-year colonial war made terrible blunders costing heavy casualties, the French generals hardly knowing how to fight an armed-peasant guerilla war and the Vietminh forces lacking experience of pitched battles. French positions along Colonial Route 4 were attacked and destroyed in the first week of October 1950 and Caobang had to be evacuated. In the following year, French troops under the remarkable but now very ill General Jean de Lattre de Tassigny, one of France's finest senior generals, forced Vietminh retreat from terrain that they held northwest of Hanoi and then occupied the strategically important city of Hoa Binh, deep in enemy territory. Shortly after de Lattre's death in France in January 1952, the Vietminh, at great loss of life, forced the demoralized French to retreat from Hoa Binh. By 1952–53 General Giap had learned to campaign more cautiously and, after Ho, was chiefly responsible for the ultimate success of the Vietminh against both the French and, subsequently, the Americans (Macdonald, 1994).

As the Cold War heated up, large amounts of ammunition and weapons came across Indochina's northern borders from communist China to strengthen Giap's supply position. The French, whose military situation slowly deteriorated, were heavily dependent upon capitalist American aid for uniforms, supplies and arms. By the end of 1953 America was funding 80 per cent of the French war effort and had supplied a total of $2,900 million in military aid. In early 1954, Giap accepted the challenge of conventional warfare at the valley of Dien Bien Phu which the last French commander, General Henri Navarre, regarded as strategically important because it was close to the Laotian border and all the communication routes with Laos, China and Tonkin. By that stage, however, French colonial forces were thoroughly demoralized and domestic public opinion pressed overwhelmingly for ending the 'dirty war' in Indochina.

The French military in northern Indochina had foolishly boxed themselves into a corner in Dien Bien Phu, believing a major defeat of Giap's forces there would be crippling to the Vietminh's military effort. Yet the unfortunate General Navarre, based in remote Saigon, had seriously underestimated the Vietminh's capacity to transport heavy artillery and position them in the surrounding hills, besieging the increasingly desperate French troops. In April and early May 1954, the use of nuclear weapons seemed to US Secretary of State, John Foster Dulles, the only way to save the beleaguered French garrison from total extermination by the Vietminh (although he well knew that President Eisenhower would be unlikely to approve). Britain refused to go along with the American plan for 'united action' because it opened the prospect of a third world war to contain 'Chinese-style' communism. The American climbdown enabled General Giap to register his greatest triumph by finally overwhelming the French at the battle of Dien Bien Phu on 7 May 1954, the eve of the Geneva Conference on Indochina. The French lost their entire garrison, which with last-minute reinforcements had totalled over 15,000 men, while the Vietminh achieved victory only at the immense cost of at least 20,000 casualties overall.

The most important consequence of the crushing humiliation of Dien Bien Phu was the collapse of any further support for the war in France itself. Cabinets fell rapidly until Pierre Mendès-France, who became premier on 17 June 1954, threatened to send out a million fresh conscripts unless some figleaf of an honourable settlement on Indochina were reached in Geneva within a month. American hints of readiness to use nuclear weapons had not been lost on China. The Franco-Vietminh peace settlement signed on 20 July 1954 temporarily divided Vietnam into two zones on the Korean model, upon a demarcation line close to the 17th Parallel, with mutual withdrawals from Laos and Cambodia and with the question of reunification to be decided by a Vietnam-wide election in 1956 (indefinitely postponed). The Vietminh reluctantly accepted the Geneva settlement, under pressure from communist allies the Soviet Union and China to take a 'peaceful coexistence' line, but rather ominously the United States merely 'took note' of the agreements.

Hence the communist Vietminh took the north of Vietnam and a pro-Western and 'independent' government under veteran nationalist Ngo Dinh Diem and his relatives took the south. Almost a million people migrated southwards in the months during which free population movement was allowed. The Geneva conference sounded the death-knell of French colonialism in South East Asia without assuring freedom to Vietnam as one nation and without guaranteeing continued peace to an already war-weary land. Eight years after Geneva, the United States were heavily entrenched as protectors of 'democracy' in South Vietnam. The buildup to another devastating and long-drawn-out American-led anti-communist war had begun that did not end until the fall of Saigon (renamed Ho Chi Minh City) to North Vietnamese troops on 30 April 1975.

Malaya: Return of British Rule

The 'second colonial occupation' of British Malaya that took place in the aftermath of the Second World War saw the creation of a viable nation-state as the culmination of the imperial mission. Malaya is about the size of England or New York State, two thirds covered by dense, tropical forest and divided by a mountain range extending down the spine of the peninsula. In 1945 it had a population, excluding Singapore, of under five million, of whom 44 per cent were Malay, 38.5 per cent Chinese, 10.5 per cent Indian, 5.5 per cent Aborigine and 1.5 per cent 'other' including European. Whereas the total number of immigrants in Burma amounted to no more than about 8 per cent of the population, in Malaya immigrant Chinese and Indians, who had flooded in from the last quarter of the nineteenth century onwards to work the tin mines and rubber plantations, actually outnumbered native Malays. This imbalance was to be influential in the devising of new constitutional arrangements by their British rulers during and after the Second World War. The plantations and mines that made Malaya such an important dollar earner for postwar Britain, explaining in part why the British were so reluctant to leave, were mainly along the western coastal plain. Prior to the Japanese invasion of 1941–42, the British had developed an odd patchwork quilt of colonial political authorities: the three Straits Settlements (Singapore, Malacca and Penang) run from Singapore as crown colonies; the Federated Malay States (Selangor, Perak, Pahang, and Negri Sembilan) each officially ruled by a legally sovereign sultan, in practice by British administrators; finally, the Unfederated Malay States (Johore, Perlis, Kedah, Kelantan and

Trengganu), less overtly under British control (Stubbs, 1993).

The sudden Japanese surrender of Malaya in August 1945 had rendered the planned allied invasion unnecessary (unlike Burma), but this made it difficult for the British to return to the peninsula as conquering heroes. For months afterwards, Malaya, like Burma, was plagued by lawlessness, guerilla war, and ethnic conflict, but the unpopular British Military Administration (BMA) were not under the same fiercely nationalistic pressures to leave as they were in Burma. Also, Britain could afford to let events in Burma take their course, given the Attlee government's conversion to independence for India (see Chapter 4). In terms of Britain's postwar economic predicament, Burma's export products were not dollar earners for the sterling area, whereas Malaya's tin and rubber were a vital source of dollar income (Smith, 1988). In 1949 and again in 1950 Labour Premier Clement Attlee insisted in the British Parliament that there would be no 'premature withdrawal' from Malaya, lest there be a flight of planters, miners and capital. 'Malaya's strategic position and its economic importance – it was the sterling area's largest dollar-earner – meant that its surrender was unthinkable to the British government' (Stockwell, 1992: 375–6).

During the Japanese occupation of Malaya it had been the Malayan Communist Party (MCP), through the guerilla groups of their Malayan People's Anti-Japanese Army (MPAJA), who formed the most effective resistance, with some assistance from the British. From April 1945 onwards over 2000 weapons were delivered by SEAC to the largely Chinese MPAJA who were trained in guerilla tactics by undercover British officers of Force 136. The non-communist Kuomintang or Chinese Nationalist resistance forces in the Overseas Chinese Anti-Japanese Army (OCAJA), cut off from supply lines, proved far less effective. Sceptics contend that the greater part of whatever fighting the MPAJA did during the occupation was with the OCAJA resistance, rather than against the Japanese. The MPAJA handed in their air-dropped weapons after Japan's surrender (a rare example of an anti-colonial resistance group disarming) but those arms not recovered, or obtained during both the British and Japanese retreats, were hidden away for future use. Malaya's communists then acquiesced in the resumption of British colonial rule, at least until after the BMA had left. On 6 January 1946, Lord Mountbatten, standing on the Singapore municipal building's wide stone steps, pinned campaign medals on the proud breasts of 16 MPAJA leaders. Only three of the group were Malays, the rest were Chinese of whom 11 saluted the Supreme Commander with the clenched fist, communist style, among them a smiling young Chin Peng, soon to become MCP secretary-general and commander throughout the lengthy guerilla war (1948–60) against the British and their Malay successors.

Despite British military rule, gang robberies and racial violence were rife in the immediate postwar period, over 600 people being murdered during communal strife in central and lower Perak, Negri Sembilan and Pahang. By the time the BMA handed over to a civilian government in April 1946, consisting mainly of prewar civil servants out of touch with recent developments, a great many Chinese and some Malays had become highly disenchanted with British rule. The incoming British-run Malayan Civil Service failed to appreciate the strong roots that the MCP, the only political party in existence at the end of the war, had put down within the rural Chinese community; preferring to exaggerate instead the threat of radical, pro-Indonesian and poorly supported groups like the Malay Nationalist Party (MNP). Malayan nationalism developed slowly, however, because until after the Second World War Malays felt more loyalty to individual states and their sultans rather than to Malaya as a country.

The setting up of the popular United Malays Nationalist Organization (UMNO) in March 1946, in reaction to the imposition by Sir Harold MacMichael of the Malayan Union Scheme, drawn up by London civil servants and published in January, saw Malay nationalism emerge almost overnight. The amalgamation of Malacca and Penang with the various Malayan states was to be named the Malayan Union, with equal political rights for Malays and non-Malays (Singapore would be retained as a Crown Colony under separate administration). The Malay masses were united for the first time in protest at this apparent threat of being submerged by the Chinese. The Union idea was hastily abandoned by the British in February 1948, in favour of the idea of a Federation of Malayan States with no guaranteed rights of citizenship for Chinese or Indians, but its principles remained as the ultimate goal for an independent Malaya (Stockwell, 1979). Yet Dato Onn Bin Ja'afar, Prime Minister of Johore and President of UMNO, remained distrustful of British rule and made his feelings clear to the Colonial Office when he visited London later that year.

The MCP was not illegal in the immediate postwar years but the British had a surprisingly ample knowledge of its activities, and subsequently captured several of its key personnel, because MCP secretary-general Lai Tek was in reality a British secret agent. Outwardly a communist, he had been working for the French in wartime Indochina, then in Malaya as a Japanese agent also in contact with the British, and ultimately as a postwar British Special Branch operative in Singapore. Without him, said a British intelligence report, 'an attempt would have been made in 1945 or 1946 to organise a more militant campaign by the Communists in Malaya' (Short, 1975: 32). Whether or not this assumption is warranted, the MCP achieved some success even with traitor Lai Tek in power, particularly in their infiltration and manipulation of the emerging trade unions, first in Singapore and then on the mainland of Malaya. Strikes and incipient riots on estates in the Malacca area were also instigated from 1947–48 by the lingering influence of the Malayan-based Indian National Army, formerly led by Subhas Chandra Bose, that had fought alongside the Japanese for the liberation of British India during the disastrous Burma campaign.

The Malayan Emergency

On 16 June 1948 three European planters were killed in their bungalows at Sungei Siput, near Ipoh, in Perak, by a gang of Chinese communists armed with sten guns. The British at last declared a State of Emergency. News reaching Marxist radicals from the February 1948 Calcutta Youth Conference that the new Soviet Cominform policy called for 'armed struggle' to fight against imperialism may have provided ideological justification but the causal links between Calcutta and decision-making within the MCP have now been largely discounted. The sudden escalation of violence appears to have been almost accidental, the work of a small radical guerilla unit which jumped the gun in the uncertain months after Lai Tek's disappearance along with MCP funds. Britain's reversal of policy over the Malayan Union Scheme, which guaranteed political equality for all races, and the increasing success of Mao's Chinese Communist Party (CCP) in its war against Kuomintang forces, were other powerful incentives for the majority-Chinese MCP to adopt a more aggressive strategy. Finally, the low wages, widespread shortages and high cost of living still prevalent must have persuaded some MCP central committee members in 1948 that they could mobilise the masses, on the basis of persuasive Marxist arguments, in a fight for national independence. The MCP had somehow started a military war against the British in Malaya that they could not possibly hope to win.

Equally short-sighted was the complacent British 'law and order' outlook that all unrest in Malaya was caused by 'extremists' or 'bandits', a view fostered by the Colonial

Office in Whitehall. Thus the success of the communist guerillas in the first few years of the so-called Emergency was as much a consequence of the colonial rulers' misguided strategy in treating them as if they were a criminal, rather than a political, problem as it was a result of the MCP's own efforts. High Commissioner Sir Edward Gent, unwilling or unable to recognize that a full-scale revolt was imminent in Malaya, categorised the long list of politically inspired murders during the first five months of 1948 as 'a war of nerves by the forces of disorder' (Coates, 1992: 204). Major-General C.H. Boucher, General Officer Commanding (GOC) in Malaya, was put in charge of the 'anti-bandit' campaign. When he claimed to have the terrorists on the defensive, two Europeans were murdered the following day. Large-scale British army 'sweeps', which worked well on Salisbury Plain, proved inappropriate to the jungles of Malaya.

Having fought communist guerillas in Greece's civil war (1944–49), Boucher believed himself an expert on this kind of warfare. 'I can tell you this is by far the easiest problem I have ever tackled', he claimed prematurely. 'In spite of the appalling country and ease with which he can hide, the enemy is far weaker in technique and courage than either the Greek or Indian Reds' (Stubbs, 1993: 70). This assessment was contradicted by the 50 European rubber planters, the majority auxiliary policemen, killed by 'bandits' on isolated plantations from 1948 to 1951. More positively for the British, these years also exemplify the successful partnership between Sir Henry Gurney, the new High Commissioner, and Malcolm MacDonald, Britain's effervescent Commissioner General for South East Asia. Together they conciliated the Muslim, anti-communist Malays, prepared for local elections, and maintained the momentum of constitutional advance (Sanger, 1995). Gurney, a distinguished Chief Secretary in Palestine and considered a far-sighted administrator, tried unsuccessfully to rein in the military by placing them under the command of the well-informed

Police Commissioner, Colonel W.N. Gray, former Inspector-General of Police in Palestine, and himself responsible to civil authority. Nearly 400 British ex-Palestinian police sergeant recruits also arrived at the end of 1948, seconded to the Malayan Police. Alas, they had no knowledge of local culture or languages, seeing every Chinese as a potential 'bandit' to be 'bashed around' like Jews or Arabs (Stubbs, 1993: 73).

Two main forces were fighting the communists: the British Army and the operational arm of the Malayan Police. Army units included regular battalions, many of them conscript soldiers, plus 10,000 Gurkhas, who had the highest rate of terrorists killed (their practice of cutting off heads for identification purposes sanctioned by the military), and from 1952 about 2800 Fijians, King's African Rifles and Sarawak Rangers. Whole Chinese villages were burnt by the British in the initial phase of the Emergency. At Batang Kali in Selangor in December 1948, some jittery young conscripts shot 24 Chinese villagers held on suspicion of aiding guerillas, an incident 'hushed up' by the colonial government but repeated on a smaller scale elsewhere – Chinese were frequently shot while running away from army and police patrols. The occupying Japanese had never burnt whole villages, arrested women and children, or deported thousands to China. In 1950 the Labour Minister for War, John Strachey, pointed out that an important aspect of the struggle was for the British to win the support of the Chinese rural squatter but that this was not going to be achieved by indiscriminate and heavy-handed military suppression. From 1950–51 Hugh Carleton Greene, brother of novelist Graham and later Director-General of the British Broadcasting Corporation (BBC), did his best to knock into shape the Emergency propaganda and psychological warfare organizations operating in Malaya (Carruthers, 1995).

After three years, not only were the insurgents undefeated, but in spite of considerable casualties their numerical strength had swollen considerably. Thus just over 2000 guerillas in late 1948 had become a guerilla army of well over 8000 by the end of 1951. Communist victory in China in 1949, and the following year's dramatic intervention of the Chinese in the Korean War, gave the MCP illusory reasons to believe that time was on their side. Meanwhile, British policy makers sensibly advocated an increase in the tempo of political change for Malaya. 'It would be unrealistic, unsafe and perhaps disastrous to work on the basis that 25 years was still available to us to accomplish the transition to self-government', warned Colonial Secretary James Griffiths at the Fifteenth Commissioner General's conference held at Bukit Serene on 7 June 1950 (PRO). The process of negotiating independence, as it turned out only seven years away, was given extra impetus by the need to conciliate moderate, non-communist Chinese and nationalist Malays.

Parallels have been drawn between British military strategy in Malaya and that of the Americans some 15 years later in South Vietnam. If anything, the British were more ruthless in draining the sea of frightened peasantry within which the communist fish were allowed to swim. Starting in 1950, under the Whitehall-backed plan of Malaya's Director of Operations, Lieutenant-General Sir Harold Briggs, Chinese squatters exposed to MCP intimidation on the fringes of the jungle were moved to new settlements or regrouped in the same locality, while the old settlements were replaced by 'New Villages' protected by barbed wire and police stations. Military success now depended on the progress of the compulsory resettlement of Chinese squatters who might provide food and assistance to the enemy. Rising American prices for Malayan rubber during the Korean War simultaneously benefited the British drive for economic improvement in the peninsula. By the end of the year, over 117,000 Chinese had been moved into 140 'New Villages' defended by Malay police and their own Chinese home guard. Two years later, in 1952, some 450,000 squatters had been resettled. It testifies to the poverty and hardship of these squatters that by the early 1960s, with the Emergency at an end, over 300,000 chose to remain in 400 'New Villages' – rather than return to their previous, less controlled way of life (Jackson, 1991).

Astonishingly, on 5 October 1951, Sir Henry Gurney, the British High Commissioner, was killed in an ambush by communist guerillas. 'The unnecessary and ironical nature of Gurney's death was a fitting epitaph to the muddled policy which the British Government had pursued since the end of the Second World War' (Coates, 1992: 186). Briggs's appointment as Director of Operations expired and, following a much-publicized visit to Malaya in December 1951 by Oliver Lyttelton, the new Tory Colonial Secretary, Colonel Gray was removed from his post as Commissioner of Police. At this low point in British fortunes, Lyttelton's diagnosis was that there was a need for the concentration of colonial authority in one man, combining both civilian administration and military command. Field-Marshal Bernard Montgomery, the victor of El Alamein, was considered for this post of both High Commissioner and Director of Operations but he wisely recommended General Sir Gerald Templer, GOC Eastern Command, to Prime Minister Winston Churchill. Some believe that what really turned the tide for the British in the peninsula was the arrival in February 1952 of this 53-year-old general, a former director of military intelligence, given greater political power in a state of undeclared war than any British soldier since Oliver Cromwell.

Between 1952 and 1954 Templer, the 'Tiger of Malaya', carried out a classic anti-insurgency campaign which broke the communist resistance, meanwhile speeding up political reform with the promise of independence. On the operational side, Templer endorsed the Briggs plan of Chinese resettlement in 'New Villages' and gave it fresh impetus, meanwhile using propaganda to win their 'hearts and minds', a phrase with which he became indelibly associated.

On the political side, Templer continued Gurney's policy of appointing prominent Malays as 'members' of the Federal government, answering for some departments in the Legislative Council of the Federation and so representing a step on the road to independence. In autumn 1954 a statement was made in the House of Commons by the next Tory Colonial Secretary, Alan Lennox-Boyd, promising independence once the anti-communist Emergency had been brought to a successful conclusion. This did much to ensure Malay support for the British anti-terrorist campaign which had successfully broken the back of communist resistance by the mid-1950s (Cloake, 1985).

A strong case can be put that the British did not win the Emergency so much as the MCP lost it. Crucially, the communist base of support was confined to the Chinese community, which made up less than 40 per cent of the total population, allowing the government to concentrate its counter-guerilla efforts on that one section of Malayan society. In addition, given Malaya's geographical position, the MCP could not count on the sort of outside material aid, supply of weapons and logistical support that China, for example, was providing to Vietnam's communist guerillas. The colonial government's tight control of Singapore meant that only the narrow south Thai border provided a land route to the outside world and a sanctuary for rest and recreation. By the early 1950s, communist guerillas were outnumbered 50 to one by British servicemen, Malay police and colonial troops and the cost of the Emergency was running at £1 million a week. The British were also able to take full advantage of their position as a long-established colonial power to redress sectional Malayan grievances by introducing social, economic and political reforms. After the first federal election was held in July 1955 they could also negotiate independence with a locally elected Kuala Lumpur government of which they approved, thus undercutting the appeal of the MCP. Finally, the British were fortunate because of the prosperity generated by the

Korean War, the price of natural rubber on the international market during the 1950s being the best for any decade since the 'boom years' of the First World War. This prosperity made the expensive resettlement of Chinese squatters possible and financed Templer's 'hearts and minds' strategy. Without the Korean War boom, and the general economic buoyancy of the period, there is little doubt that the colonial government's task would have been that much more difficult (Stubbs, 1974).

The end of French colonial rule in Indochina in 1954 had left the British isolated as the only significant colonial power in South East Asia, if we discount Portuguese East Timor and Dutch New Guinea (Irian Jaya). The changing international environment (America's insistence on the abolition of colonialism) also urged flexibility towards Malaya's constitutional development and partnership with popular nationalist movements. Before 1955 Malaya had no experience of electoral politics, except at a local level, and the British were reluctant to go further towards self-government until there was more evidence of political cooperation between the three main ethnic communities. Since 1952, however, the two main middle-of-the road communal parties, UMNO, led by Tunku Abdul Rahman, Dato Onn's successor as President, and the Malayan Chinese Association (MCA), had been in alliance. The British reasoned that this was the best multiracial movement they were likely to get. In 1953 the two parties became officially known as the UMNO–MCA Alliance and went from strength to strength. After the 1955 election gave the Alliance Party, now joined by the Malayan Indian Congress (MIC), all but one of the 52 elected seats in the Legislative Council, Lennox-Boyd agreed to negotiations about self-government. At the Baling peace talks, held not far from the border with Thailand in December 1955, Abdul Rahman confronted a communist delegation led by Chin Peng who were prepared to lay down their arms. They left empty-handed because the Alliance leader stubbornly refused to recognize the MCP as a legitimate political party that should be allowed to contest future elections. Following a constitutional conference in London in early 1956, the date for independence (or *Merdeka*) of the Federation of Malaya was fixed for 31 August 1957.

This handover was an exception in that most of British decolonization in Asia was completed by the late 1940s. Malaya did not become independent until the same year as Ghana (former Gold Coast) and a year after the Sudan. Under Abdul Rahman as Premier, British armed forces stayed on in Malaya to deal with the dying embers of the communist insurrection, confined to a few skirmishes along the Thai border (the MCP leader, Chin Peng, did not emerge from the jungles of northern Malaya until 1989). The Tunku, as the anglophile prime minister was widely known, remained in office until 1970 and kept Malaysia aligned with the Commonwealth in defence terms but from the 1960s her investment and trading patterns increasingly 'looked east' – towards Japan. These economic links proved far more significant than those with Australia or New Zealand but in 1970 65 per cent of all foreign capital in Malaysia was still British.

Singapore and Federation

The post-1948 Emergency had created a colonial environment on the island of Singapore at the tip of Malaya, with its large Chinese population, hostile to radical left-wing politics. Emergency Regulations prohibited all political parties and other organisations from holding public meetings except during election time. In a relentless effort to stamp out trade union involvement in militant politics, the colonial police force meticulously screened all union leaders and ruthlessly removed any who had previous connections with the Singapore Federation of Trade Unions (SFTU) or harboured left-wing views. The SFTU, controlled by hardcore Chinese communists, constituted the mass base of the communist movement in Singapore but even so could not withstand British repression. Under these circumstances, militant political and labour leaders went into temporary hibernation, and the political arena was left to others more acceptable to the British colonial power. This meant a reliable business and commercial elite became strongly entrenched within the island's newly representative institutions. Active political life was largely confined to a wealthy conservative minority represented by the Progressive Party. Suppression of dissent in Singapore effectively deradicalized public debate, containing Chinese noncollaboration politics until the removal of the lid that the Emergency had imposed. From 1948 until 1953 a policy of political concessions together with swift coercion succeeded in preserving British rule (Chew and Lee, 1996).

The emergence in 1954 of more popular parties, the Labour Front and the People's Action Party (PAP), together with the widening of the electorate in 1955, removed the British bulwark against more radical movements. The new parties were soon competing in militancy and radicalism, making a satisfactory compromise more difficult for the British who were determined to keep full use of Singapore as a military and naval base and to have ultimate control over the external defence and internal security of the island. Constitutional talks broke down over this in 1956 but a new round of negotiations in 1957 produced agreement under which defence and foreign affairs were reserved to the British but Singapore was to have its own prime minister, cabinet and Malayan-born head of state appointed by the Queen. Singapore achieved internal self-government in 1959 (separately from the regional design of a Greater Malaysia that would play a key strategic and economic role in the British Commonwealth) but did not become an independent state until 1963 and then only as part of the Federation of Malaysia.

Authoritarian paternalist Lee Kuan Yew, leader of the PAP, began his long period of rule as prime minister of Singapore, winning every election until his retirement in 1990, the island's 2.5 million population enjoying the highest standard of living in the region (with the exception of oil-rich Brunei). In September 1963, at his suggestion, Singapore and Malaya agreed to a merger subject to the inclusion of Sarawak and the rest of the former British North Borneo (Sabah) in a new 'Malaysian' Federation (only Brunei chose to remain outside). The period of 'konfrontasi' (confrontation) between Malaysia and Indonesia (1963–66) has been interpreted either as the latter's President Sukarno seeking an external enemy to consolidate a failing regime or as deliberately provoked by Kuala Lumpur to facilitate the incorporation of Sarawak and Sabah into Malaysia and to bring Sukarno down. Commonwealth troops, British, Australian, New Zealand, and Malaysian, were hastily assembled into an effective defence force which deterred Sukarno from further provocation on the borders of Kalimantan (former Dutch Borneo). In 1965 Indonesia's ruler was sidelined by General Suharto's military coup and Singapore opted to withdraw from the Federation and resume its independence after 9 August as a republic within the Commonwealth. Brunei, the last British possession in the area, only became fully independent in February 1984 but remained within the Commonwealth (Keay, 1997).

Conclusions

Dutch, French and British experiences of armed resistance against nationalist or communist movements in post-1945 South East Asia, and the varieties of international, metropolitan and colonial reactions, have few characteristics in common. What is perhaps significant are less the parallels, such as French and Dutch intransigence, than that 'recolonization' was attempted at all, given the pious assurances of freedom for colonial peoples enshrined in the 1941 Atlantic Charter and the 1945 United Nations Charter. Postwar French politicians were convinced that France without its colonial empire would no longer be invited to the conference table as a world power. Vicious colonial wars in Indochina and Algeria were the terrible price paid to maintain France's international role. The real task confronting returning European colonial powers following the Japanese surrender in South East Asia – how to reach political accommodation with the leaders of nationalist resistance to imperial rule without endangering future trading relations – was one of which France and the Netherlands showed only an imperfect grasp, whereas Britain's more pragmatic imperial outlook was qualitatively different.

It seems remarkable, in retrospect, that France and the Netherlands, their prestige weakened by external defeat at the hands of the Japanese and internal occupation by the Germans, not only deluded themselves that they would be welcomed in former Indochina and the NEI but had the self-confidence to return. Even those French and Dutch officials aware of the rise of Asian nationalism, encouraged to some extent by the occupying Japanese, saw anti-colonialism as merely the work of a few isolated trouble makers. The arrogant Dutch effort to restore their rule, based on the conviction that they were still much loved by their colonial subjects, has been called one of the major pieces of self-deception in the annals of empire; a dubious accolade equalled only by the French campaign to recover Indochina. In Malaya, the British also had no intention of restoring anyone to power except themselves after 1945, but it does not follow that their continuing occupancy corresponded to the return of the French and the Dutch. Guerilla warfare both retarded the prospects of British withdrawal and constrained the development of an anti-colonial Malay nationalist politics. In the context of the Cold War, after 1948 the British could justify their imperial presence as necessary until the communists had been defeated and safe passage guaranteed to a united, independent and democratic Malayan nation. The colonial state was a pivotal force in postwar Malaya and although multiracial experiments such as Union were frustrated, they left an enduring legacy for the politics of independent Malaya (Harper, 1999).

4

SOUTH ASIA, THE MIDDLE EAST AND THE MEDITERRANEAN: BRITISH RETREAT FROM EMPIRE

The effects of post-1945 economic weakness on Britain's ability to sustain Europe's largest colonial empire was a necessary, if never a sufficient, condition for decolonization. Maintaining a costly imperial presence in the vast Indian empire was also no longer balanced by the commerical and strategic benefits. Britain had little left to lose and much, it was hoped, to gain by an amicable transfer of power. American and Russian hostility to British imperialism was another significant postwar factor. This chapter looks at British withdrawal or removal from overseas possessions, mandates or occupied territories in South Asia (India, Burma, Ceylon), the Middle East (Palestine, Egypt, Aden and the Gulf States) and the Mediterranean (Cyprus, Malta and Gibraltar), whose ultimate goal was intended to be self-government within the British Commonwealth. As with India and Ceylon, the object of British policy was to transfer power on terms that would preserve a special link with the British imperial system and encourage commercial cooperation. Burma (now Myanmar) is treated here as part of the South Asia/Indian subcontinent because that was how the British viewed it, and Burma's fate was also tied up with the British departure from India.

SOUTH ASIA

British India: The Case for Departure

India was the prototype for the evolution of the rest of the British Empire, as Canada had been for the white colonies of settlement. Cautious British attempts to answer the aspirations of Indian nationalism can be charted from the 'Montagu-Chelmsford' reforms (1919), through to the Simon Commission (1927–29), and then the Government of India Act (1935). The end of British rule was accelerated by the Second World War which was crucial in determining both the timing of departure and in making it essential to resolve the imperial crisis outstanding from the late 1930s in months rather than years. During the war in Asia, India's vast subcontinent with its 300 million Hindus, 90 million Muslims and six million Sikhs had become a vital imperial source of men, money and war materials. The Indian Army expanded in size from just over 205,000 in October 1939 to over 2,251,000 in July 1945 and, after the Japanese surrender, was vital for maintaining order in Lord Louis Mountbatten's extensive South East Asia Command (SEAC).

Once the emergency of world war ended, longer-term imperial trends reasserted themselves. Cost-effectiveness suggested to Labour politicians in the British metropolis that control of a reluctant Indian empire far outweighed the commercial benefits. India's economy had ceased to balance metropolitan trading books with other parts of the world or to provide a protected market for British goods. Imperial protection and patronage were no longer necessary for British businesses, some of which were already selling out to Indian buyers. 'The general conclusion is that on the whole Great Britain should not lose, but on the contrary, may gain in prestige and even in power, by handing over to Indians', claimed Viceroy Lord Wavell in 1946 (Brown, 1985: 310). An important proviso was that a friendly and united India became a member of the British Commonwealth and arrangements were made for maintaining defence links.

The real breakdown between the Indian National Congress, the Hindu-dominated freedom movement led by Mahatma Gandhi and Jawaharlal Nehru, and the British government occurred early in 1942 with the Cripps cabinet mission. Sir Stafford Cripps, Leader of the House of Commons, had arrived in New Delhi to offer India full dominion status after the end of hostilities, or the chance to secede from the Commonwealth and go for total independence, with the proviso that no part of India could be forced to join the new state. As the Japanese swept over Malaya and into Burma, the Cripps offer was the point at which British departure from India after the war suddenly became inescapable – even arch Empire-loyalist Winston Churchill, who did little to support Cripps, recognized that there could be no retraction of the offer of independence. Yet the gimlet-eyed Cripps failed to get Congress to support the allied war effort in return, even with the Japanese bombing Calcutta. Meanwhile, the Muslim League's austere but formidable leader, Mohammed Ali Jinnah, did not oppose the British military campaign (a disproportionate 30 per cent of the Indian Army was Muslim) and Cripps dangled before him, not entirely seriously, the divisive offer of a Pakistan state.

A separate Muslim state was not predetermined, only the almost total solidarity of Indian-Muslim politics for the first time behind the League, under Jinnah's autocratic leadership, made it possible. After their rejection of the Cripps offer, the Congress leadership, with its majority Hindu support, decided to embark on August 1942's abortive 'Quit India' campaign – not because they felt the country was on the brink of a nationalist uprising or even non-violent resistance but because this action brought them together as a united movement, even if it soon slipped out of their control. Yet the British were *not* pushed physically out of India by the strength of this mass, nationalist movement, despite exaggerated claims made for Gandhi's final, most famous but 'un-Gandhian' all-India campaign. The result was often violent, extremely patchy and followed no overall plan, allowing the British to quickly regain control of storm-centres like Bihar, eastern Uttar Pradesh and Bombay. Within a year of the 1942 eruptions, Leo Amery, Secretary of State for India, could write, 'it looks as if India had never been so quiet politically as it is at this moment' (Brown, 1985: 314). Ruthless suppression and imprisonment of Congress leaders secured the Raj quite comfortably until the end of the war but the British had received a timely warning of what awaited them from any future well-coordinated Congress opposition to imperial rule.

After the war, the loyalty of Indian police and troops came to be seriously doubted, there were police strikes and mutinies in the Indian navy, while SEAC's use of Indian soldiers against Indonesian and South Vietnamese nationalists from 1945–46 became increasingly unpopular. The Indian Civil Service was also badly understaffed and in places incompetent, as the horrors of the 1943 Bengal rice famine seem to demonstrate. By 1945, the rift between the Muslim League and Congress seemed irreparable, as India slid towards civil war. 'Our time in India is limited and our power to control events almost gone. We have only prestige and previous momentum to trade on and they will not last long', commented a pessimistic Wavell in October 1946 (French, 1998: 245). The Raj was losing international legitimacy, just as its prestige and authority within India were draining away. The British public also had other priorities after 1945, a war-weary and bankrupt imperial power whose chief aim was to somehow finance a new welfare state had little enthusiasm for sending troops and money to hold, against its will, an Indian empire of doubtful value.

In March 1946 a second Cripps delegation arrived in New Delhi, eventually putting forward an ingenious tiered and federal-union plan for Indian independence within the framework of dominion status. This plan was scuppered by Nehru and Gandhi, then rejected by both Congress and the Muslim League, and with it the last opportunity to preserve the unity of India. Even so, by late 1946 the Attlee Labour government recognized that the Indian masses, international opinion, and their own voters would not stand for a reassertion of the Raj. Aneurin Bevan, the conscience of the Labour Left, pointed out that rather than a scuttle:

> withdrawal from India need not appear to be forced upon us by our weakness, nor to be the first stage in the dissolution of the Empire. On the contrary, this action must be shown to be the logical conclusion, which we welcomed, of the policy followed by successive governments for many years. There was ... no occasion to excuse our withdrawal. We should rather claim credit for taking these initiatives. (Roberts, 1995: 78)

For reasons both of national prestige and party political advantage, therefore, Labour was determined to present the surrender of India as a triumph for British statesmanship, although from the right-wing Tory point of view it was a national humiliation. Thus nationalist, international, and metropolitan pressures combined to make independence and partition take place, both to avert Muslim–Hindu civil war and also because of Britain's generally weak position in the postwar world.

Prime Minister Clement Attlee removed Wavell, whose political grasp he doubted, and made the King's overweening cousin, now Viscount Mountbatten, the 20th and last British Viceroy of India – sworn in on 24 March 1947 –

because he had plausibility and charisma, plus royal connections, which Wavell lacked. The new Viceroy's staff team
was headed by Lord Hastings Ismay, who declared that
their appointment was 'like being put in charge of a ship
in mid-ocean with fire on deck and ammunition in the
hold' (Campbell-Johnson, 1997: 35). On 6 July, Sir Cyril
Radcliffe, a secretive barrister who had never even visited
India, was appointed to head a boundary commission
charged in just five weeks with not so much the partition
of the whole of Britain's Indian Empire as the partition of
two of its 11 provinces: Punjab and Bengal, the twin
pillars on which the British Raj rested. The problem
facing Radcliffe can be seen in that three communities
made up the Punjab in India's north west: Muslims
(50 per cent), Hindus (35 per cent), Sikhs and others
(15 per cent).

Division along religious or communal lines had come
about because of rising Muslim political awareness and
the inability of the Congress party, led by Gandhi and
Nehru, to assure Muslims that they too would enjoy a
stake in the emerging India. Following the Muslim League's great setback in the 1937 elections to the provincial
legislatures and the victorious Congress refusal to include
Leaguers in new provincial ministries, Jinnah ultimately
decided that, once separate electorates had been opposed
as divisive by Congress, the only option was a separate
Pakistan. On 9 August 1946, a year before partition, 5000
people were killed in communal riots in Calcutta, Bengal,
during a Direct Action day called by the Muslim League. By
March 1947, the killing had spread to the Punjab, fanned
by the demands of Sikhs, who were the dominant landowners, for a state of their own (Khalistan). So the
bloodshed unleashed after the failure of Hindu and Muslim leaders to compromise – and by British impatience to
reach a constitutional settlement for a transfer of power –
was already well under way before Mountbatten arrived in
India as the last viceroy.

The Partition of India

Mountbatten, flamboyant yet pragmatic, arrived to oversee a final attempt to reconcile Hindu, Sikh and Muslim, declaring that he and the other leaders were present to transfer power to nearly one fifth of the human race. By 3 June 1947 all parties agreed that partition was now the only option. Nehru had already declared in a speech made on 20 April: 'The Muslim League can have Pakistan, if they wish to have it, but on condition that they do not take away other parts of India which do not wish to join Pakistan' (Pandey, 1969: 195). This meant letting the people of the six 'Pakistan provinces' – Assam, Sind, Baluchistan, North West Frontier Province, Punjab, Bengal – decide for themselves whether they wanted to join the existing Constituent Assembly of the Hindu provinces (which would mean joining the Indian union) or to form one, two or three independent Pakistan states; the non-Muslims in the Punjab and Bengal having the additional option of demanding the partition of each province and then joining the Indian union with their Hindu-majority areas of West Bengal and East Punjab. Partition having been accepted as inevitable by the leaders of the three parties (Congress, the League and the Sikhs), Sir Cyril Radcliffe's pen sliced through the burning plains of Punjab and the lush paddy fields of Bengal. The result of this map-making exercise, which was not made public until 17 August 1947, two days after the celebration of independence in Delhi and Karachi, was a nightmare for the millions of Hindus, Muslims and Sikhs who discovered themselves on the wrong side of the line.

Revisionist historians have emphasized Mountbatten's distaste for Jinnah and partiality to Congress and Nehru, with the last of whom the Viceroy's wife, Edwina, was to conduct some kind of love affair. Yet the existence of powerful anecdotal evidence does not of itself prove a charge that the Viceroy interfered with the Radcliffe Commission findings by adjusting the Punjab border to allot a nominal Muslim-majority sub-district such as the Feroze-pur salient (in the heart of the Sikh community) to India. In the absence of documentary records which could prove or disprove the circumstantial evidence on which the revision-ists rely, the historical debate will continue (Roberts, 1995; French, 1998). In any case, reducing the decision-making of 1947 to an affair of personalities, in which Jinnah was excluded from the Nehru–Mountbatten–Edwina circle, provides interesting gossip but unreliable history. Person-alities aside, there was a growing convergence of British and Hindu nationalist interests in 1947. The British needed the Congress in order to ensure a speedy transfer of power on terms which would safeguard their future economic and strategic interests in the region. The Muslim League, on the other hand, was expendable with the end of the Second World War in which, unlike Congress, it did not oppose Britain. In these circumstances, any British viceroy would have regarded Jinnah as obstructive – failing to appreciate the relentless honesty with which he pursued a Muslim homeland – and shared a closer community of interests with Nehru, even without Mountbatten's personal rapport with the Congress leader and future ruler of India until his death in 1964.

The other contentious issue regarding partition emerged during April 1947 and relates to the setting of a time-limit for the transfer of power. Should June 1948 be adhered to, as laid down in Attlee's parliamentary statement of 20 Feb-ruary, or should independence be accelerated in view of the drift towards civil war? Mountbatten decided that power should be transferred much sooner and fixed on 15 August 1947 so that the period of communal and political uncer-tainty be cut to a minimum. The speed of the handover has been linked by some commentators with the communal massacres and mass migration that followed partition. By bringing forward the political deadline for the transfer by partition from 15 to five months, Mountbatten, it has been alleged, took unnecessary and unacceptable political risks, thereby inducing enforced resettlement of the Punjab's Muslim and Sikh communities by means of vast migrations in opposite directions, involving staggering casualty lists. Alternatively, 'far from being the cause of the bloodshed and political crisis in 1947, [Mountbatten] was never much more than a spectator, sent out by a desperate Attlee to oversee and attempt to manage the imperial collapse' (French, 1998: 289).

Mountbatten's press adviser, Alan Campbell-Johnson, argues that to assert that the Viceroy rushed or bludgeoned Nehru and Jinnah without giving them time to collect their thoughts is a latter-day myth. 'The prevailing atmosphere, on the contrary, was one in which the leaders, obsessed with the dangers of delay, were pressing Mountbatten for a quick decision'. On 9 April 1947 Jinnah said to Campbell-Johnson of the Viceroy, 'His Excellency should press on with his work, reach a decision quickly and avoid exhortations'. A fortnight later, Mountbatten reported at his staff meeting that Congress leader S.V. Patel was complaining: 'You won't govern yourself and you won't let us govern' (Campbell-Johnson, 1997: 36). Equally, Mountbatten soon realized what Wavell had been trying to impress on London for so long, that unless a final solution was rapidly achieved there would be reciprocal genocide and administrative breakdown. Hence the 3 June Plan for swift British withdrawal before the slaughter grew worse and transfer of power to two successor dominions – India and a separated Pakistan in the north-west and north-east of the subcontinent, the exact boundary being drawn by Radcliffe's independent boundary commission. To the last Jinnah obstinately stressed his objections to what he regarded as a 'moth-eaten' Pakistan 'hovering on either side of India like a pair of wings' (Brown, 1985: 327), having earlier yielded his demand for a 'corridor' across Indian territory to link the 'two-winged' Pakistan.

This division of the subcontinent into India and East and West Pakistan led to one of the largest ever migrations in world history, with an estimated 12.5 million people (about 3 per cent of undivided India) being displaced or uprooted. There was further upheaval in 1971 when Bengal's eastern wing broke away from Pakistan to form an independent Bangladesh. For the people of the two divided provinces, in particular the Punjab, the north-west province most affected in 1947 by violence and killings, partition meant fear, disruption, violence and a huge transfer of population. The exodus of some six million Muslims from east Punjab to the new West Pakistan and about four and a half million Sikhs and Hindus to the land between Amritsar and Delhi began overnight in an area the size of Wales. In Bengal about one and a half million Hindus left the eastern sector (Bangladesh), while thousands of Muslims from Bihar, Calcutta and elsewhere sought the 'safe' side of the border in east Bengal. The worst violence in Lahore and Delhi did not occur until the actual time of partition, when train loads of refugees crossed the frontier in each direction and were exposed to hostile gangs from other communities who descended on the passengers and engaged in mass slaughter. In the north Indian state of Uttar Pradesh nearly 4000 Muslims a day boarded the train to Pakistan until 1950, three years after independence. The migrants into and from Punjab and Bengal left behind at least half a million, perhaps a million, dead, and memories so horrific, so stained in blood that they still haunt survivors in the present generation and in 1997 prevented them from celebrating 50 years of independence plus, in India at least, almost unbroken parliamentary democracy.

The Princely States: Kashmir

There also remained the problem of integrating into India or Pakistan the over 500 princely states which in 1947 covered more than a third of the subcontinent and comprised some two fifths of its inhabitants, or 100 million people. Hyderabad resisted integration and was absorbed into India only after a 'police action'. Jammu and Kashmir's ruler, Maharajah Hari Singh, was a Hindu ruling over a predominantly Muslim kingdom above the Punjab who held out for an independent state. He made a 'stand-still agreement' in August 1947 then, in face of Afridi tribal incursions coming from a district close to the new Pakistani border, was forced to accede to India on or about 26 October, in exchange for Indian military help and subject to a plebiscite (indefinitely postponed) of the Kashmiri people. By allowing India to invade and subsequently to annex Kashmir, Mountbatten, who was by then Governor-General, supposedly reneged on his 3 June Plan of partitioning the subcontinent according to religion. Pakistan supported the tribal invaders and the situation was only stabilized by a UN-sponsored ceasefire in January 1949 and the setting up of a Line of Control border that has split Kashmir. Pakistanis believe to this day that Mountbatten, as India's Governor General, cheated them out of territory and, because of his pro-Congress and anti-Pakistan bias, sparked off the long-running Kashmir dispute. Within Indian-administered Jammu and Kashmir, militant groups have now fragmented into pro-Pakistani, those in favour of an independent secular or Islamic republic and, since 1995–96, militants fighting to stay with India (Hewitt, 1997). May 1999 onwards saw a fresh crisis over Kashmir and a serious risk of the conflict escalating, even if India and Pakistan, as nuclear powers, wanted to avoid serious confrontation.

Burma: Collapse of British Rule

Burma, with a total population at the 1931 census of 14.6 million, includes vast tracts of hill country with long land frontiers bordering on India and China. It is an exception in the self-congratulatory record of British decolonization as the only territory where the former colonial power failed to secure its most-favoured nation position, even in an informal capacity. In no part of British Asia was the rejection of British influence so complete and the contrast with Ceylon and Malaya is striking. The reasons for this lie in Burmese suspicion of British motives in the run up to independence. Burma and Malaya were both under Japanese military occupation from the spring of 1942 until August 1945. The British had to fight their way back into Burma during 1944–45, conversely they returned to Malaya in September 1945 without a fight when the Japanese surrendered. World demand for Malayan rubber and tin was high but Burma sold a large part of its rice, teak and oil to India and almost all of its commodities within the sterling area. Burma ceased to be a prime economic asset, that is, once India in 1947 ceased to be British. 'In terms of the harsh economic realities of the postwar world, Britain could afford to let events in Burma take their course' (Smith, 1988: 48).

So the British placed a much higher value on Malaya from the point of view of the British economy, and acted with far greater determination from 1945–46 to make sure that they held on to the Malay States (see Chapter 3). The British White Paper on Burma of May 1945, promising self-government within the Commonwealth, was accepted (if not by Churchill) as Britain's long-term objective for Burma, as it was for India and Ceylon. In the interim, recourse was made to the position established by the 1935 Burmese constitution. The return of the Japanese-tolerated Burma National Army, under its popular young leader Aung San, to the British side in 1944–45 as the Anti-Fascist Organisation (AFO) and its postwar establishment as the Anti-Fascist People's Freedom League (AFPFL), a political movement with strong nationalist appeal, made the White Paper seem inappropriate (Tarling, 1983). Lord Mountbatten, at this time head of the British Military Administration (BMA), was prepared to tolerate Aung San's party, thus conferring legitimacy on a particular Burmese leader. This partiality led to acrid disputes between Mountbatten and his colonial officials, men with long experience in prewar Burma, for whom Aung San was little better than a common criminal, on whose head they intended to fix a charge for the murder in 1942 of a village headman who had organised resistance against the Japanese (Allen, 1984).

Moutbatten tried to push Sir Reginald Dorman-Smith, the traditionalist Governor of Burma in Rangoon, faster and further down the road to self-determination than he was inclined to go. Dorman-Smith's dilemma was that it would take time to build up a coalition of 'moderate' elements strong enough to counter the growing power of the AFPFL and he soon lost the political initiative to Aung San. The Myochit Party attempted to oppose the popularity of the AFPFL but its leader U Saw's record of collaboration with the Japanese, and Mountbatten's refusal to let Dorman-Smith arrest Aung San on the above murder charge, explain why its following soon declined. Neither could the colonial government, in the closing months of 1945, rely on a massive presence of British or Indian troops, given the critical situation in the East Indies and Indochina, to outface or suppress any political movement which refused to accept British authority. The real casualty of the crisis was the governor himself. Premier Attlee lost patience with a vacillating Dorman-Smith and decided to replace him with Mountbatten's *protégé*, General Sir Hubert Rance. Yet London still failed to understand the intricacies of Burmese political maoeuvering and the need for some clear initiative on the part of the British. A police strike in Rangoon soon after Rance's inauguration as governor 'revealed the poverty of British imperialism in no uncertain terms' (Stockwell, 1992: 351). Colonial government was on the verge of breakdown and the cooperation of Aung San's party, the AFPFL, had become indispensable to British control. 'The Burmese and AFPFL.....are determined to have their freedom and have it quickly', reported the new governor (Darwin, 1988: 99).

Rance became convinced that he would have to bring Aung San onto his executive council, and that the White Paper delaying independence had to be scrapped. The setting of a deadline for withdrawal from India meant that Burma's importance to Britain because of its relationship to India, or even what became Malaysia, no longer carried any weight. Thereafter, British rule was rapidly wound up. An AFPFL delegation went to London in January 1947 and reached an agreement with the Attlee government on the election to a constituent assembly to draft the constitution for an independent Burma. The AFPFL won a resounding victory in the Burmese elections in April 1947 and the British looked forward to cordial relations with Aung San as leader of a new Burma within the Commonwealth. Regrettably, the Aung San–Attlee agreement on independence triggered a struggle for the spoils between a myriad of Burmese groups, notably the AFPFL itself, the Burma Army, the Burma Communist Party, the minority Karen National Union, and others besides. The rural Burmese did not wish to return to an economic system that tied them to the world market and liability for prewar debts to hated Indian bankers and usurers. Resentment against Indian migrant labour had also become increasingly bitter during the 1930s. AFPFL leaders dared not resist this xenophobic feeling, convinced that if they did so agrarian communism would win over the rural masses. It became clear in the spring of 1947 that Aung San would insist on Burma's becoming a republic, erasing from the constitution any reference to the British crown. In 1947, though not after 1949, a republican constitution was incompatible with membership of the British Commonwealth.

Shockingly, on 19 July 1947, Aung San and seven cabinet colleagues were assassinated, allegedly at the instance of U Saw, former leader of the Myochit Party, removing the one nationalist leader who might have had a chance of uniting Burma and maintaining close links with Britain. U Saw, a defector from the AFPFL, wanted a more revolutionary programme, perhaps expecting to blame the murders on the British and then to lead a general uprising. He was tried and executed. U Saw's links with renegade British personnel who had supplied him with arms made Aung San's surviving colleagues suspect British complicity at a higher level (Allen, 1991). The AFPFL remained in office under Aung San's successor, U Nu, and fashioned the constitution for an independent Burma but its commitment to both republicanism and centralism ensured that it would not remain within the Commonwealth. To British officials in Rangoon and Singapore, Commonwealth membership would have been a visible symbol of Burma's loyalty to the British connection and so her secession as a republic (like the Sudan in 1956) was a damaging blow to British prestige and power in South East Asia and an encouragement to anti-British nationalism everywhere. The new AFPFL government also met with the hostility of Burma's minorities, especially the Karens who had insisted from the first on their desire to be separate from the Burmans. Following independence in January 1948, U Nu was unable to impose his authority effectively beyond Rangoon. Civil war, communist uprisings, military rule (from 1958) and Karen, Kachin and Shan secessionism, engulfed the ill-fated Union of Burma.

The legendary Aung San's daughter, Nobel Prize winner Daw Aung San Suu Kyi, formerly married to an Oxford academic and held under house arrest for almost six years by the military, now leads the main opposition party, the National League for Democracy (NLD), in its campaign against General Ne Win and Burma's (Myanmar since 1989) State Law and Order Restoration Council (SLORC) military government. Ms Suu Kyi felt unable to visit her husband in England before he died in 1999, fearing that if she left the country the military would manufacture an excuse to exile her.

Ceylon: Progress to Dominion Status

The leaders of the Sinhalese majority in the Crown Colony of Ceylon (in 1972 renamed Sri Lanka) were fearful of Indian domination and so were anxious to maintain close ties with Britain but movement towards self-government was also influenced by large minorities of Tamils and Indian immigrants as well as other small communities who made up some 30 per cent of the population. The demand for rapid progress towards cabinet government and dominion status was voiced largely by the Sinhalese community, whose politicians were almost all extremely rich and conservative landowners hoping to exercise power through control of a parliamentary majority. Between the two world wars, the British Colonial Office had tried to discourage the growth of communally based political parties through a constitution linking ministerial responsibility to a committee system modelled on English local government practice. The rise of racial tensions and an unwillingness to operate this system, even before the outbreak of war, made constitutional reform necessary; pressures increased by the impact of war in Asia that made Ceylon, after the fall of Singapore to the Japanese, of vital strategic importance for British imperial defence. Dominated by Don Stephen Senanayake, the island's nationalist leadership insisted that Ceylon's contribution to the war effort should be rewarded by a pledge of dominion status. In 1942 Ceylon's assembly or State Council followed suit and in May 1943 London responded with an assurance of internal self-government but with external relations, defence and currency questions reserved to British control.

In October 1945 the report of Lord Soulbury's Ceylon Commission on Constitutional Reform endorsed these proposals but did not recommend dominion status on the grounds that Ceylon's defence and external affairs remained of vital imperial importance. The Soulbury report sought to preserve Britain's full control over Ceylon as a military and naval base, while delaying rapid constitutional change before normality was restored. In a crucial concession, both the control of Indian immigration and restrictions on the franchise were, however, to be treated as internal matters over which the British would have no authority. At the time the report was published, with political change in both India and Burma on the agenda, the new Labour government added a promise that Ceylon should proceed to full dominion status in a comparatively short interval. Senanayake, the leading Sinhalese politician, attempted to ease British concern about minority interests by creating a political party, the United National Party (UNP), that would appeal to both the Tamil and Muslim communities. At the September 1946 elections the UNP emerged as the strongest grouping in the Ceylon Parliament but without Tamil and Indian support failed to win an outright majority.

More serious for Senanayake and London was the success of the communists among the Sinhalese, especially in urban areas that had expanded during the war. The communists and their allies, who demanded complete independence outside the British Commonwealth, formed an opposition controlling over 40 of the 100 or so seats in the lower house. Social unrest and strikes followed between October 1946 and June 1947 as jobs were lost among transport workers, government and municipal employees and tea and rubber trade workers. Fear that Ceylon might fall behind Indian independence drove Senanayake to London to ask for an immediate promise of independence within the Commonwealth. The British cabinet gave way in order to bolster the forces of moderate nationalism. Ceylon was to become a model dominion provided that cooperation in defence and foreign affairs could be satisfactorily negotiated. Agreements that guaranteed Anglo-Ceylonese cooperation were concluded in November 1947 and loyal Ceylon smoothly became an independent dominion on 4 February 1948 (Darwin, 1988).

THE MIDDLE EAST

Palestine: Britain's Mandate

The British, anxious to avoid nationalist fervour spreading to their own mandates in the Middle East, forcibly intervened in Damascus on 30 May 1945 to encourage the subsequent ending (in 1946) of French rule in Syria and the Lebanon. In Britain's own former League of Nations mandate of Palestine, however, Labour politicians confronted the impossible task of satisfying both Jews, who desired to establish an independent homeland, and Arabs, who saw continuing Jewish immigration as inflicted on them in November 1917 by the Balfour Declaration promise to 'favour the establishment in Palestine of a national home for the Jewish people', provided it did not 'prejudice the civil and religious rights of the existing non-Jewish [viz. Arab] communities' resident there (Fraser, 1980: 18). British room for manoeuvre was limited because after 1945 Palestine became an international and not a purely imperial problem. For Britain to remain the dominant regional power, both Arab cooperation and American support were vital, without them British influence would decline, not only in the Middle East but also in the rest of the world. There was the additional complication that any local settlement would require the sanction of the United Nations, since Palestine was a mandate and not a colony. Partition was the least satisfactory option, as far as Foreign Secretary Ernest Bevin was concerned, because a divided Palestine would exacerbate the problem of Arab nationalism and destroy Britain's paramount Middle East position. It might also create a Jewish Palestine that could be absorbed, so Bevin feared, into the system of Soviet satellites.

Under Labour from 1945 to 1948, the Foreign Office and the Colonial Office shared responsibility for the British mandated territory of Palestine, the former for the international dimensions of the problem, the latter for the mandate's day-to-day administration. The Foreign Office under Bevin (solution: a binational state) feared for Britain's strategic position in the Arab world, the Colonial Office under Arthur Creech Jones (solution: partition) wanted to preserve some semblance of administrative control until an orderly withdrawal could be announced. The Foreign

Office took the lead in deciding the future in Palestine largely because of the international repercussions of any wrong step. Britain had to win support for any solution from the new American superpower and the United Nations. Former trade union leader Bevin, who was strongly pro-Arab and anti-Zionist, told the British Defence Committee meeting in January 1947 that Palestine, conveniently situated for control of the Middle East, was strategically necessary to retain Britain's position in the region.

Facing the Mediterranean but entrenched in the Middle East, Palestine was vital to British efforts to improve Anglo-Arab relations. If badly handled, it could also create a common Arab front against Britain and thus endanger British bases in Transjordan, Libya, the Sudan and Egypt. British oilfields in Iraq, the port of Haifa, and the friendship of Ibn Saud, the king of Saudi Arabia, had to be protected. Bevin also needed to retain Arab goodwill in face of a potential Russian threat to the Middle East, particularly after the Palestinian-Arab insurrection of 1936–39. On the other hand, American sympathy for the Zionist cause of restoring Palestine to the Jews (a return to Zion) and postwar British dependence on American friendship and economic support had to be taken into account. The British could not support an independent Jewish state without alienating the Arabs, upon whose goodwill they were dependent strategically and militarily. Nor could the British impose a settlement acceptable to the Arab countries without antagonizing President Harry Truman's pro-Jewish advisers in Washington.

The salient feature of 1946–47 was the persistent effort on the part of the British, especially Bevin, to support the Arabs and thereby sustain British power in the Middle East. British defence requirements in the region, including maintenance of essential oil supplies and communications, required the cooperation of the Arab states, who must not be allowed to gravitate towards Russia. 'As a case study in decolonization, Palestine demonstrates the convergence of ethical sympathy for the Arabs and political calculation of how best to maintain British influence' (Louis and Stookey, 1986: 15). When it became clear in mid-1946 that Britain's armed forces might be withdrawn from Egypt, the Chiefs of Staff attached emphatic importance to the retention of strategic rights in Palestine. For in the case of war, a semi-independent Egypt would hold the key British position in the Middle East, and it was necessary to hold Palestine as a screen for the defence of Egypt.

In 1945 British policy in Palestine was still based on the famous White Paper of 1939, the terms of which had been designed to allay Arab fears that the Palestinian mandate would be swamped by the Jewish immigration set in motion by Hitler's genocidal policies in Europe. No more than 75,000 Jews were to be admitted over the following five years and further Jewish immigration would require Arab acquiescence. An independent Palestine was also promised within ten years but the Jews would remain a minority and the new state would be predominantly Arab. The Zionist dream of a separate Jewish state was hence ruled out by the 1939 proclamation which was designed to appease Arab hostility to Jewish immigration. Churchill denounced this as a breach of faith with the Jews but made no change when in office. After 1945 Foreign Office objectives remained pro-Arab but, with the Nazi Holocaust creating thousands of European Jews desperate to go to Palestine, there were now other pressures – international, nationalist and domestic – on Britain's vacillating Labour government.

Three such were mainly responsible for the British decision to abrogate its mandate: American pressure and intervention on behalf of the Jewish cause; the undermining of British rule in Palestine itself by Jewish terrorist organizations; and the escalation of illegal Jewish immigration. The recommendation in April 1946 of an Anglo-American Committee of Enquiry set up by Bevin was that the Palestinian state should be neither Arab nor Jewish but have a large degree of autonomous self-rule. They also called for the immediate admission of 100,000 Jewish refugees or displaced persons (DPs). President Truman quickly and publicly accepted this last part of the report without first consulting Britain. What was intended to be American support for a Zionist–British compromise was taken by the British to be Presidential backing for partition and final evidence that the Americans, rather than offering practical help, could not even be relied upon to restrain the Zionists.

The British were also forced to retreat because their mandatory rule was undermined in Palestine itself by Zionist terrorism, more particularly by Irgun Zvai Leumi (IZL) and the Stern Gang. The most dramatic terrorist incident since the assassination in 1944 of British ambassador Lord Walter Moyne in Cairo, occurred when the IZL blew up the British military headquarters at the King David Hotel in Jerusalem on 22 July 1946 with some 92 British, Arab and Jewish dead. During the course of 1947, illegal immigration to Palestine became another rock against which the mandatory regime foundered, in particular Zionist propaganda made out of the embarrassing *Exodus* ferry affair, during which 5000 would-be immigrants she carried, survivors of the Nazi murder camps, ended up being sent forcibly back to Germany in British ships. 'The pressure of terrorist violence, the pressure of Arab relations, the pressures of the Anglo-American relationship, the pressure for economy and demobilisation, all drove the British remorselessly' (Darwin, 1988: 117).

Palestine: Britain Ends its Mandate

The deteriorating security position and the threat posed to the status quo by the escalation of illegal immigration led to great pressure from the administration in Palestine to terminate the mandate at the earliest date possible. In February 1947 Britain announced that she was referring the Palestinian question to the UN and in May the United Nations Special Committee On Palestine (UNSCOP) was set up with broad powers of investigation. The British decision to withdraw was triggered by the majority UNSCOP report drawn up in August which recommended partition into an Arab and a Jewish state, with the city of Jerusalem remaining under international trusteeship. As the mandatory power, it would fall to Britain to carry this plan through if it were approved by the UN General Assembly. Whatever else, Bevin was determined that Britain should neither carry out such a policy nor be implicated in it, because partition into separate states would obviously lead to strong Arab resistance.

The only answer was to resign the mandate and leave: a conclusion endorsed by the British Cabinet on 29 September 1947. The twin issues of security and illegal immigration were making British rule in Palestine untenable. In the aftermath of the transfer of power to India, Attlee was determined to liquidate Palestine as an economic and military liability, 'an act of abdication for which there was no imperial precedent' (Darwin, 1988: 119). The date of withdrawal was eventually fixed for the expiration of the mandate on 14–15 May 1948 but after September 1947 the influence of the British diminished considerably. On 29 November 1947 came the historic UN General Assembly resolution in favour of partition, acknowledging the legitimacy of a Jewish state. When the remaining British left, the Jews under Prime Minister David Ben Gurion declared independence as the state of Israel on 14 May 1948, followed next day by the outbreak of the first of a series of Arab–Israeli wars that were to redraw maps of the Middle East.

Unexpected Jewish military successes from 1948–49 further destabilized the politics of the Arab world but at least Britain escaped the Foreign Office nightmare of a general Arab campaign against her interests in the region. An earlier American suggestion (March 1948) of a UN Trusteeship for a unified Palestine instead of partition had as its only effect to quicken the efforts of the Jews to win land in the war. They needed to seize and hold more territory and thus force the issue of partition, lest the international community support some alternative plan. If they should hold the land, it would be difficult to avoid creating two states. The steady withdrawal of British troops created the way for new offensives and Eastern Bloc arms helped turn the tide. The Jews began scoring gains, so that the course of battle and not the UN promised to determine the fate of Palestine.

Truman abandoned the idea of a UN Trusteeship and recognized the new state of Israel, as did the Russians. There was no Arab unity: Egypt, Syria, Transjordan, Lebanon and Iraq, failed even to coordinate their battlefield strategies. The Israelis succeeded in expanding well beyond the territory originally reserved for a Jewish state under the UN partition plan but the Arabs of Palestine, who had lost their birthplace, were unable to establish an autonomous state of their own. Instead, the armistice agreements between Israel and the intervening Arab nations provided that Transjordan (renamed Jordan) and Egypt should divide the territories of Palestine that the Israelis had not conquered. About 700,000 Palestinian Arabs thus became displaced refugees in Jordan, Egypt (in the Gaza Strip), Syria and Lebanon. This left roughly 150,000 Arabs who remained behind in Israel. No Arab nation accepted this outcome as permanent, so Israel remained surrounded by hostile neighbours. Palestinian Arab refugees now took the place of the Jews as a people without a homeland and a major source of instability in the Middle East.

Egypt: The British Foothold

Since 1922, when the British protectorate officially ended, Egypt was nominally an independent state under a constitutional monarchy but in reality British troops remained in occupation until 1954, so important was the Suez Canal

87

regarded. The British residency shared power with the King and Egyptian nationalist leader Saad Zaghlul's party the Wafd, at least until the assumption of power by Gamal Abdel Nasser. Whenever there was a free election, the Wafd invariably won a sweeping victory. King Fuad, and later his playboy son Farouk, would then seek ways of ousting the detested Wafd from power and ruling without them. This might succeed for a time but the Wafd would always return because the King lacked political support or the British wanted the Wafd back in power to preserve the semblance of parliamentary democracy. When the Italians invaded Abyssinia (Ethiopia) and Libya, the Wafd returned to power and in 1936 signed a treaty with the British to protect them against Italian fascist ambitions in North Africa. British occupation was formally ended by the Anglo-Egyptian Treaty, although some 10,000 troops were withdrawn to the Suez Canal Zone which was to remain in British hands for another 20 years. On the outbreak of war with Germany, practically all the advantages won by the 1936 treaty were revoked when, once again, Egypt was occupied by a huge imperial army to fight the German Afrika Corps and the Suez Canal became a vital shipping lane for allied forces.

After the Second World War, a vast British military base, whose garrison now boasted some 80,000 men, was not withdrawn from the Canal Zone, owing to Cold War fears of Soviet interference in the Middle East. As well as its importance to imperial military strategy, more than two thirds of the traffic through the Canal came from Britain's merchant fleet, trading with Australasia, the Far East and the oil states of the Gulf. Utilizing a plank in the platform of the Wafd party, King Farouk and premier Nahas Pasha were determined to assert Egyptian rule over the Anglo-Egyptian condominium (otherwise British control) in the Sudan. In October 1951 the Wafd forced the issue and unwittingly committed political suicide by abrogating the 1936 treaty and proclaiming Farouk the King of Egypt *and* the Sudan. The British took the view that only the Sudanese themselves could choose whether or not to join Egypt or become independent. Despite Farouk's new nationalist credentials, he was unable to prevent mobilization of the militant Muslim Brotherhood, devoted to driving the British out of Egypt and establishing an Islamic state.

In January 1952, determined to disarm the vexatious auxiliary police, British tanks attacked a police barracks, killing 41 Egyptians, the next day anti-foreign riots swept Cairo and elsewhere, including the burning of the famous Shepheard's Hotel. The incompetent and corrupt Wafd government, unable to maintain order, now saw the initiative for anti-colonial struggle pass out of its hands. The Egyptian army mutinied, following exposure of profiteering by government officials. In a bloodless coup, a revolutionary council of young Free Officers led by General Mohammed Neguib and Nasser overthrew King Farouk, banishing him into exile, where he became well known as a French Riviera playboy. Nasser bestrode the Arab world from 1954, when he displaced Neguib to become prime minister, until his death in 1970, and also did much to rid it of the relics of British domination. Unusual as an anti-colonial leader with whom London could not strike a bargain, Nasser's portrait hung for years on almost every poor Arab wall in the Gulf states, along with that of the local ruler (Balfour-Paul, 1991).

The new Egyptian military regime of relatively junior officers came to terms with Britain over the Sudan, which in 1956 became independent, in exchange for which the British agreed to leave the Canal Zone. The Suez Agreement of October 1954 guaranteed the withdrawal of all British bases from the Suez Canal area, hitherto the centrepiece of British military power in the Middle East, within a period of 20 months. The last British troops had only just left before, on 26 July 1956, President Nasser 'nationalized' the Suez Canal, effectively concluding the 74-year period of Egyptian subjection to Britain. America had refused to assist Egypt's revolution by financing the building of a hydroelectric dam on the River Nile, leading Nasser to seek revenue from a nationalized canal to pay interest on loans to build such a high dam. British Premier Anthony Eden was determined not to 'appease' Nasser, whom he likened to an Egyptian 'Mussolini' with pan-Arab ambitions, 'a Caesar from the Atlantic to the Gulf.... It is either him or us' (Louis and Robinson, 1994: 479).

Britain's subsequent invasion of the Canal Zone early in November 1956, in collusion with France and Israel but without American backing, was the only serious intrusion of colonial politics into British life. For the Conservative government was compelled to ration petrol to British motorists until the Egyptians had cleared war debris from the canal and reopened the shipping lines to the oil refineries. President Eisenhower forced Britain and France to end their military invasion by threatening economic sanctions, including the blocking of Britain's drawing rights on the International Monetary Fund (IMF). Macmillan, Britain's Chancellor of the Exchequer, feared a 'run on sterling' and withdrew his previous support from the prime minister. Eden, having deceived parliament that British forces had been sent from Cyprus to prevent an Arab–Israeli war, now resigned from office on the pretext of illness (Kyle, 1991).

In retrospect, the Anglo-French invasion of Egypt was a disastrous miscalculation that weakened both of the leading European colonial powers, strengthened the influence of the two superpowers in Africa and made the Egyptian nationalists in power in Cairo into heroes throughout much of the Arab and colonial world. Yet the humiliation of Suez did not lead to a sudden revulsion against colonial rule among British policy makers, since arrangements for the independence of the Gold Coast and Malaya in 1957 were well in hand *before* Egypt was invaded. The greatest threat Nasser represented to European imperialism was his potential undermining of the weak, Western-oriented Arab elites of the Middle East – Libya, Saudi Arabia, Iraq, Jordan and Lebanon – as well as the sheikdoms of the Gulf to which we now turn.

Aden and the Gulf States

In the years after Suez, Britain's Middle Eastern presence was reduced to the Aden Protectorate on the southern fringe of the Arabian peninsula and the Crown Colony of Aden (now in south Yemen), guarding the entrance to the Red Sea, plus the administered, treaty and protected territories of the Gulf (Kuwait, Muscat and Oman, Bahrain, Qatar, Trucial Sheikdoms). The loss of Suez rapidly promoted Aden into Britain's principal military centre in the Middle East and the number of British servicemen stationed there quadrupled from 1957 to 1960. Britain's informal empire in the Middle East also suffered from the wider effects of the Suez crisis. Nasser and Arab unity had become almost synonymous after 1956, so to the north the Syrian Ba'ath Socialist Party turned to him as the man most likely to achieve Arab unity and in February 1958 Egypt and Syria joined in a single centralized state, the United Arab Republic. On 14 July that year King Feisal of Iraq and British ally Nuri as-Said were murdered, the monarchy was overthrown and a republic set up under General 'Abd al-Karim Kassem.

Fear that the regimes of President Chamoun of Lebanon and young King Hussein of Jordan might also topple led to American and British troops being landed in answer to their respective appeals for help. Worried about Soviet influence in the region, President Eisenhower appeared before the UN General Assembly on 13 August 1958 to make a plea for Arab isolationism and non-alignment; subsequently Kassem's Iraqi regime joined neither the Soviet bloc nor the Nasser-dominated Arab League. Britain's attempt in the 1960s to head off Egyptian penetration in South West Arabia through the Yemen, on the other hand, seemed to attract little American enthusiasm. Relations with oil-rich Kuwait were more successful (by 1960 Kuwait was supplying 37.6 per cent of Britain's total crude oil import) and on 19 June 1961 complete independence was smoothly delivered. Britain's continuing close relationship with Kuwait was soon put to the test when General Kassem declared that the new oil-rich state was an 'integral part' of Iraq. Troops were speedily landed from a British commando carrier sent via Aden, without UN approval, and the danger from Iraq was averted. Nearly 30 years later, Iraq military dictator Saddam Hussein's troops invaded Kuwait for real in late 1990, provoking American-led UN forces to launch the high-tech Gulf War (1990–91) against poorly-trained Iraqi forces who were killed in vast numbers.

Peace and stability in the oil-producing states of Arabia and the Gulf region were seen as vital for the West but within Aden itself the growth of Nasser-inspired Arab nationalism, encouraged by labour union strikes and election boycotts, was beginning to present problems for its British colonial administrators. When Lord Lloyd, Under-Secretary of State for the Colonies, visited Aden in May 1956, he was pressed to speed up progress towards self-government but the port's growing strategic and commercial importance was such that the British were not yet inclined to leave. In 1958 the officially-nominated majority in the Legislative Council was abolished and Arabic was permitted as an alternative to English. A federation of the small states or emirates under the nominal protection of the British in the Aden Protectorate was also suggested, the better to resist incursions from the Yemen, but this met opposition to archaic feudal rule from various nationalist factions.

Aden itself was nothing like as prosperous as Kuwait, while the emirates of the Protectorate and the sheikdoms of the Gulf were underdeveloped and lacking in resources. On 11 February 1959 the Western States of the Aden Protectorate signed a treaty of federation, each state to elect six members to a Federal Council, the British promising protection and financial aid. Matters became more complicated in September 1962 when civil war broke out in the Yemen and Egyptian troops were sent in by Nasser to assist the Marxist 'revolutionary' government. Then in January 1963 Britain attached Aden Colony to the federated tribal states of the Western Protectorate, hoping to prevent further disruption by Yemeni nationalists; a move unwelcome among those in the port who disliked being linked with the desperate poverty of the interior. The Eastern Protectorate of Hadhramut states, twice as large as the Western region, remained outside the new Federation of South Arabia. Competing Adeni nationalist parties like the fundamentalist Front for the Liberation of South Yemen (FLOSY) and the Marxist National Liberation Front (NLF) became the targets of Egyptian propaganda and sponsorship, exacerbating a terrorist campaign which culminated in an attempt to assassinate High Commissioner (Governor) Sir Kennedy Trevaskis at Khormaksar airfield on 10 December 1963. In the interior, the new federal state infringed Arab tribal autonomy, leading to a violent insurrection in 1963–64. Sir Richard Turnbull, the next High Commissioner, who had been instrumental in putting down the Mau Mau revolt in Kenya, suspended Aden's constitution in August 1965 and reverted to direct rule to halt the terrorist campaign but this met with the disapproval of a UN Mission.

The British Defence White Paper of 1965 indicated that both Aden and Singapore would be retained to maintain the Labour government's 'imperial position east of Suez' at a cost of £317 million annually – or 15 per cent of Britain's total defence budget. Yet Aden was to be abandoned when the South Arabian Federation became independent, according to Defence Minister Dennis Healey's 1966 White Paper, in order to hold down spending on the 'overstretch' of Britain's defence capabilities. The UN Colonial Committee passed a resolution in June 1966, meanwhile, declaring that the rather shaky federal government was unrepresentative. Rioting in Aden grew worse in the spring and summer of 1967, making Britain's embarrassed tenure of the exposed port and base increasingly fragile and a considerable drain on manpower. In May Sir Humphrey Trevelyan, a diplomat experienced in Arab affairs, had been called out of retirement to become the colony's last High Commissioner. After several months of notably brutal repression of the insurgent population, during which the NLF came out on top as a contender for power, and despite the unauthorised retaking of the central Crater district of Aden by the First Battalion of the Argyll and Sutherland Highlanders, Trevelyan announced recognition of 'the [NLF] nationalist forces as representatives of the people' (Williams, 1968: 140). From the British point of view, a group more fanatical but also more popular than the former federal government had emerged just in time for a dignified but abrupt withdrawal on 29 November 1967.

When the decision to leave Aden was made public, the Foreign Office hastened to reassure the sheikdoms of the Gulf that Britain intended to maintain her presence there, despite having removed the strategic pivot on which their defence had hitherto rested (as British protection from Iraq given to Kuwait in 1961 had demonstrated). The Labour government's long-deferred devaluation of sterling on 18 November 1967 was soon followed by defence spending cuts and a hotly-contested British cabinet decision in January 1968 to withdraw militarily from 'east of Suez' by the end of 1971, despite the rulers of Malaysia, Singapore and the Gulf region begging for a postponement of British departure. The British cabinet had already agreed to postpone the pull-out by nine months under American pressure. Foreign Secretary George Brown reported a 'disturbing and distasteful discussion' in January with Dean Rusk, US Secretary of State, at which Rusk had accused the Labour government of 'opting out of our world responsibilities' and 'implied that it was the end of co-operation'. 'For God's sake act like Britain!' Rusk had thundered (PRO).

The last region in which Britain had retained a world power status, the Indian Ocean, was to be given up and with it the renunciation of that status. Further east, the reconciliation of Malaysia and Indonesia in 1966 had already ended the danger of Malaysia and Singapore being overrun and absorbed into a Greater Indonesia. The argument for a British military presence was also weakened in the Gulf region, where the 1960s had seen a rapid growth in the wealth and power of Iran and Saudi Arabia, the two main Gulf states. Britain's treaty obligation to defend the tiny Gulf sheikdoms (Bahrain, Qatar, Abu Dabi, Sharjah) now came to seem an encumbrance out of all proportion to its benefits, whereas cultivation of the main Arab states was increasingly in Britain's long-term interests. Partial withdrawal from military and colonial responsibilities east of Suez had been transformed into a steady retreat from both the burdens and privileges of imperial power. The 1968 Labour cabinet decision hammered the final nail into the coffin of Britain's Middle Eastern empire.

MEDITERRANEAN FORTRESS COLONIES

Cyprus

Cyprus, Malta and Gibraltar have been labelled as 'fortress colonies' in the Mediterranean because of their strategic and military value to the British Empire. Cyprus had been leased by the British from the Sultan of Turkey in 1878, then annexed to the British Empire in 1914 when war with Turkey broke out. In 1931 there was a Greek Cypriot uprising in favour of ENOSIS, or union with Greece (about 500 miles away): Government House was burnt down, martial law declared and 2000 were arrested.

In 1948 violence erupted again in clashes between communist and right-wing Greek Church groups on the island (Anderson, 1993). Meanwhile, with the retreat from Palestine in 1947–48 and then from the Suez Canal Zone after 1954, Cyprus had become the general headquarters for British land and air forces in the Middle East, an intelligence 'listening post' and military garrison of immense tactical and political importance for Britain and for NATO. From the British point of view, Cyprus had become too important to surrender, 'the fact that the British strategic stakes in both Egypt and Palestine were simultaneously under pressure meant that the imperial value of the island was rising rather than falling' (Holland, 1998: 15).

Some 80 per cent of the Cyprus population were Greek in language, culture, religion and politics; 20 per cent were Turkish. The island's Greek Orthodox Church was the most powerful social and political force and had agitated since the earliest years of British rule for ENOSIS. The presence of both Greek and Turkish communities in Cyprus and Greece's latent historical claims to the island made the future of Cyprus an international question, with the strategic considerations of British imperialism and NATO also holding centre stage through to independence. On the other hand, the colonial nature of the Cyprus emergency of the 1950s was equally important because Cyprus was a colonial possession within the British Empire, administered through the Colonial Office, and policed like other colonies where the British were confronted by armed guerilla insurrection, notably Palestine, Malaya and Kenya. It was regarded, however, as not a 'normal' colony because it cut across relations with Greece and Turkey (about 40 miles away), thereby giving the Foreign Office a stake, as also with Malaya.

On 28 July 1954, while debating new proposals to increase local autonomy, Colonial Office minister Henry Hopkinson made the notorious House of Commons statement that, owing to its 'particular circumstances', the island could 'never expect to be fully independent' (Porter and Stockwell, 1987: 322) and thereby invited the Greek premier to raise Cyprus as an issue at the UN. New constitutional proposals were rejected by the Greek Cypriots in this unhelpful atmosphere as 'something for Zulus' (Darwin, 1988: 215). During this climate of rising tension, with British Premier Anthony Eden under heavy international and domestic pressure, Archbishop Makarios III, the black-garbed and bearded Greek Orthodox patriarch who after 1950 had emerged as the leader of the Greek Cypriot community, authorized recourse to armed struggle by the National Organization of Cypriot Fighters (EOKA) led by Colonel George Grivas (alias Dighenis), a right-wing, royalist and staunchly anti-communist Greek Cypriot leader. On 1 April 1955 the terrorist campaign against British rule in Cyprus and for unification with Greece got under way, bombs went off in Nicosia and an attempt was made on the life of the governor, Sir Robert Armitage.

On 30 June 1955 Eden invited Greek and Turk representatives to a conference in London but little came of this and so Field Marshal Sir John Harding, who had served against the Mau Mau in Kenya, was sent to replace Armitage as Governor, arriving on 3 October. A state of emergency was not declared until 26 November 1955. For the next four years, the British were facing a terrorist enemy in EOKA which, while incapable of driving them out of Cyprus, threatened over time to erode the British public's willingness to support the military and financial costs of maintaining the imperial presence. British officials were also unprepared for the commitment to ENOSIS by violent means of youthful Greek Cypriots, even schoolchildren, particularly in the capital of Nicosia. Makarios' ability to arouse international sympathy, the highly effective Grivas-controlled EOKA guerilla terrorism, and the open support of Athens, made this a British colonial problem more intractable than any other in the late 1950s (Holland, 1985).

Despite the military strain and periodic atrocities of the EOKA campaign, which tied down some 25,000 British troops, at no point did London consider yielding to the Greek Cypriot demands for ENOSIS. America's President Eisenhower favoured the Anglo-Turkish view of the Cyprus problem, which raised the spectre of future partition of the island between Greek and Turkish Cypriots, but he also put pressure on Greece to honour its NATO commitments. At the close of February 1956, Governor Harding, Archbishop Makarios and Colonial Secretary Alan Lennox-Boyd met in Nicosia but negotiations collapsed, given British obstinacy over ENOSIS. On 9 March 1956 Makarios was arrested and exiled to the Seychelles. 'Black November' 1956 followed with 416 incidents and 216 British soldiers and civilians killed. Indian boundary commissioner Lord Cyril Radcliffe's long-awaited constitutional proposals for Cyprus were unveiled on 19 December 1956 and envisaged a local legislature with wide internal autonomy but with foreign affairs and defence reserved to British control (see the discussion of Malta below). Proposals drawn up by a British jurist were unlikely, at this stage, to persuade Greek Cypriot leaders to renounce their goal of ENOSIS. Makarios' release from detention to an Athens hotel, to encourage discussion during a truce in March 1957, prompted right-winger Lord Salisbury to resign from the Conservative government, 'the only resignation from the British Cabinet on a colonial issue during the "end of empire"' (Holland, 1998: 179).

Earlier in 1957, the British had captured important EOKA figures in Nicosia but Grivas once again avoided capture and the experienced General Joseph Kendrew had assumed responsibility for all anti-EOKA operations. Governor Harding was also replaced – by the new Conservative Prime Minister, Harold Macmillan – with the more liberal Sir Hugh Foot, who remained in Cyprus until independence. The ENOSIS struggle now widened into a communal conflict between Greek and Turkish Cypriots, the

Cyprus problem threatening to break up NATO's precarious solidarity in the eastern Mediterranean. The succeeding year, 1958, saw Turkish-Cypriot riots in Cyprus, followed in the summer by intercommunal rioting between Greek and Turkish Cypriots which left a hundred dead and starkly revealed the full extent of British dependence upon Turkish police. The communalization of Cypriot politics was henceforward to bedevil the future of the island. Macmillan had proposed a scheme in June for each community to have its own legislature and, after a further seven years of British rule, joint Greek and Turkish sovereignty. This was rejected by Turkey which would accept nothing less than partition. On 3 October 1958 two British women were shot by EOKA terrorists in Famagusta and the security forces retaliated by arresting local Greek Cypriots who were roughly treated, resulting in at least two deaths. If this represents the nadir of British rule, the following year was to see the opening of discussions about eventual withdrawal (Hitchens, 1984).

Makarios and Grivas were now outflanked by the wily Macmillan who recognized that the key to defeating ENOSIS lay in associating Greece and Turkey with the negotiations of Cyprus' future role. Macmillan's internationalizing strategy, subsequently modified, forced Makarios publicly to abandon ENOSIS or integration with Greece for separate independence on 22 September 1958. Only the 60-year-old Grivas remained intransigent, and in October and November he unleashed one last futile and bloody wave of terror. In January 1959 an independent Cyprus, ruling out both ENOSIS and partition, was discussed in Paris by the newly reconciled Greek and Turkish foreign ministers, followed by the Zurich agreement of 10 February 1959, which brought together their respective prime ministers. Later that month a formal conference of interested parties gathered at Lancaster House in London, the traditional British meeting place before the granting of independence. Cyprus, which seemed so much a part of the British Empire in 1954, became largely dispensable only a few years later owing to London's delayed adjustment, enforced by the 1956 Suez disaster, to changing strategic circumstances (among them the shift towards nuclear weapons after the 1957 defence review).

Under the new plan Cyprus would remain independent within the Commonwealth, jointly guaranteed by Greece and Turkey, but its constitution would allow the two communities almost complete autonomy. London agreed provided it secured a treaty that preserved British sovereignty over the military bases at Dhekilia and Akrotiri in perpetuity. Faced with this diplomatic *fait accompli* and the blunt warning that the alternative was partition, the Greek Cypriot leadership reluctantly acquiesced and Makarios added his signature not long after, returning to Cyprus to great acclaim on 1 March 1959. In accordance with the Zurich agreement, EOKA handed in its weapons on 13 March and Grivas left Cyprus the next day for Greece, having conducted four years of untiring guerilla warfare against the British. Sir Hugh Foot, the last British governor of Cyprus, left the island with little ceremony the following year and an independent Republic of Cyprus was declared under President Makarios from 16 August 1960.

Cyprus did not leave the news, however, because from Christmas 1963 to February 1964 hundreds were killed during clashes between Greek and Turkish Cypriots, following Makarios' provocative abolition of the 70:30 ratio in the island's civil service and town councils. A UN peacekeeping force replaced British troops at the end of March 1964, separating Greek from Turkish Cypriots for nearly ten years. Then, on 15 July 1974, an armed coup engineered by the military junta in Athens overthrew parliamentary rule and Archbishop Makarios. Turkey saw this ill-advised Greek seizure of power as threatening its own interests in Cyprus. Ignoring the UN Security Council, on 20 July 1974 Turkey mounted a police action which on 14 August turned into an invasion. The independence of a unitary Cyprus had lasted for only 14 years, despite all the promises made by Britain and the international community. In effect, Cyprus has been partitioned since 1974 with the Turkish Cypriots now occupying the entire northern third of the island. In 1983 the setting up of the Turkish Republic of Northern Cyprus was announced, constitutionally separate from the Greek south, but this was not internationally recognised.

Malta

Rapidly changing British attitudes towards Malta between 1956 and 1964 closely reflected Whitehall's changing estimate of its strategic value and sudden demotion in the 1962 Defence White Paper. The Maltese retained close cultural, sentimental and economic links with Britain, on whose naval spending they were overwhelmingly dependent. Internal self-government had been permitted since 1947 but the Nationalists, a Catholic clerical party, pressed in 1954 for full independence within the Commonwealth, reacting to an increased American military presence. The opposition Malta Labour Party (MLP), led by the flamboyant Dominic Mintoff, won the February 1955 election on a platform of 'integration' with the United Kingdom (rather like Jersey). A round table conference was convened in December which, rather surprisingly, recommended that Malta should be offered direct representation in the Westminster parliament (as French colonies were represented in Paris). The British government accepted this unprecedented proposal in March 1956 and it was endorsed, despite the hostility of the Catholic Church in Malta, by a local referendum. Subsequently, the MLP fell out with the British over the scale of economic aid that would be forthcoming and Mintoff's call for integration turned into a demand for outright independence. In 1959, after fruitless negotiations, the Maltese constitution was suspended, and direct British rule imposed.

In 1960 a British commission visited Malta to find some way out of the impasse, publishing a report in 1961 whose recommendations were quickly accepted by Iain Macleod, the Tory Colonial Secretary. The Maltese were offered wider local autonomy and encouraged to participate in defence and foreign affairs but these powers would be 'concurrent' with those of London and the British parliament would retain its right to legislate on behalf of the island. Both the main Maltese parties rejected the proposed new constitution but the Nationalist Party won the elections of February 1962 and took office with the promise of making certain constitutional amendments, while preserving British control of defence and external relations. Failure to agree, as before, on economic aid led the Nationalist premier, Borg Olivier, to demand full independence in August 1962 and London, convinced of Malta's declining strategic value, conceded rapid progress towards complete self-government. Malta became fully independent in September 1964 but Britain was allowed to station her forces there for another ten years in return for grants and loans of some £50 million over the same period, 'a redundant stronghold at a low rent' (Darwin, 1988: 280). Mintoff soon returned to dominate Maltese politics, using his long years in power for a sustained onslaught against the Church.

Gibraltar

Gibraltar, ceded in perpetuity to Britain under the Treaty of Utrecht (1713), is only two and a half square miles with a loyal population of around 26,800, mainly of Genoese stock, that retains a sense of separate British identity. Connections with the surrounding Spanish region have always been close, with commercial contact and intermarriage, but Britain's possession of the Rock was inevitably a sore point for patriotic Spaniards. In 1950 the concession of greater local autonomy and representation provoked a campaign of Spanish harassment at the frontier post, when Madrid's request for negotiations over the colony's status was rejected. On the eve of further constitutional changes in 1963, Gibraltar became an issue at the UN and further exchanges took place between Britain and Spain, the latter concerned that the greater the degree of local independence, the harder it would become to effect a simple territorial transfer. The British government responded to further Spanish pressure at the UN by holding a referendum in September 1967 allowing 12,762 registered voters to choose between association with either Britain or Spain: 12,182 voted of whom only 44 opted for Franco's Spain.

In May 1969 the Rock was declared no longer a colony but, as the City of Gibraltar, 'part of Her Majesty's dominions', thus circumventing a UN resolution calling for the end of Gibraltar's colonial status by October. A new constitution also emphasized British allegiance with the governor responsible for defence, external affairs and internal security. General Franco's government responded by closing the frontier with Spain (not reopened until 1985). By the 1970s Gibraltar had become of marginal importance as a naval base but was still an important fuelling station that required a large British subsidy to survive, because all direct links with Spain had been cut off after the referendum. In October 1980 Gibraltarians were granted the right to retain full British citizenship. Britain could not tolerate Gibraltar's involuntary transfer to Spanish rule, even in the disguised and unlikely form of self-determination, since that would amount to an undignified retreat. As the millennium approaches, only Gibraltar remains of British colonialism in the Mediterranean but clashes over smuggling, frontier controls and sovereignty can still present an intermittent problem. During 1997 tensions arose over the long-standing refusal by Spain to permit British and NATO military aircraft to cross Spanish air space on their approach to Gibraltar airport. A new diplomatic row between Britain and Spain in February 1999, prompted by disputes over fishing rights in waters around the Rock, escalated swiftly because of Spain's continuing desire for (joint) sovereignty. 'Between the irresistible and the immovable, Gibraltar remained in suspended animation, a colony in all but name' (Darwin, 1988: 310).

Conclusions

The British Raj left the subcontinent of India nine years before independence was conceded to a single British colony in Africa. So the 'wind of change', which dislodged various other European colonial rulers in subsequent years, blew in from the Indian Ocean. The achievement of independence by India in 1947 represents one of the most remarkable acts of decolonization in the twentieth century and was followed closely by Burma and Ceylon (Sri Lanka). Partition was a bitter and partial solution to the problem of India's independence which satisfied none of the parties involved. For the British it meant failure to preserve a united India and the almost complete reversal of prewar policies. For Jinnah and the League, it was a 'moth-eaten' Pakistan rather than the full six Muslim provinces claimed. For Congress and Nehru it meant the end of the dream of a single free, socialist and secular republic which had driven their campaign for independence since the 1920s.

British withdrawal from its Palestinian mandate in 1948, little influenced by events in India, owed a great deal to international and American pressures, Jewish terrorism and the refugee problem. After the 1956 Suez shambles, Britain's Middle Eastern presence was confined to Aden and the Gulf region but even these protectorates and sheikdoms had become untenable ten years later. Nationalists compelled a hasty departure from Aden in 1967 and Britain's intention, announced early in 1968, to withdraw militarily from Malaysia, Singapore and the Gulf by the end

of 1971 meant that she would no longer be able to inter-
vene east of Suez. This has been called the most far-reach-
ing change in Britain's world position since her departure
from India over 20 years before. Alongside the important
military bases of Aden and Singapore, Britain faced growing pressure in the 1950s for political change in Malta and
Cyprus, her island 'fortress colonies' in the Mediterranean.
Cyprus presented particular difficulties because of the
Greek-Cypriot demand for ENOSIS or union with Greece.
Fortress Gibraltar also became a touchy issue after 1945,
especially since Britain's decline as a Mediterranean power,
and a new approach to its colonies, encouraged Spain's
hopes of recovering the territory at its apex.

5

AFRICA AND THE CARIBBEAN: WINDS OF CHANGE BLOW

The nature of the confrontations across various African colonial possessions in the post-1945 period was determined to a major degree by the particularities of British, French, Belgian, Spanish and Portuguese responses to resurgent or unaccustomed nationalist demands. The relatively rapid decolonization of French and Spanish North African protectorates from Morocco to Eritrea, in the ten years following the Second World War, set an awkward precedent that was not to be followed in Algeria and other colonies with a strong European settler presence (see Chapter 6). Former Italian possession Libya, after 1945 placed partly under British, partly under French, administration, became independent at the end of 1951 with a monarchical form of government under King Muhammed Idris, overthrown in 1969 by Colonel Muammar Gadhafi (Gadafy). Sudan, Tunisia and both French and Spanish Morocco were all decolonized in 1956. In Sudan the British handed over power to the Riverain Arab elites in the north, thereby alienating the non-Arab, and largely non-Muslim, people in the south, while in French Morocco the situation was complicated by conflicts between the supporters and opponents of the sultan. British rulers on West

Africa's Gold Coast confronted popular nationalism after 1949 with the mass mobilization of Kwame Nkrumah's Convention People's Party (CPP). The Gold Coast went through various constitutional stages to become, as Ghana, an independent state within the Commonwealth in 1957, effectively setting the pace for British and French decolonization in Africa.

On 3 February 1960 in South Africa, British Prime Minister Harold Macmillan gave his now famous 'wind of change' speech, a phrase first used by him in Accra to little attention, almost three years after the Gold Coast had been blown out of the Empire. The intention was to explain to the Cape Town parliament about the decolonizing process in Africa:

> ... the most striking of all the impressions I have formed since I left London a month ago is of the strength of [this] African national consciousness. In different places it takes different forms, but it is happening everywhere. The wind of change is blowing through this continent, and, whether we like it or not, this growth of national consciousness is a political fact. We must all accept it as a fact, and our national policies must take account of it. (Ovendale, 1995: 476).

He advised the Afrikaners to moderate their 'separate development' or 'apartheid' segregationist policies and temper white rule that weighed heavily on the black majority of the population.

South Africa's white supremacist politicians were unmoved by this advice. When a mass demonstration was organized on 21 March 1960 against the oppressive pass laws that controlled all aspects of black life, the police at Sharpeville, south of Johannesburg, panicked and opened fire with live ammunition, killing 69 unarmed African demonstrators and injuring another 180. Worldwide anger made it difficult for Macmillan to steer the Commonwealth through the ensuing crisis (South Africa withdrew from membership a year later). Sharpeville was followed in October 1960 by the independence of the Federation of Nigeria, exemplifying that decolonization was not entirely driven by fierce nationalist pressures. The same momentous year for African colonial independence (16 new African states entered the United Nations in 1960) also saw Belgium's precipitate departure from the Congo, closely followed by the international repercussions of a bloody civil war and the unhappy involvement of the United Nations.

The British congratulated themselves that, even when the pace of political change was accelerated, the basic notion of a prepared decolonization, a constitutional progress towards African self-government, would remain generally acceptable to candidates drawn from an educated black elite who were to inherit the privileges, perquisites and, it has been argued, authoritarian rule of their former colonial masters (Mamdani, 1996). Of course, decolonization did not happen quite so smoothly as the above would suggest. Thus in 1951 the British Colonial Office lost patience with the 'legalistic particularism' of the ageing Kiros leaders of Sierra Leone's National Council and imposed its own constitution. The legislative council was reconstituted with an African majority and ministers nominated by the ruling Sierra Leone People's Party began to assume departmental duties. Despite violent demonstrations in both Freetown and the Northern Province against these nominations, and a marked lack of urgency on the part of Prime Minister Sir Milton Margai, the transfer of power continued unchecked and was eventually completed in April 1961 (Hargreaves, 1988).

The Economics of African Decolonization

In January 1957, only two months before Ghana's independence, Harold Macmillan, who had just succeeded Eden as British Tory premier, called for a dispassionate reassessment of the colonial situation. As Chancellor of the Exchequer in 1955–56, he had already attempted to cut spending on colonial development. Now he asked the government's official committee on colonial policy for a pragmatic cost–benefit analysis, devoid of imperial fervour, 'to see something like a profit and loss account for each of our colonial possessions, so that we may be better able to gauge whether, from the financial and economic point of view we are likely to gain or to lose by its departure'. When the committee gave the Cabinet its reply to Macmillan's request in September, it concluded that the economic considerations of decolonization 'tend to be evenly matched and the economic interests of the United Kingdom are unlikely in themselves to be decisive in determining whether or not a territory should become independent'. In effect, the economic dangers of delaying decolonization where it was suitable were far greater than any risk from independence negotiated, as in Ghana and Malaya, 'in an atmosphere of goodwill' (Cooper, 1996: 395–6).

This conclusion followed a balance sheet of the cost of keeping colonies – £51 million per year for the regular Colonial Office budget, the Colonial Development and Welfare Act, and the Colonial Development Corporation. East Africa had a substantial overall deficit, partly due to the cost of fighting Mau Mau in Kenya, and the combined commercial importance of African colonies to Britain was still less than that of the Union of South Africa. On the benefit side, British colonies together contributed £1.3 billion to sterling balances at the end of 1956. Ultimately, Britain stood little more risk from devolving power than from trying to retain it, because she could in most cases get hardly more economically out of direct colonial rule than out of keeping ex-colonies in the Commonwealth and the sterling area. Indeed, the overall consensus was that the essential aim should be to secure the goodwill of those who would eventually succeed to political power.

In any case, political and strategic considerations were often more significant to the official mind, for as Sir Roger Stevens put it in 1961, 'in spite of our substantial commercial and other interests in Africa, the latter's chief political importance for the West derived from the Cold War' (Fieldhouse, 1986: 8). Political doubts about Britain's colonial inheritance had also preceded Macmillan's 1957 cost–benefit analysis. Equally, the surge of unrest in southern and central Africa from 1959–60, France's precipitate colonial retreat from west and equatorial Africa in 1960 and the Congo anarchy of 1960–62, subsequently 'challenged the assumptions of the 1950s about the inevitability of gradualism in colonial affairs' (Darwin, 1988: 256) and hastened a British desire to construct regimes to whom power could be transferred safely. The prime minister was certainly swayed by the policies pursued by the other European colonial powers, particularly the Belgians in the Congo, but above all by the failure of French policy in Algeria (Ovendale, 1995).

After 1945 France saw colonies as essential to its economic recovery, increasing metropolitan investment through the state in a desire to maximize intra-imperial trade at a time when hard currencies were in short supply. Public officials could not foresee that the metropolitan economy would itself experience a postwar recovery (industrial production more than quadrupled between 1945 and 1958) second only to that of Germany. By the mid-1950s the chief function of French investments in sub-Saharan Africa (including Madagascar which had seen a nationalist rising suppressed from 1947–48 at a cost of thousands of lives) was evidently to enable colonies to run enormous deficits in their balance of payments. Hence, for the franc zone as a whole, colonial deficits with France were 621.1 billion francs in 1958, which were more than offset by French public transfers of 666.7 billion. Who were the beneficiaries of this massive overseas aid? The French official mind became convinced that the colonies provided no special benefit to the *métropole* as a consumer, while only the least modern and uncompetitive French industries found important artificial markets in these highly protected colonies. British example tended to suggest that France might retain economic advantage in its colonies once it no longer had the responsibility for financing and governing them.

On returning to power as prime minister in June 1958 after a lengthy absence, Charles de Gaulle, soon to become President of the Fifth Republic, weighed up the economic pros and cons of Empire. De Gaulle's main concern was metropolitan: building up the general strength of the French economy took precedence for this Flanders-born Frenchman over the 'kith and kin' appeals deployed by Algeria's hard-pressed white settlers to enlist support in Paris and the south of France. De Gaulle's other focus was on European union, to ensure that the European Economic Community (EEC) initiated by the Treaty of Rome (1957) turned upon French leadership. For this to happen, French resources, economic and military, had to be switched from North Africa to the European mainland and the French Army oriented towards a modernized, continental and nuclear role. 'The least one can say is that Africa costs us more than it benefits us', de Gaulle pronounced in April 1961, identifying himself as usual with France. 'Our own progress has now become our great national ambition and is the real source of our power and influence. It is a fact that decolonization is in our own interest and is therefore our policy' (Fieldhouse, 1986: 17). The ending of the Algerian war in 1962, with built-in safeguards for France over Saharan oil, released more men for yet further domestic economic expansion. As growth opportunities and full employment beckoned in the 1960s, maintaining the French colonial empire seemed to represent only increased taxation costs and continued military commitments without real economic benefits.

The Gold Coast: Under British Rule

The Gold Coast in West Africa, sandwiched between the Ivory Coast and Togo, was seen by British liberal imperialists at the Colonial Office during the Second World War as an ideal testing place for gradual decolonization. It was the second biggest dollar earner for Britain after Malaya, supplying about a third of the world's cocoa beans, and so was vital to the health of sterling. There were no troublesome white settlers, a tactful colonial government, a local elite composed of traditional chiefs and a small class of Western-educated African politicians remarkable for their loyalty and cooperative nature. The southern provinces had a relatively prosperous commercial economy due to the rising price of cocoa and there were high levels of schooling and health services. Governor Sir Alan Burns (1941–47) secured support in 1944 from the well-established political elite for the first stage of a measured constitutional progress but his successor, Sir Gerald Creasy (1947–49), a Colonial Office planner, discovered that the reformers had been over-confident. Because of delays in drafting the necessary statutory instruments, the constitutional changes approved in 1944 had not been put into effect until 1946, by which time they no longer appeared quite so progressive. These changes were meant to bind the coastal and inland regions more closely together and to provide for a larger representation of local opinion, the first step in a gradual, 'carefully timed march towards the distant horizon of self-rule, perhaps a generation or more away' (Darwin, 1988: 175).

The Burns constitution, by bringing the inland region of Ashanti and the coastal 'colony' under a single legislature, exemplified that if local and other African interests were to be protected against the interference of British rule, political influence at the capital, not personal influence with the local district commissioner, was henceforth the key. So wealthy lawyer J.B. Danquah formed the United Gold Coast Convention (UGCC) in 1947 to mobilise the small class of businessmen and lawyers in the coastal towns who felt that the new constitution would give too much power to traditional rulers and chiefs who disliked Western, demo-cratic ideas and had been preserved artificially by the Brit-ish. The colonial administration, exhausted and depleted by its wartime duties, failed to identify, or even to satisfy, rising expectations in many sections of Gold Coast society.

Several major grievances fed unrest in this previously model British colony. In rural areas, the spread of com-mercial cocoa farming led to social and cultural upheavals, and wealthy businessmen nursed grievances at the priv-ileged position of the local chiefs. In the rapidly growing towns like Kumasi and Accra there were an increasing number of 'verandah boys', unemployed young men who had received some Western-style schooling but were unable to gain the prestigious non-manual jobs to which they aspired. Food shortages and inflation, particularly serious in the towns, were also blamed on government and Euro-pean traders. Attempts by the British to control swollen-shoot disease attacking the cocoa trees, upon which the colonial economy depended, by destroying diseased trees, further enraged farmers who did not believe official expla-nations for its necessity. Thus when, on 28 February 1948, the commander of a small police detachment in Accra fired on a procession of protesting unemployed ex-servicemen, killing two, widespread rioting and looting in the city spread to three other towns, including Kumasi in the Ashanti region, rural heartland of the cocoa industry. Twenty-nine were killed and well over 200 injured, a heavy price to pay in order to restore imperial order.

The British suppressed the disturbances, for which Crea-sy's Whitehall training had ill-prepared him, but they were startled by the success with which Danquah and the UGCC mobilized popular support. In response, the influential Colonial Secretary, Arthur Creech Jones (1946–50), set up an all-African 38–member commission under Judge Hen-ley Coussey to recommend constitutional change that

113

would both prevent further unrest and encourage traditional and more Westernized politicians to come to terms. The report of Coussey's committee in August 1949 produced a new constitutional formula calling for a much larger elected legislative assembly, universal suffrage and devolution of the Gold Coast's internal affairs to an executive council made up of African ministers. The British accepted these recommendations, hoping to restore a moderate, socially conservative coalition of chiefs and urban elite that would help sustain British rule. Sir Andrew Cohen, Colonial Office policy maker and future governor of Uganda, minuted on 17 June 1948 that political advance in West Africa was going to be 'more rapid...than the capabilities of the people would justify on merit'. He became anxious to increase public investment through agencies like the Colonial Development Corporation, so that 'as the West African territories get greater political freedom they should be more closely linked to the UK economically, both for their own advantage and ours' (Hargreaves, 1988: 117). A cost-cutting British government, on the other hand, felt gradual constitutional advance would have to be a substitute for generous economic assistance.

Nkrumah's Populist Nationalism

The real beneficiary of Judge Coussey's commission, however, was to be Kwame Nkrumah's Convention People's Party (CPP) that emerged in June 1949 out of the Committee on Youth Organization, formed as a militant spearhead of the UGCC, with an appeal to popular nationalism in the south and its doctrine of 'positive action'. Nkrumah, a Catholic-trained schoolmaster, did not initiate the Accra riots, but the heavy-handed British response widened his base of support. In 1947, he had been brought back from studying at the London School of Economics to organize as general secretary the UGCC campaign and build a popular base for it by drawing in trade unions, farmers, traders and

114

other interest groups. A Marxist-influenced, Pan-African activist, Nkrumah went too far for the UGCC's middle-class leadership by organizing the 'verandah boys' as well. When the UGCC attempted to destroy his power base, Nkrumah retaliated by forming the popular organisation he had created into a new party, the CPP, claiming to be the true voice of Gold Coast nationalism and demanding 'Self-Government NOW'. A campaign of 'positive action' – strikes, boycotts, and demonstrations – heightened conflict with the British. The collapse of a general strike in January 1950 led to Nkrumah's imprisonment and the new and last Governor of the Gold Coast, Sir Charles Arden-Clarke (1949–57), tried to fill the political vacuum by rallying 'moderate opinion' in favour of the Coussey constitution.

Unfortunately for the Governor, the CPP, unlike the UGCC 'moderates', was already well organized to follow the 'constitutional road' of manhood suffrage and on 9 February 1951 won an astonishing 34 of the 38 elective Assembly seats. Assuming approval from Creech Jones, the Governor summoned Nkrumah, 'Great Leader of Streetboys', from prison and with as much grace as he could muster invited him, as Leader of Government Business, to nominate colleagues for ministerial office. Arden-Clarke made the most of Nkrumah's willingness to give an extended interpretation to 'Self-government NOW' – the six years of CPP–British government that followed seems protracted in retrospect but was far shorter than the Colonial Office had expected. During this time rising cocoa prices, stimulated by the Korean War, increased government revenues by over 50 per cent and so made several newly prosperous black ministers more willing to accept British advice about how to administer a modern state as a parliamentary democracy. By accepting office, Nkrumah avoided any further open confrontation with London and sought self-government within the Commonwealth and the rules of the sterling area.

Despite Africanization, the number of British officials actually increased after 1951. The smoothness of Anglo-Ghanian cooperation owed a great deal to Nkrumah's success in imposing the authority of the CPP all over the country and in checking the rise of regional or tribal movements. In return, the British turned a blind eye to CPP misuse of official funds and were willing to concede full internal self-government and then independence. Once Nkrumah had won another election in 1954, the target-date for full independence was set for December 1956. Conservative British ministers, worried by the growing counter-nationalist opposition in the north, and particularly in Ashanti which feared exclusion from the benefits of southern-led rule, required Nkrumah to face the test of a third election. When the CPP won another victory, on a reduced poll, the British Cabinet approved legislation which made the former Gold Coast as Ghana into an independent state within the Commonwealth on 6 March 1957. As ruler of the first British colony in Africa (if we exclude the Anglo-Egyptian Sudan) to achieve freedom, Nkrumah insisted Ghanaian independence was not a mere merit award for a 'model colony' but a turning-point in the history of the vast African continent.

French West and Equatorial Africa

Crucial differences, as well as occasional borrowings, separate the British decolonizing experience in West Africa from that of the French in West and Equatorial Africa. The latter were less inclined than the British to accede to and prepare for unconditional independence. Yet nationalism had become more prominent in French colonies after the Second World War in the form of political movements, thanks to increasing literacy and education, the militancy of trade unions and leadership from charismatic, Western-educated, so-called *évolués* ('evolved ones') who spoke French and held European-style office jobs or similar

116

employment. Indigenous white-collar workers were seen as proof of French success in *la mission civilisatrice* but also provided most of the nationalist leaders who campaigned for greater African access to political decision-making. Whereas British policy makers conceded in the 1940s that at some time far in the future independence *might* be offered to 'moderate' successor regimes acceptable to British strategic and commercial interests, the French assimilationists saw their African possessions as irremovable parts of an indivisible whole. To the French colonial mentality, the Empire was vital, 'in order to resist subordination to *les anglo-saxons*, whatever the rest of the world might think' (Clayton, 1994: 3). Politicians also insisted on the importance of the French colonial empire to guarantee France's postwar role as a great power.

In January 1944, six months before the Normandy invasion of occupied France, de Gaulle had convened a colonial conference at Brazzaville, in the French Congo, attended by French governors and administrators from all over French North and sub-Saharan Africa. No Africans were present. While the conference recommended the phasing out of various abuses, such as African forced labour and the harsh *indigénat* (judicial code), it held out no prospect of any advance to self-government or independence. René J. Pleven, the Gaullist commissioner for the colonies, declared that:

> the goals of the task of civilisation accomplished by France in her colonies rule out any idea of autonomy, any possibility of evolution outside the French bloc of the empire; the eventual creation, even in the distant future, of 'self government' [in English in the text] for the colonies is to be set aside. (Wilson, 1994: 62)

This inflexible attitude presents a marked contrast with the contemporary British willingness to at least consider 'self-government' for African colonies 'in the distant future'.

The most important nationalist party to win inter-territorial support in French West Africa was the *Rassemblement Démocratique Africain* (RDA) or African Democratic Rally organized by Félix Houphouët-Boigny, arguably the most significant Francophone black leader, who became president of the Côte-d'Ivoire (Ivory Coast) from independence in 1960 until his death in 1993. Although Houphouët-Boigny and his party initially allied with the French Communist Party (PCF) and took up Marxist ideas, he was primarily a nationalist who called for autonomy for the individual African states which made up French West (AOF) and Equatorial Africa (AEF) and Cameroon. Chief among his opponents, either because they disagreed with his communist alliance or opposed the splitting up of the French African federations into separate countries, were Dahomey's Sourou Migan Apithy and Senegal's Léopold Sedar Senghor, supporters of the French Socialist Party who joined other African members of the French Assembly in setting up the Overseas Independents' Group (IOM). African politicians throughout Francophone black Africa generally allied with one or other of these groups, sometimes switching between them (Aldrich, 1996).

Strong African leaders gradually established political authority in the different colonies of French West and Equatorial Africa, gaining election to local assemblies and to the National Assembly in Paris. The major figure calling for reform in French Guinea was Ahmed Sékou Touré, an influential trade union organizer; in Congo-Brazzaville it was Abbé Fulbert Youlou, an RDA priest; in Togo, Sylvanus Olympio, an intellectual businessman; and in Cameroon, Ruben Um Nyobé, a communist public servant. Protests were generally peaceful but a violent incident occurred in February 1949 at Treichville, a working-class suburb of Abidjan, Côte-d'Ivoire, where riots were followed by 400 arrests. Demonstrations culminated in Dimbokro, where French soldiers shot and killed 20 Africans and wounded 100 more. Houphouët-Boigny broke with the communists in 1951, as did most of his RDA colleagues, subsequently becoming a junior minister in the mid-1950s French government and a favoured link with black Africa.

When Olympio dropped his plan for unification of Togo with the Gold Coast (Ghana), the French allowed his government greater autonomy than elsewhere in Africa. Militant nationalist Um Nyobé, leader of the *Union des Populations du Cameroun* (UPC), refused to follow Houphouët-Boigy's lead in abandoning communism and became increasingly doctrinaire, in 1955 taking to the jungle to organize a Mao-style revolution. Riots broke out and French forces restored colonial order, with up to 100 deaths, also banning Um Nyobé's party. In response the UPC launched a sabotage campaign at the end of 1956, terminated by the killing of Um Nyobé in September 1958. Evident moves towards independence henceforth did much to defuse nationalist feeling.

A new Socialist government emerged in Paris early in 1956 concerned about future progress in French West and Equatorial Africa but thankful for the relatively quiet situation compared to North Africa. It decided to give greater autonomy to the remaining African colonies under the Defferre law, a *loi cadre* (legislative decree) passed in June 1956 and named after Gaston Defferre, the Minister for France Overseas. This enabling legislation established electoral equality and ministerial responsibility for black French men and women in colonies where European residents formed only a tiny minority, now deprived of their privileged position. France had gone further than any other imperial power in decolonizing its African possessions without according them outright independence. This largely satisfied the moderate African nationalists, and in elections in early 1957 the RDA had great success. Black governments now took office and Paris told French colonial officials to cooperate with their new leaders. All this was overshadowed in March by the declaration of Ghana's independence from Britain under Nkrumah, hence more radical African leaders such as Sékou Touré campaigned for a similar outcome. Senghor and the IOM meanwhile chafed at the breakup of French West and Equatorial Africa into separate states and old rivalries came to the surface once again.

The Defferre law had been in effect for only a year before the Algerian crisis returned de Gaulle to power and brought down the Fourth Republic (see Chapter 6). De Gaulle substantially changed the 1956 *loi cadre*, preserving the different statuses of overseas *département*, *territoire* and associated state, but greatly reducing the powers given to colonial assemblies and government councils – 'what had been given in 1956 was taken away in 1958' (Aldrich, 1996: 302). For the French Union, de Gaulle substituted a new Community (without the adjective 'French'), in which France would still preserve its dominant role in foreign affairs, defence, economic and financial policy, and so on. On the other hand, each 'colony' would vote on whether to remain as such, be fully integrated into the French Republic as a *département*, or go its own way as an independent state with or without association with France. The catch was that if an African state voted to separate from France, it would forgo all French financial or technical assistance, a powerful deterrent for poor countries on the economic 'periphery'. On the other hand, the French were far more willing than the British to commit substantial resources, even troops, to maintain special relationships with African colonies once they had attained self government.

De Gaulle's blueprint for French decolonization meant the creation of numerous small autonomous African states that would each be individually tied to Paris, thereby adopting the patriotic 'discourse' of nationalism while preserving in French hands the realities of military and financial power (Birmingham, 1995). Most nationalist politicians, their Francophile vanity flattered, lobbied for a 'yes' vote for continued French territorial status (rather than federation) in the new Community as campaigns got under way for a referendum to be held on 28 September 1958 throughout French Africa and in the Comoros, Djibouti, French Polynesia and New Caledonia. The only strong opposition came from Sékou Touré in Guinea and Djibo Bakary, a trade unionist minister in remote and undeveloped Niger, who followed Touré in calling for rejection. French administrators had no difficulty in turning the vote against him. Pouvana'a a Oopa, rejectionist leader of a Polynesian nationalist movement, also failed to convince the electorate of French Polynesia, whereas Touré's efforts succeeded. Guinea hence became independent and departing French officials took with them almost everything that was movable, hoping to demonstrate the consequences of Touré's option for 'poverty in liberty [over] wealth in slavery'. The new republic survived with support from neighbouring states, plus the Soviet Union, and thereby helped to encourage African independence elsewhere.

The remaining French territories celebrated the birth of the new Community in Paris on 14 July 1959, yet this was 'the last gasp of the policy of assimilation' (Chipman, 1989: 107) and only served to increase pressures within the black African states for complete independence. In September, the African heads of government asked de Gaulle to transfer total authority to them, as permitted under the powers of the Community constitution. After some discussion, particularly on the future of a federation set up among four West African states (the Mali Federation of Senegal, the Soudan [Mali], Dahomey and Upper Volta), the French government agreed. In mid-1960, 'almost as quickly as French officials could fly from one capital to the other for the lowering of flags and appropriate speeches' (Aldrich, 1996: 303), the former colonies of French West Africa (Senegal, Mauritania, Mali, Upper Volta [Burkina Faso], Niger, Dahomey [Benin], the Côte-d'Ivoire) and French Equatorial Africa (the Moyen-Congo, Gabon, the Central African Republic, Chad) as well as Cameroon, Togo and Madagascar (Malagasy Republic), secured recognition of what de Gaulle preferred to call their 'international sovereignty'.

France had decolonized its black African colonies in one fell swoop and the Community disappeared to become a set of fragmented but sovereign nations, allowing France to turn its attention back to North Africa for the final two years of the Algerian war. Not only was French influence preserved with the new independent states through co-operation and military agreements. France was also praised by African leaders for the liberal spirit which it seemed to display in the decolonizing process, in contrast to the tragedy of Algeria. On the other hand, European powers often bequeathed parliamentary systems without the legal and civil institutions necessary to support them, and after decades of undermining pre-existing social structures. Post-colonial independence in Africa could mean fragmented states that were not economically viable and many were caught in vicious civil wars or became an arena of the Cold War struggle.

Nigeria: Under British Rule

In British Nigeria conditions were markedly different from the Gold Coast or Sierra Leone in terms of the huge size of the territory, its cultural and religious divisions, politics and social organization. 'Nigeria', remarked Chief Obafemi Awolowo, a prominent Yoruba local politician, in 1947, 'is not a nation. It is a mere geographical expression' (Darwin, 1988: 179). The Muslim north, which contained over half Nigeria's population and covered three quarters of its confines, was a different world, with its Fulani aristocracy and its landed estates, from the provinces south of the Niger–Benue line where Western, Christian and commercial influences were far stronger. This division had been in some ways exacerbated by British administrative policies. To further complicate matters, the southern provinces were divided between the Yoruba people of the west and the

Ibos of the east, not to mention the large number of minority tribes scattered across the middle and south. The objective of British policy after 1945 was to transform this vast and loosely articulated collection of provinces into a modern, self-governing state, to improve its administration and develop its economy. Ten years later, the leisurely progress towards self-government contemplated in 1945 had become an unseemly rush, culminating in independence in 1960.

The effects of the emergence of Nigerian nationalism were significant but limited, for 'the popular notion that colonial rule was expelled from Africa by the rise of African nationalism can only be applied to the largest country in black Africa with the heaviest qualifications' (Darwin, 1988: 180). There was even danger that the powerful traditional rulers in the north would refuse to participate in a constitution increasingly geared to the aspirations of Western-educated politicians in the south. Separatism and disintegration, not nationalism, frightened the British Colonial Office most, whereas the growth of a sense of Nigerian nationhood was to be positively encouraged. This is not to say that there was no black opposition to colonial rule and colonial government fears, much exaggerated, of communist influence. Between 1945 and 1950 the southern region was disturbed by a succession of upheavals: the 1945 general strike of public workers protesting against inflation; the abortive campaign against the 1946 constitution; the more violent campaign of nationalist 'extremists' between 1947 and 1950; and the Enugu colliery dispute of November 1949, when police opened fire and killed 21 miners. Local traders also resented the power and influence of large European firms, especially in postwar conditions of shortage, while the growing number of educated Nigerians resented their exclusion from top government and bureaucratic posts.

Before 1950, however, there was little enthusiasm for the creation of a Nigerian nation except among small professional circles in the coastal towns (Nigeria had only 150 lawyers, 160 doctors and 786 clergy in a population of 40 million), and even here African politicians had been divided by Ibo–Yoruba antagonism. The main political association, the National Council of Nigeria and the Cameroons (NCNC) led by Dr Nnamdi Azikiwe, dominated by the Ibos, failed to extract constitutional concessions from the Colonial Office and abandoned in 1947 its boycott of the new legislative council. In 1949, addressing the Ibo State Union, Azikiwe made his famous declaration that 'it would appear that the God of Africa has specially created the Ibo nation to lead the children of Africa from the bondage of the ages'. A year earlier, Chief Awolowo had joined with prominent Yoruba from Lagos to launch the Egbe Omo Oduduwa society into Nigerian public life, 'to accelerate the emergence of a virile modernised and efficient Yoruba state within the Federal State of Nigeria.... [and] to unite the various clans in Yorubaland and generally create and actively foster the idea of a single nationalism throughout Yorubaland' (Wilson, 1994: 94). The uninhibited assertions of ethnic pride by both Awolowo and Azikiwe in the immediate post-1945 period were to prove politically embarrassing at a later date, being identified as hindering national integration when quoted against them by rivals or denounced as 'tribalism'. On the other hand, in the 1940s and 1950s the drama of 'competitive mobilization of ethnicity was one of the most important means by which rival political leaders "nationalized" the political process within a given colonial framework' (Wilson, 1994: 95).

A shift in British policy none the less took place in 1948, as on the Gold Coast. It was thought unwise to refuse concessions granted to the latter and British officials in Nigeria were anxious to anticipate any hardening of the educated class against them, which 'liberal' Governor Sir John Macpherson and the new Chief Secretary Hugh Foot (future governor of Cyprus) saw as the main cause of trouble on the Gold Coast. Higher administration was to be opened up to Nigerians (University College, Ibadan, received its first students in 1947); and local government in the east was reformed at the expense of traditional 'native authorities' in order to benefit the educated 'new' men. Above all, the constitution was to be revised by an elaborate system of consultation culminating in 1951 in a somewhat contentious 'general conference' which had the effect of utilizing chiefs and local notables from west and north to restrain the rise of populist nationalism. The Macpherson constitution formalized the political identity of the three existing regions, giving each an assembly based on complex systems of indirect election and manhood suffrage and an executive council, with Nigerian ministers taking over responsibility for education, planning and local government.

Nigeria: The Federal Solution

The original intention of the British was to stage further instalments of self-government at a pace which would preserve overall British control until political differences between north and south became less marked and a strong federal government could be set up with the consent of all three regions – the Yoruba west, the Ibo east and the Hausa–Fulani–Muslim north. There was, of course, no Nigerian equivalent of Nkrumah's CPP capable of enforcing its choice of ministers at federal level but natural majority parties quickly emerged in each region. In the south east it was the NCNC; in the south west the Action Group, political heir to the Egbe Omo Oduduwa, achieved a less secure supremacy; in the north the Northern Peoples' Congress (NPC) developed as an openly regional party, sustained by the power of the Muslim aristocracy. Delegations from each region made up the central legislature and executive but united action at the centre was difficult to achieve. The Colonial Office was determined to forestall the emergence of populist nationalism by devolving power to a federal government within which reliable northern conservatives would exercise a controlling influence. It was precisely the impossibility of persuading the three regions, particularly the north, to cooperate in a federal government and to agree upon its powers that led the British to accelerate self-government and promise in 1957 that full independence would be the reward for agreeing to work a proper federal system.

The London constitutional conference in May and June 1957 began to face the problem of how the 200 large and small 'primary nations' of Nigeria (based on language as a criteria of nationality) might organize themselves into an independent state. Chairman Alan Lennox-Boyd, Conservative Secretary of State for the Colonies (1954–59) – who wanted to postpone Nigerian demands for independence as far as possible – was against restructuring the federal authority by creating new regional governments, since this would favour the NCNC and reduce the leverage enjoyed by the traditional Muslim rulers of the huge Northern Region and their NPC spokesmen. 'This is the dilemma with which we are faced', he informed the British Cabinet committee on colonial policy on 14 May 1957:

> Either give independence too soon and risk disintegration and a breakdown of administration; or hang on too long, risk ill-feeling and disturbances, and eventually to [sic] leave bitterness behind, with little hope thereafter at our being able to influence Nigerian thinking in world affairs on lines we would wish. (Cooper, 1996: 397)

Meanwhile, the principle of regional self-government having already been conceded, Colonial Office officials were anxious to complete the transfer of power as soon as possible, rather than, as earlier on the Gold Coast, to delay it by further tests of African opinion. With the agreement of the constitutional conference, four distinguished British public servants were appointed as commissioners to find out about the fears of minorities in any part of Nigeria. They proposed to allay such fears, whether well or ill founded, by setting up a Bill of Rights and other minor constitutional adjustments, supremely confident that Nigeria meant to follow the road of liberal democracy and parliamentary government. 'Lennox-Boyd like a clever general drew the line of battle and baited the Nigerian delegates into accepting battle on his own grounds', commented an African participant at the talks (Hargreaves, 1988: 163).

Thus reassured, Macmillan's Conservative government was able on 1 October 1960 to transfer power to a surprising coalition of Northern Muslim NPC and Eastern Ibo NCNC (Azikiwe became President), which was initially unwilling to grant its former rulers limited military facilities, despite having signed an Anglo-Nigerian Defence Pact. Britain continued, nevertheless, to provide nearly half of the new Federation of Nigeria's imports and also took nearly half of her exports. Some 75 per cent of Nigeria's foreign capital remained British or from the sterling area. 'Decolonisation was embarked upon, at least in part, to make the world a safer place for British business', writes an historian of the late colonial state in Malaya. 'Economic decolonisation was a much slower process than the transfer of political power' (Harper, 1999).

The new Nigerian government emphasized its hostility to communism and its loyalty to Britain but was soon being attacked by the Yoruba Action Group in the south west as a client and lackey of British neocolonialism. British economic links, such as sterling reserves, were rapidly being run down, a republican constitution was drawn up and defence assistance sought elsewhere. In 1966, the year of a Commonwealth conference in Lagos, the first of many Nigerian military coups took place. The vast Muslim community in the north has generally favoured military governments as a way to limit the power of the Christian-dominated south. Nigeria's Eastern region, stronghold of the Ibo population, seceded in May 1967 and declared itself the independent republic of Biafra. This was the

beginning of a terrible and drawn-out civil war, until secession was crushed in January 1970 by the Nigerian military
government.

The Central African Federation

Successive British governments attempted to decolonize in
central Africa in the 1950s by handing over power to white-
settler regimes, thereby avoiding African majority rule.
Afrikaner dominance of post-1948 South Africa allowed
the sentiment for amalgamation between the white-dominated governments of Northern Rhodesia (now Zambia) and
Southern Rhodesia (now Zimbabwe) to gain strength. In
1950, Northern Rhodesia's 36,000 settlers were surrounded by 1,849,000 Africans and, unlike Southern Rhodesia's 129,000 whites who had enjoyed almost complete
internal self-government since 1923, were administered
directly by the Colonial Office. The north's rich copper
mines run by expatriate British pitmen lording it over
underpaid blacks had received an enormous boost during
wartime, which added to the argument for locking together
an English-dominated unit in central Africa. Amalgamation
of the two Rhodesias would also make it easier for the
white-settler minority to handle the growing economic
and political aspirations of Africans.

There was an enormous increase in British migration to
the two Rhodesias after the end of the Second World War
which led to evictions and peasant hatred of white rule but
black servants were cheap and the austerity of Labour's
Welfare State Britain was remote from the sunshine of
central Africa. 'In the UK you're always fetching coke and
coal and doing the washing up – here others do it for you.
It gives you more spare time', explained an ex-Royal Air
Force migrant (Caute, 1983: 302). In 1948 the election of
Dr Godfrey Huggins of the United Party (UP) in the Southern Rhodesian white-settler elections and of Roy Welensky
– the volatile, aggressive, half-Jewish and half-Afrikaner

voice of Rhodesian whites – in Northern Rhodesia's Crown Colony served notice that the British government would be compelled to take the initiative in central African affairs. The aggressive white vision of a modern European state being carved out of the central African bush did not seem too remote in the immediate postwar years.

Federation, not amalgamation, was Colonial Secretary Arthur Creech Jones's preference, since this would continue to give the colonial bureaucracy in Northern Rhodesia the power to bargain on behalf of the Africans. The Colonial Office wanted to see a triangular federation that would include Nyasaland (now Malawi), partly in order to offload the colony's debt on to shoulders other than the British taxpayer, partly to bring European and African power more toward a multiracial mix, since Nyasaland had only a marginal settler presence. Policy makers in London's Whitehall and Rhodesian white settlers came closer together on central Africa's future after 1949. The chief representative of the Colonial Office, Andrew Cohen, compelled to minimize British expenditure during a period of anti-Soviet rearmament, had to do a deal at a London conference in March 1951 with Huggins and Welensky. The settlers would accept federation instead of amalgamation, while the Colonial Office agreed that the federal legislature should have significant powers. While African leaders like Harry Nkumbula in Northern Rhodesia were uniformly opposed to federation, Southern Rhodesia's nearly two million Africans feared absorption by the Union of South Africa even more. Ultimately, federation was 'a geopolitical construct' designed 'to erect a counterpoise to the expansion of South Africa, especially by checking Afrikaner immigration' (Hyam, 1987).

The British Conservative Party victory in October 1951 boded well for Huggins and Welensky, but the new Colonial Secretary, Oliver Lyttelton, who from his business interests well understood the imperial significance of the copperbelt, held out for a triangular federation. Lyttelton resisted a unified civil service, through which the Southern Rhodesians could achieve regional dominance, and also insisted on some African representation in the federal legislature. The real problem for London was who was to have key control over the various African populations – the territorial bureaucracies or the federal power? Welensky, a burly former railway engine-driver and ex-heavyweight boxer, had already organized a powerful lobby in Britain which played on the assumption of conservative paternalists that federation would be run by the whites until the black majority became – in the whites' eyes – 'civilized'. Some Labour supporters were also persuaded by the lure of institutionalized multiracialism as a progressive force for regional economic development. In April 1952 a new conference assembled in London at Lancaster House, the Southern Rhodesian delegation achieving several victories in regard to African affairs, followed by a rubber-stamping convention at Carlton House Terrace throughout January 1953. Then on 14 July 1953 the Rhodesia and Nyasaland Federation Act received the Royal Assent, and the Central African Federation (CAF) began its brief but tempestuous history.

The few African representatives in the new federal and territorial legislatures, dependent on white patronage, commanded little confidence among populations increasingly aware of what was happening elsewhere in Africa. The African National Congress (ANC) grew in strength both in Northern Rhodesia and Nyasaland by articulating fears of increasing settler power becoming widespread at all governmental levels. Both protectorates saw a series of strikes, riots, boycotts and other protests. In Southern Rhodesia, where federation brought some minor improvements to middle-class Africans, there was less evident unrest but from 1957 fears grew that the constitutional review conference which the British had fixed for 1960 would complete the transfer of power into settler hands. The reconstituted Southern Rhodesian ANC was banned in

February 1959 and its exiled leader Joshua Nkomo, hitherto a rather lonely spokesman of moderate resistance, found himself drafted in October 1960 into the presidency of a more militant replacement, the National Democratic Party (NDP), itself proscribed (after rioting) by Prime Minister Edgar Whitehead in December 1961. There were now the nuclei of strong militant parties in both Rhodesias dedicated to the prevention of a white-dominated central African dominion. The British Conservative government continued, meanwhile, to express confidence in the good intentions of Rhodesian whites but, with growing evidence of African dissent, Labour Party and missionary critics became increasingly distrustful. In the long run, Colonial Office expectations that white-settler regimes in central Africa would prove liberal in policies towards their black majorities were far too optimistic.

Central Africa: The Emergence of Nationalism

Nevertheless, the prospect until 1959 seemed to be of a further entrenchment of European authority, based on the dynamic growth of Southern Rhodesia and its ability to absorb a large influx of mainly British immigrants. White politicians in the Federation legislature were not so sanguine about the future, convinced that further advance towards independence from British control had to be made before the 1960 conference. Welensky, who had succeeded Huggins as Federal Prime Minister in 1956, was also well aware that if the CAF were to acquire self-government, the local Europeans had to show London some proof that African political rights would not be permanently withheld. Welensky's subsequent attempt to recast the Federal franchise appeared to suspicious Northern Rhodesian and Nyasaland blacks as the first stage in a drive to create a segregationist *fait accompli* before 1960. The emergence of African nationalism in the CAF between 1957 and 1959 was, therefore, partly a response to the evolving tactics of

131

white federal politicians. Black leaders throughout the CAF became aware that time was not on their side if they were to avoid permanent white domination.

By 1958 the bulk of African opinion had become convinced that it was the local white leaderships, not the British government, who were effectively shaping federal realities, and that nationalism was the only method of preventing further decline in their position. It was to meet these pressures that the Nyasaland African Congress (NAC) called Dr Hastings Banda back from his London medical practice in mid-1958 to assume the leadership and campaign for an African majority on the Legislative Council. Black Rhodesian nationalists could not afford to be left behind by the NAC and so stepped up their own level of political activity. Then, in January 1959, widespread disturbances broke out in Nyasaland and a 'murder plot' against Europeans was alleged. On 21 February Welensky, as CAF premier, announced that federal troops were en route to Blantyre to assist the British colonial administration in protecting whites; five days later, Whitehead declared a state of emergency in Southern Rhodesia and arrested 500 ANC leaders.

Welensky's federal action had compelled the Governor of Nyasaland, Sir Robert Armitage, to declare a full state of emergency in his own territory. Dr Banda and other NAC leaders were arrested on 3 March 1959 and flown to various prisons in Southern Rhodesia – 51 Africans were killed by security forces and 79 wounded. One week later, the colonial authorities in Northern Rhodesia banned the Zambian ANC and similarly imprisoned its leaders, Harry Nkumbula and rising star Kenneth Kaunda. As a result of the three 'Emergencies', hundreds of African leaders from each territory were imprisoned without trial. White-settler leaders Welensky and Whitehead had successfully 'coerced British colonial governments into snapping shut the lid on African political protest in central Africa'. The only risk in this strategy was that the British government, seeing that the local white politicians in Salisbury (Harare), Southern Rhodesia, had made 'such a crude shove towards the driving seat, might decide to reaffirm its own power to decide in which direction the rickety colonial vehicle was headed' (Holland, 1985: 224–5).

British Prime Minister Harold Macmillan could not allow Rhodesian and Nyasaland affairs to slip from British supervision, or his government would be made vulnerable to Labour charges of complicity in the machinations of white minorities in the CAF. The broader strategy of African decolonization, not least in East Africa, had to be protected, or British prestige, under restoration following the Suez setback of 1956, would once again suffer. Macmillan thus appointed Sir Patrick Devlin, a British High Court judge, to head a Royal Commission to look into the Nyasaland Emergency. Devlin's report in July 1959 criticized the security forces and concluded that 'no doubt only temporarily' the colony had been made into 'a police state' (Ovendale, 1995: 471). Nyasaland's colonial government stood accused of using South-African-style repression in an African-majority colony, thereby damaging Britain's image as a liberal world power.

Macmillan designated a fresh Royal Commission led by his close friend Lord Walter Monckton to investigate the future of the CAF which marked the beginning of a massive and irreversible alienation between metropolitan politicians and Salisbury federalists. The Monckton Commission arrived in Southern Rhodesia in February 1960, the same month in which Macmillan gave his 'wind of change' speech to the South African parliament in Cape Town before travelling on to the Rhodesias and Nyasaland, where he became convinced of the strength of black resistance to the CAF, took the decision to free Hastings Banda and 'to begin stuffing the genie of white hegemony back into the Central African bottle from which it had escaped under cover of the emergencies' (Holland, 1985: 227). In effect, the British government, by giving the Nyasaland ANC the freedom to resume their operations, were signalling that they were no longer convinced of the Federation's humanizing multiracial mission and that the demand for secession was now open to negotiation.

The white minorities in the CAF became further isolated from British political culture by events such as the Transavaal's 1960 Sharpeville massacre; Northern Rhodesian support for Tshombe's Katanga breakaway (1960–63) from the new post-colonial Congo; and the publication of the Monckton Report in October 1960, recommending African majorities in territorial legislatures and the right of individual states to reconsider membership of the CAF. 'Almost without exception its recommendations play into the hands of African extremists', fulminated Welensky to Colonial Secretary Iain Macleod. 'The secession proposals are the final straw... We are in the midst of events which I believe will, if not very carefully handled, lead to the end of civilized and responsible government in this part of Africa before very long' (Welensky, 1964: 272). When the long-awaited Federal Review Conference was finally convened at Lancaster House on 5 December 1960, Sir Roy said the Federation was fine and should be left alone, Dr Banda said it was rotten and should be broken up and then staged one of many protest walk-outs. Both sides awaited the outcome of simultaneous negotiations on revised territorial constitutions for both Southern and Northern Rhodesia that would determine the place of whites in central Africa. Whereas Southern Rhodesian negotiators meeting in London in February 1961 managed to defer black majority rule into the distant future, when enough Africans attained the necessary franchise qualifications, Northern Rhodesia's white representatives were persuaded by the British Colonial Office to accept its imminent arrival.

Welensky, striving to keep some kind of quasi-federation alive, put pressure on London policy makers by hinting that any 'sell-out' to Northern Rhodesia's black nationalists would spark a republican coup by the federal power in that territory and thereby a white-settler declaration of independence from London throughout the region. In October 1961, as a sop to pro-Rhodesian right-wing opinion in the House of Lords, Macmillan removed the progressive Macleod from the post of Colonial Secretary during a cabinet reshuffle. No other concessions were made and in February 1962 the new Northern Rhodesian constitution was finalized along the lines of that in Nyasaland. After territorial elections held in October an African nationalist majority was installed in the Legislative Council, though divided between Harry Nkumbula's ANC and Kenneth Kaunda's breakaway United National Independence Party (UNIP). Full independence could not be long delayed, particularly after Nyasaland's right of secession was confirmed in December 1962.

Despite attempts by white federalists to win over the ANC, Kaunda and Nkumbula formed a coalition which, in March 1963, demanded and received Northern Rhodesia's right of outright secession from the CAF. Subsequently Nyasaland became Malawi, a self-governing African state ruled autocratically by Hastings Banda, and Northern Rhodesia became independent in October 1964 as the republic of Zambia with Kaunda assuming the presidency. Southern Rhodesia's separate path from the mid-1960s and throughout the 1970s as an outcast white-settler governed state is dealt with elsewhere (see Chapter 6). The British government announced the prospective breakup of the CAF on 28 March 1963, by which time it had long been discounted by all the parties involved, although not formally dissolved until 1 January 1964. The great Zambian copper mining interests set out to establish a working relationship with Kaunda as if the CAF had been but a temporary aberration.

The Congo: Independence and Civil War

The whole process of decolonization in the million-square-mile Belgian Congo, with its 100,000 Europeans in a sea of

14 million Africans, was telescoped into eighteen months, compared to at least a generation in what became Ghana. The Belgians had done the least of all the post-1945 European colonial powers to extend any political training or experience of government to Africans in what was, in essence, 'a giant interlocking complex of mining and plantation companies held together by an armed police force' (Birmingham, 1995: 60). Two universities were established from 1954–56 but the large majority of students were children of white officials and at independence there were in total only 16 Congolese graduates. Missionary churches took Africanization more seriously, by 1960 there were some 600 Catholic priests and about 500 formally ordained Protestant ministers; literacy levels were also quite high among the missionary-school educated Congolese. The paternalistic Belgians were working to a 30–year plan for gradual 'emancipation' which had not been running for very long when African patience finally ran out.

In January 1959 ex-postal worker Patrice Lumumba, striking pan-African leader of the *Mouvement National Congolais* (MNC), announced on returning from the All-African Peoples' Conference in Accra that his objective was immediate independence. *Alliance des Bakongo* (ABAKO) leader Joseph Kasavubu, the first tribal leader to stand out against the Belgians, followed suit in Léopoldville (Kinshasa) where his party was in the ascendancy. The conflict in Kasai province between the Baluba and the Lulua, which was later to intensify and contribute so much to the prevailing chaos, came into the open during 1959. Following serious riots in the capital, which were in origin partly economic (growing unemployment), partly political (the banning of a political meeting), the King of the Belgians, Baudouin II, abruptly announced on Belgian radio that the Congo was to be extended full independence.

The MNC refused to take part in a Round Table Conference held in Brussels from 20 January 1960 until Lumumba, who had been sentenced to six months' imprisonment in Stanleyville for inciting riots, was released and allowed to attend (he arrived in Brussels on 26 January). The day after his arrival, six months ahead was fixed as the timetable for the handover. Even so, anti-Belgian rioting in the Congo grew progressively worse. In Brussels, Lumumba stood for a strong unitary state but businessman Moïse Tshombe of Katanga (Shaba), pro-Western leader of the Lunda group's CONAKAT party, insisted on a federal structure and wanted the Congo to remain linked with Belgium. As agreed in Brussels, government was grudgingly transferred on 30 June 1960 to the Democratic Republic of Congo-Kinshasa under President Kasavubu, representing the moderate, Christian cultural tradition of the west, and Prime Minister Lumumba, the radical bureaucratic tradition of the north.

The political collapse of the newly independent Congo began almost immediately. In early July the former Belgian *Force Publique*, now renamed the Congolese Army, mutinied against its Belgian officers, and Europeans were attacked in Léopoldville and elsewhere. Belgian troops were subsequently landed, uninvited, at a number of airfields and the port of Matadi but in Katanga, the prosperous copper province in the south-west, where the mutiny had also spread, the provincial government headed by Tshombe invited Belgian troops in to restore order and protect the white population. In Katanga there seemed a chance of Belgians continuing to run affairs in the name of the new African rulers, a process of dependence they had hoped to perpetuate in the Congo as a whole. On 11 July 1960 Tshombe's government proclaimed that Katanga had seceded as a separate state, partly to prevent its profitable mining resources being taken over by a centralized regime in Léopoldville, to the evident approval of the mighty *Union Minière du Haut Katanga* and other Belgian capitalist and settler interests. Tshombe also refused permission to land at Elizabethville (Lubumbashi), in the southern half of the province, to a plane containing Kasavubu and

137

Lumumba, who were rushing around trying to rally different parts of the fractured country they had inherited (Hargreaves, 1988).

Lumumba appealed for support to fellow African leaders, to the United Nations, the United States and the Soviet Union (from whom he received funds), thereby threatening to make the Congo into a theatre of the Cold War. UN Secretary-General Dag Hammarskjöld hoped his organization would in effect take over the role of preparing the Congo for self-government which Belgium itself had handled so badly. Implementing this policy was to require three years of armed intervention by a large and unpopular international force. Lumumba's coalition government, meanwhile, under severe strain because of army mutiny, covert foreign interventions, and various secessions, was dismissed on 5 September 1960 by President Kasavubu. Three months later, deposed premier Lumumba was captured by hostile Congolese while trying to join follower Antoine Gizenga (who had formed an alternative pro-Soviet government in Stanleyville), taken to Katanga, and in January 1961 shot by an execution squad supervised by a Belgian captain, probably under the auspices of the CIA (Kanza, 1972).

There was no effective central government of the Congo for almost a year but by August 1961 the United Nations, with American support, had promoted a new pro-Western national government in Léopoldville with Cyrille Adoula as premier and reconstituted the Congolese army. The UN's representative in Katanga, Irishman Dr Conor Cruise O'Brien, then ordered strong UN action against the separatist *gendarmerie* and their mixed bag of mercenary supporters in Elizabethville to enforce a UN Security Council resolution calling for their withdrawal in order to prevent civil war. The use of force by the UN on 13 September received a bad press in some Western capitals; the official British view being that 'there was no mandate for the removal of essential foreign civilians which might lead to the breakdown of the administration of Katanga' (Kyle, 1995: 24). So Hammarskjöld decided to fly personally to Ndola, just over the border in the Zambia copperbelt, where Tshombe had agreed to meet him to negotiate a ceasefire. While approaching Ndola late at night on 17 September 1961 the Secretary-General's plane crashed in the bush and all but one of its passengers were killed (a bodyguard died later). Ever since, there has been speculation by O'Brien and others that Hammarskjöld was unintentionally shot down by two mysterious aircraft in the pay of the European industrialists who controlled Katanga, but convincing evidence remains scarce.

Tshombe's regime continued, until the termination of Katangan secession in January 1963, to collect revenues from *Union Minière* with which to pay for mercenary soldiers and their Belgian officers, apparently serving as a reliable protector of foreign investment against communist penetration. As pro-Western elements gained the upper hand in Léopoldville, secured by General Joseph Mobutu's command of the Congolese army, the Russians became more interested in provincial revolts, while even communist China provided support to a rebellion of rural radicals in southern Kwilu. Soviet-oriented groups in control of Lumumba's former home districts around Stanleyville were only suppressed in November 1964, after an American airlift of Belgian parachutists. The resilient Tshombe, having replaced Adoula as premier and now operating out of Léopoldville, gained control of the whole country from 1964 but was then deposed by President Kasavubu, in turn overthrown by an army coup in November 1965 led by skilled political operator Mobutu. The new military regime ensured a precarious stability 'in conditions more satisfactory to *Union Minière* and the Americans than to followers of the martyred Lumumba' (Hargreaves, 1988: 182). This helps to explain why the corrupt, tyrannical and self-serving Mobutu managed to survive in power for over 30 years, while systematically bleeding the Congo (renamed Zaïre 1971–97) dry.

THE CARIBBEAN

British West Indies

The prewar West Indian Royal Commission (1938–39) chaired by Lord Moyne had recommended that the islands of the British West Indies, most of whose populations could trace their descent from African slaves, should be abandoned. In the late 1950s and early 1960s African independence ceremonies further acted to propel decolonization. Loyal to crown and empire, yet without evident strategic or economic value, the Caribbean islands and islets which, with two mainland South American colonies (British Honduras and British Guiana), made up the British West Indies presented a baffling problem for the Colonial Office, scattered as they were over thousands of miles of distant ocean. West Indian federation under 'moderate' political leadership was the preferred British option because it would make for a more viable economic partner in both a colonial and a post-colonial situation. A conference of Caribbean politicians at Montego Bay, Jamaica, in 1947 had endorsed such a closer association and the Jamaican assembly voted unanimously for federation in August 1951. This initially made sense to West Indian leaders, often drawn from trade unionism, because only a government capable of mobilizing resources over the whole of the British Caribbean could tackle the urgent need for economic development. Yet the Federation Act passed through the British Parliament in 1956 was very limited in extent because it had to allow for the strong local patriotism and cultural differences of islands like Jamaica, Trinidad, Barbados and Grenada.

In the first West Indian federal general election held in 1958, federal supporters did badly on the two major islands of Jamaica and Trinidad. The mainland colonies of British Honduras and British Guiana also rejected federation for a variety of reasons, including a fear that they would be called upon to subsidize the poorer islands. Jamaica, the largest and strongest island, was the first to withdraw, despite Prime Minister Norman Manley extracting from London the promise of full self-government in exchange for continued membership of the federation. Harold Macmillan's visit to Kingston in March 1961 had little effect and in August 1962 Jamaica received her independence. Trinidad followed separately in the same month (with Tobago) but Barbados did not become independent until 1966. Frustrated by inter-island rivalries, West Indian federation lasted for barely five years and so represented a failure for Whitehall planners, demonstrating that the British were not always in control of the decolonization process.

The remaining islands were linked with Britain in 1967 as 'associated states', which meant that they had internal self-government while Britain remained responsible for defence and foreign affairs. All but one, Anguilla, subsequently opted to become completely independent: Grenada (1974), Dominica (1978), St Lucia and St Vincent (1979), Antigua and Barbuda (1981), St Christopher (Kitts) and Nevis (1983). The twin island state of Antigua and Barbuda was run by the corrupt Vere Bird family dynasty and several of these small islands now rank among the biggest transshippers of South American cocaine to Europe. On the mainland, British Guiana, inhabited by the descendants of Indian indentured labourers, African slaves, Portuguese and Chinese traders, and indigenous Amerindians, became independent (after London introduced a new constitution to remove Marxist former dentist Cheddi Jagan from office) as the state of Guyana in May 1966. The former crown colony of British Honduras, autonomous since 1964 under the anti-British People's United Party (PUP) and renamed Belize in 1973, waited longer for independence because of a long-standing boundary dispute with neighbouring Guatemala that required the continuing support of British troops. In 1981, while remaining part of the Commonwealth, Belize became the last Central American state to become independent.

French and Dutch West Indies

Violent post-1945 events in the French Antilles (West Indies), including the killing of striking workers in Martinique, emphasized political discontent in the Caribbean but provoked only a strong-arm response from the French state. The first pro-independence groups, nearly all Marxist or Trotskyist, emerged in banana-growing Guadeloupe and Martinique from 1959 onwards in the wake of Castro's revolution in Cuba, the Algerian war and the steady progress of world decolonization. Supported largely by young middle-class students and intellectuals, these anti-colonial parties enjoyed limited though not negligible popular support but performed well in elections only when independence was not the main issue. The arrival of Mitterrand's Socialist government in France in 1981 appeared to offer the prospect of change but, despite some decentralization of power, independence parties still lacked widespread working-class support, with the exception of the well-organized *Union Populaire pour la Libération de Guadeloupe* (UPLG).

Unwilling to participate in the existing democratic institutions, many *indépendantistes* turned to political violence and sought to gain legitimacy by identifying parallels with New Caledonia in the South Pacific (see Chapter 7), but otherwise there was little to unite their disparate movements in a global struggle against French colonialism. Terrorist attacks against 'the occupying power and the symbols of colonialism', as the 'Algerian way' *Alliance Révolutionnaire Caraïbe* (ARC) termed it, multiplied in the first half of the 1980s, primarily bombings in Guadeloupe. After 1986 the

Chirac government sought to bring the Caribbean *Départements d'outre mer* closer to France, primarily through more
economic aid and less emphasis on decentralization, and
minority socialist pressure for full independence receded
(Aldrich and Connell, 1992). In 1995 severe hurricanes
struck the islands, causing widespread devastation to Guadeloupe's dependencies: the French part of Saint-Martin
and Saint-Barthélemy. The island authorities of Saint-Martin, the smallest island in the world to be divided between
colonial powers (France and the Netherlands), used the
natural catastrophe as a pretext to repatriate illegal Haitian
immigrants. The Netherlands Antilles (Curaçao, Bonaire,
Sint-Maarten, Sint-Eustatius and Saba) remain Dutch
dependencies, although they have a small federal parliament and have been largely self-governing since the 1954
Realm Statute. The island of Aruba left the Antilles to
become a separate territory, although still within the Kingdom of the Netherlands, on 1 June 1986.

Conclusions

The year 1960 has been called 'the year of wonders' in
French, as in British, decolonization in black Africa. In
1960 the transfer of power speeded up as French West
and Equatorial Africa rapidly became Senegal, Mauritania,
Guinea, Burkina Faso, Côte d'Ivoire, Mali, Benin, Togo,
Chad, Niger, Moyen-Congo, Gabon, and the Central African Republic, almost all governed by *évolués*, or Westernized black leaders sympathetic to France. The following
years in East Africa also saw British colonial rulers depart in
Tanganyika (1961), Uganda (1962), Kenya (1963) and Zan-
zibar (1963), the last uniting in April 1964 with its neighbouring state of Tanganyika to form the United Republic of
Tanzania, with austere socialist and former school-teacher
Julius Nyerere as president. Kenya is dealt with in the next
chapter in relation to the Mau Mau uprising of the 1950s

143

and white-settler-dominated colonialism. As we have seen, the ill-considered and precipitate way in which colonial powers like Belgium withdrew from Africa intensified the birth pangs of independence and often caused political instability that led to vicious civil wars.

Almost everywhere, colonial rule in Africa came to an end far more quickly and far less satisfactorily than the Europeans, in London, Brussels, Paris or on the spot, had intended. Colonial Secretary Iain Macleod (1959–61), who oversaw the independence of many British territories in East and West Africa, admitted that the British had left rather faster than might have been thought to be ideal, from the point of view of preparing the new nations for self-government; but he later insisted that 'any other policy would have led to terrible bloodshed in Africa'. Britain's territories could not have been held by force: 'Of course there are risks in moving quickly. But the risks of moving slowly were far greater' (Low, 1993: 246). The leisurely British timetable for self-government envisaged immediately after the Second World War had been rapidly overtaken by events. Whatever the other effects of rapid decolonization might have been, British leaders like Macmillan congratulated themselves that they did not leave behind in East Africa the bloodshed of either a Congo or an Algeria, an important negative achievement.

For a French public disillusioned by the war in Algeria, departure from sub-Saharan Africa had been made possible by the *loi cadre* of 1956, providing for a large extension of representative government in each of the colonies, although within a continuing French-dominated federal structure. The Defferre law may have given black French men and women electoral equality and government posts but this was soon overshadowed in 1957 by the complete independence of Ghana from Britain under Nkrumah. If the French were initially less willing than the British to concede and prepare for outright independence, they have sought to demonstrate since the 1960s that Francophone Africa still lies within their military sphere of influence. Paris has deployed its soldiers on some 20 occasions, with the ostensible justification of protecting French lives and property, in the Comoros Islands, Gabon, Chad, Djibouti, Mauritania, the Central African Republic and Togo, as well as in the former Belgian colonies of Zaïre (Congo) and Ruanda. In 1996 France enjoyed a trade surplus with Africa worth more than £20 billion. Cultural and linguistic connections form another aspect of France's influence with her former colonies that far exceeds any lingering British presence, albeit that nearly all of the new military leaders in Sierra Leone, Ghana and Nigeria after 1966 were trained in Britain's Royal Military Academy at Sandhurst.

6

WHITE-SETTLER AFRICA: RELUCTANCE TO CONCEDE MAJORITY RULE

No other 'colonial' war divided opinion in the metropolis and threatened domestic political instability more than that of Algeria. By contrast, neighbouring Tunisia and Morocco becoming independent made little impression on the indifferent mass of French public opinion. The tenacity with which the French Army and French settlers sought to hold on to their Algerian possessions in North Africa was reflected on a smaller scale by white-settler intransigence in British Central and East Africa. For the British, particular difficulties arose from the Mau Mau rising in Kenya during the 1950s, a primary goal of which was to restore Kikuyu native lands occupied by white settlers and pro-British chieftains. In the timetable laid down in 1959 by the British Colonial Office for East African independence, Kenya was to remain a colony until after 1975. From this perspective, the hasty bargains made between the British and nationalist politicians like Kenya's Jomo Kenyatta, under which the British agreed to give up their colonial rule in 1963, were little more than last-ditch attempts to ensure a dignified departure and leave some semblance of order behind.

No African nationalism caused more trouble to the British than the white-settler nationalism of central Africa. The illegal seizure of power by whites in Southern Rhodesia (Zimbabwe) in the mid-1960s placed embarrassing strains on successive governments in the metropole because of Commonwealth and international criticism of British inaction. Prolonged African resistance, the collapse of Portuguese Mozambique, and the withdrawal of South African support, were all needed to ensure the removal of the white-settler regime in Rhodesia by 1980. Angola and Mozambique had an extensive Portuguese-settler presence when armed anti-colonial struggle broke out in the early 1960s. In the period from 1950 to 1968 the white population of Mozambique quadrupled from 50,000 to 200,000. The ability of tiny and impoverished Portugal to hold on to its huge African colonial empire until the mid-1970s, heedless of international and UN condemnation, fuelled right-wing British and French critics of their own governments' rapid decolonization. The recent history of South Africa is touched on here because in 1994, with the dismantling of apartheid and the arrival of black-majority rule, it became the last African white-settler state to hand over power.

Algeria: Under French Rule

The French occupation of Algeria went back to the 1830s and by the end of the Second World War there were some 1,250,000 European settlers, mostly French but also Spanish, Italian and Maltese, surrounded by some nine million Muslim Arabs. The Martinique writer Frantz Fanon, who served as a doctor with the Arab nationalist resistance, singled out the French settler as the chief enemy of the Algerian people, the creator of the colonial situation who, planter-like, had appropriated the land, displacing the *fellahs*: landbased and backbent Arab peasants whose nationalism was 'felt between their toes'. Faced in Algeria with the challenge of postwar Arab nationalism, French

147

colons (colonizers/landlords) and *pieds-noirs* (nickname for peasant farmers wearing cheap black shoes) made common cause to defend their threatened patrimony.

The resident European minority of colonial city dwellers and farmers on the land behaved as a political and social majority, largely controlling Algerian affairs and enjoying a privileged position, in that as French citizens they were directly represented in the French parliamentary system and did not have to rely on spokesmen in Paris to lobby for them. Muslims could only acquire citizenship by renouncing Islamic practices. Technically, Algeria was not regarded as a colony but had been incorporated into metropolitan France and was represented in the National Assembly – this made it particularly difficult to surrender government to the majority Arabs. As a province of France, Algeria had been divided into three *départements* separated from the vast and sparsely settled 'Territory of the South' where the Algerian nomadic way of life persisted and where the French ruled in a pronounced colonial manner. Yet Algeria was vastly under-administered by the French. Many Algerians in remote mountain areas had never seen an European before the outbreak of colonial war.

One outstanding feature of the period 1954–58 was the extent to which French military cadres came to identify with *Algérie Française*. Military 'honour' became irretrievably committed to the preservation of French Algeria. The angry attitude of the French Army, more particularly the parachute regiments, towards the leaders of the Fourth Republic has to be placed in the context of a series of postwar military humiliations which made resistance to Algerian nationalism ever more bitter and intransigent (Kelly, 1963). The French Army had fought an exhausting and demoralizing war in Indochina (1946–54) against Ho Chi Minh's Vietminh guerillas, leading eventually to the disastrous loss of military 'honour' at Dien Bien Phu in May 1954 which eliminated France's Asian Empire (see Chapter 3). The French government fell after this traumatic defeat – the first time a metropolitan government had fallen on a colonial issue in Europe since the Second World War.

Only four months after the subsequent ceasefire in Indochina, sporadic fighting broke out in Algeria, intertwining metropolitan and colonial politics even more closely. The Army and nationalist opinion in France, the latter embracing a wide political spectrum from Left to Right, felt that the dreary sequence of defeat and retreat had gone far enough. The French Army's sense of self-esteem was bound up with the maintenance of French rule in Algeria. Imperial footholds in South East Asia had been abandoned, Tunisia and Morocco (with few French settlers) were to receive their independence in 1956 but Algeria signified the last line of imperial defence. Decolonization was so drawn out and bloody in Algeria because it had become 'a part of the sentimental geography of the French Army' (Girardet, 1972: 146).

Algeria: Armed Insurrection

In May 1945 an attempted nationalist uprising centred on the Algerian village of Sétif was crushed with several thousand fatal casualties, many of them the result of indiscriminate 'pacification' by the French forces. A new Algerian constitution was drawn up in 1947 granting greater civil and religious liberties to Arabs but requiring a two thirds majority in the National Assembly in Paris which was never forthcoming. 'There was probably no significant colonial entity whose internal problems received *less* intelligent and sensitive analysis than French Algeria in the late 1940s and early 1950s' (Holland, 1985: 165). Once the inadequate nature of France's postwar reforms became apparent, middle-class nationalist Algerians like Ferhat Abbas, who might have been prepared to accept assimilationist solutions sincerely offered, were overshadowed by younger leaders, resolved to seek independence by revolutionary means.

In impoverished regions of Kabylia and the Aurès mountains men with previous wartime experience slowly regrouped their military organization. It remained for the *Front de Libération Nationale* (FLN) and its fighting arm, the *Armée de Libération Nationale* (ALN), to launch an armed revolt in Algeria on the early morning of All Saint's Day on 1 November 1954 that was finally to lead to independence, after nearly eight years of savage fighting, massacres, torture and repression.

The FLN wanted the diverse communities of the Algerian population to be impressed with its strength, determination and omnipresence but used ruthless terror tactics to intimidate them. Specifically, it attempted to prevent ordinary Arabs from betraying its members to the French and to force them to aid the organization in acts of sabotage. Drawing on Vietminh practice, the FLN with its six-member cell structure and *wilaya* commands, such as the Algiers area, benefited considerably from the terrain of Algeria, particularly in the north, where most of the war was fought: from east to west ran a chain of large mountain ranges, the Ouarsenis, the Kabyles, the Hodna, the Aurès and the Nementcha, with numerous other small hill ranges. Few roads entered the mountain areas and scrub-covered hillsides provided ideal cover for guerilla ambushes. On 20 August 1955 ALN regulars struck on the coast in the environs of Philippeville leading to the massacre of 71 Europeans and 61 Algerians, the latter not necessarily loyalist but known to oppose violence. The incensed French Army responded in a cycle of reprisals that exceeded the barbarism of the ALN, resulting in the deaths of probably two to three thousand alleged 'rebels' (Clayton, 1994).

As this sequence was repeated elsewhere, local insurrections escalated into revolutionary war, and Algerians not initially involved – followers of Messali Hadj's banned *Parti du Peuple Algérien* (PPA), communists, even the moderate Ferhat Abbas – were induced, by reason or by violence, to accept the leadership of the FLN. The latter resolutely opposed all compromise, and those moderate Algerians who were foolhardy enough to become candidates for public office under the French were treated as legitimate targets. The FLN's terrorism against the local population, its most significant target, did not attract much notice beyond Algeria, one exception being the Melouza village massacre of 1957. The threat of violence was thus both pervasive and continuous throughout the war, there were bombings and shootings in public places frequented by both *colons* and Algerians, such as markets, cafes, and in Algiers, cinemas. Anyone who was not actively pro-FLN risked being labelled a traitor, then being killed, usually after mutilation, since the FLN did not feel mere neutrality was sufficient after a certain point (Hutchinson, 1978).

By the end of 1955 the French had 400,000 troops in Algeria, most of them conscripts engaged in protecting the villages of rural Algeria, while crack para-formations pursued active FLN units with little regard for legal niceties. French governments which intended to combine military repression with genuine social and political reforms, as the British were doing simultaneously in Malaya, were driven into counter-terrorism by the fury of over a million settlers, fearful for their lives and property. Under a socialist resident minister, Robert Lacoste, the Army's strength in Algeria was raised to half a million, including raw French conscripts, Muslim *tirailleurs* and Senegalese mercenaries, as well as frustrated veterans of the war in Indochina. Years of bitter fighting followed in which terrorism, torture and bombings were employed by both sides, inviting somewhat misplaced parallels with another internecine struggle – Northern Ireland's 'troubles' from 1968 onwards (Horne, 1972).

In March 1956 the National Assembly in Paris voted with near unanimity to give sweeping emergency powers in Algeria to the government of socialist leader Guy Mollet, exemplifying the intensity of French nationalist feelings and the pressures of public opinion. Even the communists supported this vote which led to the extension of the war in Algeria into a crusade against Arab nationalism. The Anglo-French and Israeli conspiracy to invade Egypt from October to November 1956, in order to secure the Suez Canal from being nationalized by Colonel Nasser, was one disastrous outcome of this crusading mood. The French were hoping to punish Egypt for what little support it had given to fellow Muslim FLN guerillas. General Jacques Massu's elite 10th Parachute Division returned from Suez with victory withheld by UN and American intervention. Massu was then given an order by French hard-liner Lacoste to thwart a planned labour strike in Algiers and to clear the city of the FLN.

The Struggle for Algiers

The infamous 'battle of Algiers' was fought early in 1957 between the 8000–strong 10th Paras and the FLN network in the casbah. The FLN carried out bombing attacks on favourite *pieds-noirs* haunts, assassinated 'loyalist' Arabs, and sought to bring Algiers to a standstill by taking advantage of a perfect ground for urban guerilla activities. General Massu replied with a massive military intervention that led to the internment, torture and murder of suspects. This marked not only a victory for the *pieds-noirs*, who had long been demanding better protection, but also for the FLN, who saw it as broadening the 'interface' of Franco-Algerian friction. If the Army's ruthless counter-revolutionary tactics succeeded militarily, the FLN expanded its political support, and the general colonial situation steadily deteriorated. In the short months of its duration, '"the battle of Algiers" encapsulated the dilemmas and brutalities of decolonization more powerfully than any comparable situation of modern times' (Holland, 1985: 169). Italian Gillo Pontecorvo's outstanding pseudo-documentary movie, *The Battle of Algiers* (1965), presents an interesting contrast with Hollywood's inclusion of the same dramatic events in Mark

Robson's action-adventure film *Lost Command* (1966) that focuses on a Para commander (Anthony Quinn) seeking to recover French pride lost at Dien Bien Phu. A direct outcome of Massu's temporary triumph against the FLN in Algiers was the Muslim uprising there a year later.

In the following two years (1957–59) the cancer of Algeria spread out to infect political and social life in France itself. Probably a majority of French citizens still favoured protecting the interests of the *colons* whatever the price. Increasingly, the French Army and police were morally compromised by the use of torture interrogations and the adoption of psychological warfare techniques in Algeria, whose exposure reinforced UN and international disapproval. After the fall of Mollet, the French military believed that weak and unstable governments in Paris would sell Algeria down the river. On 13 May 1958 the *pieds-noirs*, who had staged a general strike and seized the main government building in Algiers while the Army watched, nominated a 'Committee of Public Safety' which Massu was asked to head and grudgingly accepted, later claiming he did so only to prevent further disturbances. Massu's action none the less indicated that the French Army in Algeria had now joined with the settlers in open defiance of the government in Paris. Despite an earlier plot to assassinate him by *colon* extremists, Army Commander General Raoul Salan also pledged military support to the *pieds-noirs* leaders and added a loud 'Vive de Gaulle!' to a speech made on 15 May to a large crowd in Algiers. Two days later, left-wing Gaullist Jacques Soustelle, a former governor-general of Algeria popular with the *colons*, arrived to add further fuel to the hysteria.

The danger of a military coup directed from Algiers was only averted by the political re-emergence of General Charles de Gaulle, the charismatic but aloof French wartime leader widely greeted as the saviour of *Algérie Française*. He was voted in as prime minister in the Paris Assembly on 1 June 1958, despite vociferous communist protests, by a majority of 329 to 224 votes. The Fourth Republic had gone into voluntary liquidation with the threat of a military take-over hanging over it but de Gaulle had secured political legitimacy and so was not beholden to the Army. In Algiers on 4 June, he was presented to a vast crowd, including Muslims as well as settlers. With arms outstretched in a V-sign de Gaulle opened by declaring resoundingly: *'Je vous ai compris'* but did not reveal the nature of his enigmatic understanding. Each faction in Algeria chose to believe he supported them (Williams, 1995: 382).

The Surrender of French Algeria

The new regime in Paris was soon monopolized by de Gaulle who created a less than democratic Fifth Republic that was to achieve a final solution to the Algerian problem but not as the Army expected by reasserting French power over Algeria. Influenced by Britain's 1957 decolonizations in Ghana and Malaya, de Gaulle, whose main concern was always metropolitan, did not want France to get left behind. Salan, who had moved closer to the settlers during the May 1958 crisis, was replaced as commander in Algeria by General Maurice Challe who vigorously set about the task of destroying the nationalists. At the end of 1958 the ALN were approaching military defeat; by mid-1959 that defeat was almost total. De Gaulle's position in any future negotiations with the FLN was undoubtedly strengthened by the military success of Challe's offensive operations (Clayton, 1994).

Yet French public opinion on Algeria was more deeply divided than ever before and war-weariness was becoming increasingly evident in the *métropole*. Early in 1960 de Gaulle took control of the situation, when the *colons* again took to the barricades in central Algiers but this time without military support, by picking out and replacing the imperialist generals, settler leaders and civil servants who had defeated the peace-making efforts of his predecessors.

The French President appeared on television on 29 January 1960. On this occasion, rather than making his usual delphic utterances seeking to pacify both the Army and Algerians he declared that 'the Algerians shall have free choice of their destiny' and that there would be no concessions to those 'who dream of being usurpers' (Williams, 1995: 402).

On 4 November 1960, de Gaulle at last came off the fence and declared that the new course he had followed since his return to the Presidency now 'leads not to an Algeria governed by metropolitan France but to an Algerian Algeria. This means an emancipated Algeria in which the Algerians themselves will decide their destiny...' (Betts, 1991: 111). On 20 December the United Nations, now with many new African members, recognized Algeria's right to self-determination. A referendum was held on 6 January 1961 in which the French nation voted overwhelmingly in favour of de Gaulle's position, further displeasing the already discontented *pieds-noirs* and those generals whom de Gaulle had reposted because of their support for the settler cause. Subsequently, in April 1961, the First Foreign Paratroop Regiment seized control in Algiers and there was yet another threat of military insurrection.

The conspiring generals, Challe, Jouhaud, Zeller and Salan, prepared an ill-defined *coup d'état* to overthrow de Gaulle which failed (the air force refused to join in) and with it any attempt at forceful change of national policy. Outside the Algiers area the plotters had found little support but there was extravagant talk during the state of emergency of paratroopers from Algeria landing on the mainland and surrounding Paris. The officers involved were isolated and disciplined, leaving behind only the colonial irreconcilables who went underground in the *Organisation de L'Armée Secrète* (OAS), led by Salan and Jouhaud, to fight FLN terrorism with counter-terrorism, a sort of armed resistance to de Gaulle's self-determination policy for Algeria (Henissart, 1973).

The reactionary OAS launched a savage campaign against the Muslim population of Algeria, designed to provoke a reaction that it was hoped would oblige the French Army to reassert authority. Such desperate tactics, including plots to assassinate de Gaulle and bombings in France during the autumn and winter of 1961–62, accelerated the psychological rupture with the French colonial past, bringing the diehards into direct confrontation with the Army and *les barbouzes* (the 'false beards', former policemen and criminals, sent from France to fight the OAS). These mounting horrors produced a revulsion in France that allowed independence negotiations with Houari Boumédienne and Mohammed Ben Bella, representing the provisional republic, at the French-Swiss spa town of Evian in 1962 to be received with both gratitude and relief. Salan was captured in April and on 1 July 1962 Algeria officially became independent of France. Joint arrangements for the exploitation of newly discovered Saharan oil were agreed which lasted until 1970.

The ALN had achieved the first complete victory over a colonial power ostensibly through force of arms in the postwar period, if we exclude the only partial (North Vietnam) victory of the Vietminh in 1954. Yet the scars remaining, the cost of up to half a million Arab lives and the involvement of over half a million French troops, the deaths of over 3000 European civilians, plus the continued killings of the OAS, were not easily healed by the treaty signed at Evian. The French estimated that 50,000 Algerians were killed between April 1961 and the ceasefire, followed by anything from 30,000 to 150,000 revenge killings of loyalists and Arab auxiliaries or *harkis* who had served under the French. After the OAS and FLN agreed a truce, a mass exodus of some 1,450,000 people, mostly *colons*, but also including many loyalist Arabs, left Algeria's ports *en route* for southern France or elsewhere, carrying only the permitted two suitcases per person.

Kenya: Under British Rule

Wherever there was a sizeable white-settler community struggling to preserve its authority, surrounded by a sea of hostile or indifferent African or Arab faces, violent confrontation that could involve the metropole was an ever-present possibility. One of the twentieth century's most sustained and bloody risings against white colonial rule in sub-Saharan Africa took place in Kenya. Britain's policies during the 1950s in East and Central Africa were contrary to those in the Gold Coast and Nigeria (see Chapter 5), where the Colonial Office was more flexible and accommodating to African trends. The imperial position was markedly different in Kenya because of the existence of a self-confident white-settler population capable of mobilising political support at home, plus the greater strategic import-ance of East Africa for the protection of British interests in the Middle East and the Indian Ocean.

Kenya was by far the most valuable and important of Britain's East African possessions, unlike Uganda open to extensive white European settlement since the 1890s. Because Kenya remained under Colonial Office supervision, prosperous white settlers had so far failed to turn the colony into a self-governing settler state on the model of Southern Rhodesia since 1923 or the Union of South Africa since 1910. The white settler population of Kenya were, nevertheless, deeply entrenched by the late 1940s in the political and economic life of the country, despite the presence of five million Africans. This dominant position was confirmed by settlers taking prominent posts in the colonial government during the 1939–45 wartime emergency and the incorporation of settler bodies, such as the Kenya Farm-ers' Association, as legitimate governing institutions within the colonial state.

Because of this wartime retreat from the citadels of power by the Colonial Service, by 1945 the settlers had become much more powerful than before the war. From

1945–48 some 8000 white immigrants came out to Kenya, actively encouraged by the British government (bringing the total of settlers to 30,000). The 'White Highlands', a great block of some 16,700 square miles in the heart of Kenya, were reserved exclusively for settler use, a colony within the colony, the 'tribal homeland of the whites' and guarantor of their political and economic survival. The existence of this powerful stratum of European settlers meant that there was less scope for constitutional reform than in West Africa. In 1948 Kenya's first postwar British governor, Sir Philip Mitchell, who had previously served in Tanganyika, and as governor in Uganda and Fiji, dismissed self-government for Kenya as fantastic, 'as practicable a proposition as it would be to set up in the United States an entirely autonomous, self-governing Red Indian Republic' (Bennett and Smith, 1976: 110).

Thus the Mau Mau revolt was as much the product of the Kenya government's strategy of denial of black rights as of the determination of the militants within the Kikuyu to fight to the death. The Kikuyu, the largest and most successful tribe in Kenya, making up some 20 per cent of its population, held a tribal 'land unit' bordering the 'White Highlands'. They were divided between 'collaborationist' white-educated Christians and potential candidates for the new Mau Mau blood-sacrifice oathing ceremonies drawn from a growing, disenchanted tribal population in search of new homesteads, squatters driven off white farms and, in Nairobi and Mombasa, a new elite of unemployed clerks and *askaris* (Kikuyu who had served overseas in allied forces). Recently doubt has been cast on the view that returned soldiers were particularly important in African nationalist movements, upwardly mobile ex-*askaris* were in any case more likely to become involved in constitutional politics than to join the Mau Mau.

The Kenya colonial government was convinced that the real cause of land hunger and overcrowding in the Kikuyu reserve was environmental: the deterioration of the land through overstocking of cattle, and poor agricultural methods. The imperial solution hence became compulsory destocking, improved veterinary practices and soil conservation through the terracing of eroded hillsides. Compulsory African labour was needed to achieve these ends which benefited the 'collaborationist' large yeoman farmer far more than the poor peasant. Opening the 'White Highlands' to African peasant farmers at the expense of European commercial agriculture was to be avoided at all costs. The colony's white rulers believed it would destroy the whole basis of the Kenyan economy and put an end to development. The Kikuyu land grievance was made worse by the return to the reserves of numerous squatters squeezed off European farms, and of landless Kikuyu from other areas.

Kenya was unique in British East Africa for having had, even before the Second World War, some overt African political activity. As early as 1929 the Kikuyu Central Association (KCA) had put forward a demand for an eventual African majority on the Legislative Council. In 1944 the first African member, the Kikuyu Eliud Mathu, was nominated to the Council, and a new political group, the Kenya African Union (KAU), was formed to support him. There was also an impressive expansion of the African press in Nairobi and the black educational initiative of the Kenya Independent Schools Association (KISA) in the Central Province, as well as the postwar return to civilian life, with rising expectations, of ex-*askaris*. Nairobi grew from some 40,000 in 1938 to more than 95,000 in 1952; already by 1948 half of Kenya's African wage labour was non-agricultural. A closely integrated Kikuyu peasant society was in the process of breaking up because of land fragmentation and the problems of adjustment to a wage economy in cities like Nairobi. The split with moderate, middle-class nationalism in the KAU and the squatter agitation of 1946–47 indicated that Kikuyu activists mostly fought and died for land and not for some abstract concept of nationhood (Throup, 1987).

Kenya's postwar British governor, Sir Philip Mitchell, believed in a paternalistic, multiracial government, a gradualistic doctrine of trusteeship shared by the Colonial Office, to oversee 'the great mass of the people in this region [who] are still in a state of ignorance and backwardness' (Bennett and Smith, 1976: 113). In Kenya and Tanganyika, the British embarked on 'a bold experiment to frustrate African nationalism through an elaborate mechanism of power-sharing labelled multiracialism' (Darwin, 1988: 194). In Tanganyika, where from 1952 equal representation was achieved on the Legislative Council, 'immigrant' settlers (many of German or Greek origin) were given an influence on government out of all proportion to their numbers. In Kenya, it is unlikely that the British Colonial Office originally intended their multiracial constitutional reforms to lead to independence just over ten years later under the vibrant leadership of Jomo Kenyatta, former president of the KAU. More likely, Whitehall civil servants hoped a moderate multiracial or white-dominated party would be the beneficiary with the decolonized state bound closely to Britain.

Kenya: State of Emergency

From mid-1952, after Mitchell's departure as governor, there was a three months' interregnum, during which the rate of murders and cattle-maiming in the Central Province rose alarmingly – the leisurely break before the next governor arrived is itself indicative of British complacency. The climax came early in October 1952 with the murder in broad daylight outside Nairobi of Senior Chief Waruhiu wa Kungu of Kiambu, a Kikuyu and a strong supporter of the government. An exotic system of chieftanship had been imposed on the Kikuyu tribe for the convenience of the British administration. Chiefs were nominated, paid for, and dismissed by British district officers and hence were not popular. Loyalist chiefs were, therefore, in an invidious position, paid less than taxi drivers in Nairobi, seen as a foreign invention and, consequently, prominent targets for the Mau Mau. Finally, under pressure from vociferous white settlers, on 20 October a State of Emergency was proclaimed by the new Governor, Sir Evelyn Baring, not to be lifted until 1959. This declaration saw the colonial government raising the stakes in Kenya by seizing the initiative but also closed all avenues of protest other than armed rebellion, because no African political activity (public meetings being banned) was allowed for the duration of the Emergency.

'Operation Jock Scott' led almost immediately to the arrest of 130 suspected Mau Mau leaders, including Kenyatta, whom white settlers convinced Baring to be responsible for the rising. 'There is clearly no doubt that Kenyatta is the mainspring of the movement and the KISA Teacher Training College at Githurguri its primary instrument', Baring informed the Colonial Office (PRO). The Governor had short-sightedly adopted the view of Kenya's white settlers, unable to credit uneducated, 'primitive' Kikuyu with initiating organized protest. 'Indoctrination of the young' was to be prevented by closing down KISA schools and the training college. A rigged trial was held by the British in 1953 at Kapenguria, a remote town near the Ugandan border in north-west Kenya, to secure Kenyatta's conviction for organizing Mau Mau and he was sentenced to seven years' imprisonment. Yet if the KAU was used as a cover by the young militants of the Mau Mau central committee, Kenyatta himself was always careful to avoid direct participation (Lapping, 1985).

Whether Mau Mau represented a narrowly tribalist affair without a genuine nationalist dimension is open to debate. One Africanist (Throup, 1987) believes they failed to become a truly nationalist movement, alienating the non-Kikuyu elements in the African population as well as the Kikuyu moderates. Another (Furedi, 1989: 108–9) claims Mau Mau represented 'a radical force combining some of the characteristics of militant nationalism and an underground peasant movement, motivated by specific local grievances and led by a group of activists becoming increasingly national although forced to operate in secret'. A third consensual view is that they were a 'tribally-based peasant revolt originally formed on the fringe of a nationalist movement' (Hargreaves, 1988: 131). In the contemporary British media Kenya's rebellion was depicted as an outbreak of African savagery, illustrated by bloodthirsty oathtaking and the indiscriminate murder by *panga* (long knives) of numerous unprotected white settlers on isolated farms that threatened the stability of a prosperous British colonial possession (see the British film *Simba*, a 1955 Dirk Bogarde vehicle). In reality only 32 white civilians were killed during the Emergency. In an attempt to criminalize the Mau Mau, British propaganda went to great lengths to portray them before world opinion as waging a civil war within the Kikuyu, or as an irrational force of evil, dominated by bestial oath ceremonies (Carruthers, 1995).

The first six months of the Mau Mau rising, apart from a number of isolated murders, were spent mainly in building up forces on both sides. Governor Baring was convinced by 24 November 1952, having received advice from the head of British intelligence, Sir Percy Sillitoe, that the situation in Kenya had moved from a limited police operation into a small-scale guerilla war. Imperial measures to fight and win such a war had become necessary, forestalling the settlers taking drastic action on their own which could provoke fullscale civil war, so Baring recalled units of the King's African Rifles from other parts of East Africa and a battalion of the Lancashire Fusiliers was flown in from the Suez Canal Zone (Throup, 1992). Meanwhile, thousands of Kikuyu took to the forests on the slopes of Mount Kenya and in the Aberdare range, at the height of the Emergency in mid-1953 they may have numbered some 15,000. Baring's policy to repatriate at gun-point Kikuyu 'squatters' found on European farms to the Kikuyu Reserve only served to create more recruits for the Mau Mau.

The second phase of hostilities brought a more positive and concerted Mau Mau effort against isolated guard posts and 'loyalist' villages, such as the Lari settlement massacre of 26 March 1953. Some settler leaders, like Michael Blundell, expressed real concern over the possible outcome of the struggle, despite the overwhelming military superiority of the British. Every Kikuyu was a Mau Mau within this 'pathological atmosphere' and visiting British critics of settler Kenya were seen as agents of the Kremlin. In May 1953 General Sir George Erskine was appointed Commander-in-Chief and, like Templer in Malaya, did much to reinvigorate the British military campaign. The rotund Erskine, a friend of Churchill, had little time for the settlers ('middle-class sluts') because they were 'loathed' by Africans and he also despised Sir Evelyn Baring, whose indecision owed much to ill-health. General Erskine disciplined British soldiers who killed and tortured suspected Mau Mau but could do little to prevent similar atrocities committed by Home Guards and the King's African Rifles or the volunteer, settler-dominated Kenya Police Reserve and Kenya Regiment. Volunteer forces showed little restraint in the indiscriminate killing of Kikuyu: 92 'died in custody' and 430 were shot 'resisting arrest' or 'trying to escape' during the first six months of the Emergency (Clayton, 1976).

By early 1954 the security forces had decisively gained the upper hand, because with the introduction under Emergency regulations of Kikuyu 'villagization', internment and communal punishment they ensured that Mau Mau activists would be cut off from their supporters and would eventually become isolated. When Police Commissioner Richard Catling arrived in Kenya in April, after serving in Palestine and Malaya, there were some 78,000 Mau Mau suspects (one in three of adult male Kikuyu) behind barbed wire in detention, rehabilitation and work camps. Detention camps used white 'screening teams' to force political detainees to confess that they had taken a Mau Mau oath. A former police officer who served on such a team took a harsh but typical white view: 'The Mickeys were hard men and only hard methods would work with them. It was a war to save white civilisation in Kenya and in war people get killed' (Edgerton, 1989: 200). British government officials, by institutionalizing violence or the use of 'compelling force', only assured the failure of their efforts to 'rehabilitate' the Mau Mau through confession of oath taking. (Survivors announced in April 1999 that they were to sue the British government, demanding £3 billion compensation for human rights abuses committed during the uprising.)

There followed a long period in the mid-1950s during which the forest groups were progressively isolated by the concentration of the Kikuyu of the reserves into large fortified villages, with Home Guards, watch-towers and spiked ditches (a resettlement tactic familiar from the New Villages in Malaya). The Mau Mau guerillas were also worn down by the bombing of their camp sites: the British dropped 50,000 tons of bombs on the forests and fired over two million machine gun rounds on strafing runs before the Emergency was over. During March and April 1954 'Operation Anvil' saw the police and army detain 20,000 suspects and interrogate virtually all male Kikuyu living in Nairobi, upsetting lines of communication between supporters in the city and the Mau Mau forest gangs. A series of large-scale military operations during the first three months of 1955 disorganized and scattered the major Mau Mau units, forcing them increasingly on to the defensive and making it possible to withdraw troops from the Kikuyu reserves. 'Villagization' and the effective isolation of the fighters in the forests had established the clear superiority of the security forces. Mau Mau insurgents killed were estimated officially in 1956 at 11,503, to which must be added another 900 wounded and more than a thousand executions (as opposed to 63 white security force members killed). The offensive was now carried into the forests themselves and this went on until the Emergency was finally declared over in November 1959, although even then hundreds of Mau Mau fighters remained hidden in the forests.

On 3 March 1959 at the notorious Hola detention camp in the Kenya Coast Province, reserved for Kikuyu who still refused to confess oath-taking, African guards on a British work detail killed 11 detainees and hospitalized another 20. This incident was debated in the British Parliament and led to the Fairn Committee report demand that 'shock treatment' and violence by 'screening teams' to compel confessions in the camps must end. Alan Lennox-Boyd was replaced as Colonial Secretary in the autumn by Iain Macleod, a progressive Tory profoundly offended by what had happened at Hola and prepared to apply a drastic solution to resolve the Kenyan political impasse. The four-year-old recommendation of the East Africa Royal Commission for the ending of the 'White Highlands' reservation was now belatedly accepted. The new governor, Sir Patrick Renison (1959–62), made it clear that it was the Ghana solution, not the Rhodesian one, that was to be prescribed by Macleod for Kenya. Majority rule was to replace white-dominated multiracialism. Diehard whites felt betrayed by Macleod, probably the most effective Colonial Secretary since Joseph Chamberlain, who was determined that Britain should not be left behind as the pace of decolonization quickened elsewhere in Africa in the late 1950s and early 1960s.

The traditional Lancaster House Conference was held in January 1960 to discuss Kenya's future with African delegates calling for early independence or freedom ('Uhuru') but demands that Jomo Kenyatta should attend were refused. The Kenya African National Union (KANU) won 67.4 per cent of the vote at the 1961 election and insisted on Kenyatta's release from prison which the governor, bowing to the inevitable, granted in August 1961. For nearly two years the members of the dominant Luo–Kikuyu alliance worked steadily to establish KANU as a monolithic national party under Kenyatta's magnetic leadership which in the 1963 elections won a decisive victory. On 1 June 1963 Kenyatta became Kenya's first black prime minister on the attainment of self-government and upheld the virtues of reconciliation between the nation's ethnic groups. Some 1500 Mau Mau fighters came out from the forests of Mount Kenya and laid down their arms. Yet a broad national base eluded Kenyatta, as non-alliance Kenya African Democratic Union (KADU) supporters refused to join the KANU-led government. Decolonized Kenya with, in effect, a single political party, moved towards presidential rule. Land from the 'White Highlands' was not confiscated but purchased with British aid and redistributed to prosperous KANU entrepreneurs. Numerous land-hungry former 'freedom fighters' emerging from the forests were left to seek their fortunes in the growing slums of Nairobi. Kenyatta's government presided over an expanding economy but also introduced political assassination, the rise of ethnic favouritism and increased financial corruption before the first president's death in 1978 (Kyle, 1999).

Southern Rhodesia: Towards UDI

In Southern Rhodesia's white-settler regime in central Africa some basic contradictions within European political ranks had appeared in 1953 with the succession of Garfield Todd to the premiership, a cautious white liberal who sought to go at least some of the way towards meeting African demands. Fearful that Todd's leadership would prompt white voters to switch their loyalties to 'purist' right-wing alternatives, the United Federal Party (UFP) ousted him from the leadership early in 1959 and installed Sir Edgar Whitehead as premier. At the general election which soon followed, the UFP retained a mere five-seat majority, while the conservative Dominion Party (DP) actually won more of the popular vote. On the basis of the February 1961 constitution enfranchising only a small percentage of adult Africans, Whitehead realized that full independence under white-minority rule would only take place roughly at the same time as in the neighbouring African states (on the assumption that there was little real difference between these various decolonizations) if it was coupled with some improvement in African social and political rights. For settlers had systematically replaced local laws and customs with laws aimed at increasing financial rewards for whites, racial discrimination was still rife, wage differentials between whites and Africans were insisted upon by European unions, and the fundamental injustice of the Southern Rhodesian land settlement remained undisturbed (Hargreaves, 1988).

Like Garfield Todd before him, however, Whitehead risked alienating white voters from the UFP should he proceed too rapidly with improvements in African education, access to land and political representation. Indeed, a new ultra-right 'populist' party, the Rhodesian Front (RF) led by Winston Field, emerged in March 1962, expounding the view that Whitehead had been manoeuvred by the British into a sell-out of the white-dominated Central African Federation (CAF; see Chapter 5), not only in regard to copper-rich Northern Rhodesia but within Southern Rhodesia itself. At the end of 1962, veteran nationalist Joshua Nkomo, founder of the recently banned Zimbabwe African People's Union (ZAPU), and his followers did their best to prevent qualified blacks from registering as voters for territorial elections, trying to make the 1961 constitution look unworkable. This boycott by most of those Africans whom Whitehead had enfranchised led to his defeat when the RF won 35 seats against the UFP's 29 and proceeded to form a new hard-line white government.

The spotlight was now on Field, in particular whether he would attend the CAF dissolution conference which the

United Kingdom intended to convene at Victoria Falls in June 1963. Both Field and his Treasury Minister, Ian Smith, ultimately attended, claiming later that they had received British assurances that Southern Rhodesia would be allowed to move to white self-government at the same time as Northern Rhodesia (Zambia) and Nyasaland (Malawi) adopted African-majority rule. It is more likely that they attended the conference in order to make sure of securing the CAF's military assets, putting the RF leadership in a position to threaten a unilateral declaration of independence (UDI). British delegates privately approved of this brandishing of the UDI card because it might induce black nationalists into a compromise, pushing them into settling for something less than one-man, one-vote. Winston Field visited London in January 1964 for talks with Macmillan's replacement as Tory Prime Minister, Alec Douglas-Home, requesting independence on the basis of the existing franchise. Either self-government or UDI was the option facing Whitehall. On grounds of diplomatic pragmatism, what was needed was some move to soothe the Afro-Asian Commonwealth. 'Sir Alec', concluded a Rhodesian cabinet paper in February, 'made it very clear that he wanted a facade as it was a question of presentation to the world. He was quite cynical about this' (Darwin, 1988: 316). There was little flexibility on the white Rhodesian side and Field, who had never been anything more than a figurehead, was replaced as RF leader by hardliner Ian Smith on 3 April 1964.

In May 1964 Smith called a general election from Salisbury (Harare) and obtained an overwhelming white majority supporting his intransigence. Smith made economic and security preparations for UDI, negotiations with the UK now being nothing more than a charade, then at the British general election on 15 October 1964 the Labour Party won a majority and Harold Wilson became Prime Minister. Smith visited London, largely in order to launch an appeal over Wilson's head to the British public through the media and also to get access to oil and other raw materials for a post-UDI regime. In late 1964 the Southern Rhodesian government went through the motions of organizing an *Indaba*-plus-referendum of chiefs and headmen to elicit African opinion which predictably 'approved' the acceptability of the existing franchise. Wilson made a last-ditch attempt to prevent UDI in late October 1965 when, for the benefit of the British media, he flew to Salisbury to meet Smith's cabinet and African leaders temporarily released from detention camps. Smith none the less pressed the UDI button on 11 November 1965 with language emulating that of the American declaration of independence in 1776, albeit omitting 'all men are created equal'.

UDI was demonstrably an illegal coup taking place in a dependent British colonial territory. African governments demanded that Britain should exercise her sovereignty by bringing this rebellion to an end but only Barbara Castle, a junior member of Wilson's cabinet, was in favour of intervention. In any case, no British government of whatever political hue was likely to retaliate against UDI by sending British troops to manhandle Southern Rhodesian whites into handing over power to black Africans. Not only would a British invasion directed against our 'kith and kin' upset working-class voters in the metropole but it also risked a covert military rising by senior army officers with personal links in Rhodesia against the instructions of the civil power. The logistical difficulties of assembling superior forces were also formidable, argued Defence Secretary Denis Healey – although vast distance did not prevent the Falklands invasion 17 years later. Wilson had prematurely disclosed his hand in a speech made in Salisbury on 30 October 1965 when he excluded military intervention: there would be no 'thunderbolt hurtling through the sky...in the shape of the Royal Air Force' (Boyce, 1999: 229). Yet he also maintained a steadfast refusal to consider recognizing Rhodesian independence without further concessions to the African majority. Economic sanctions against

Rhodesia were endorsed and made mandatory by the UN but white South Africa paid them little attention, neither did the Portuguese rulers of Mozambique and certain important multinational companies.

Smith's illegal regime survived and strengthened its control over signs of African resistance, despite repeated warnings of impending collapse. Wilson, desperate to appease his Commonwealth and foreign critics, agreed to meet Smith aboard warships of the Royal Navy in 1966 and again in 1968 but the rebels showed little inclination to accept the proposed Commonwealth Office formula for a settlement of 'no independence before majority rule'. Wilson's government was turned out of office, still deadlocked in its Rhodesian policy, in June 1970. After UDI failed to find support among the African population, the well-armed white security forces were left in secure control. Sanctions were being evaded and attacks on settler farms launched from Zambian bases by both Nkomo's Ndebele-led ZAPU and a break-away formed by the Revd Ndabaninghi Sithole in August 1963, the Shona-led Zimbabwe African National Union (ZANU), were easily contained by the RF regime. Under its new (March 1970) republican constitution (Southern) Rhodesia was still prosperous enough to attract thousands of white immigrants. Alec Douglas-Home, back at the Foreign Office under Prime Minister Edward Heath, visited Salisbury in November 1971 and persuaded Smith to make constitutional changes which opened theoretical possibilities of African majority rule but in a far distant future.

White Rhodesia: Black Resistance

A commission led by a judge, Lord Pearce, revealed that grassroots African opinion generally understood and totally rejected the Douglas-Home proposals to defer black aspirations, contrary to Smith's expectation of African passivity. The African National Council (ANC) founded in

December 1971 to contest the proposed settlement, brought former members of both ZANU and ZAPU into temporary alliance under the benign leadership of Bishop Abel Muzorewa of the United Methodist Church. ZANU militants had also entered into close alliance on Rhodesia's eastern borders with Mozambique Liberation Front (FRE-LIMO) guerillas and learned from them how revolutionary Marxism might be applied in the political education of rural Mashonaland. On 21 December 1972 a small ZANU force launched the first attack on a white farm in Rhodesia for six years, so opening an increasingly effective guerilla war or, from the white perspective, a 'terrorist war' of attrition against the 'civilized standards' and 'Christian values' of the Rhodesian Way of Life.

In July 1973 Smith began new negotiations with Muzor-ewa, the most pliable African leader who still commanded broad support. The danger of a bloc of revolutionary states under Marxist influence extending across central Africa from Angola to Mozambique was now creating consider-able alarm abroad, particularly in Washington. White Rho-desia's paranoid anti-communism was also exploited by right-wing British MPs who demanded an end to economic sanctions. Britain's Labour government elected in 1974 proved incapable of effecting the transfer of power and so the attempt to negotiate the final decolonization of Rhode-sia now became an international exercise whose first initi-atives were made by two unlikely collaborators: Kenneth Kaunda of Zambia and B.J. Vorster of South Africa. In August 1975 Smith reluctantly attempted to open negoti-ations with Joshua Nkomo (ZAPU), Revd Sithole (ZANU) and Bishop Muzorewa (ANC) in a railway carriage above the Zambezi River, but the talks were soon abandoned.

The nationalist and guerilla leaders were bitterly divided but in October 1976 ZANU and ZAPU agreed to ally in a Patriotic Front (PF). Significantly, Robert Mugabe had taken over from Sithole as the recognized leader of ZANU. Mugabe was a dedicated and ambitious radical who secured the confidence of the guerilla forces and of Samora Machel, now President of Mozambique. White Rhodesia, meanwhile, had been engaged since 1972 in a bitter, and ultimately humiliating, war of counter-insurgency, secret executions, detention without trial, press censorship and martial law; to the outside world appearing a racial elite fighting to maintain its privileged position. From 1977–79 Patriotic Front guerillas killed 348 white civilians, allegedly 2751 black civilians and the security forces admitted to killing 3360 black civilians (Caute, 1983). This increasingly bitter guerilla war took place against the background of international attempts to secure a peaceful settlement. In 1976 pressure was exerted upon the obdurate Smith by both Prime Minister Vorster of South Africa and America's Secretary of State, Henry Kissinger, the arch exponent of 'shuttle diplomacy'. The success of this international decolonization exercise turned on whether Smith, subsequently under strong economic pressure from the new American President Jimmy Carter, would concede to 'moderate' African leaders a transition to majority rule sufficiently attractive to withdraw popular support from the more 'extreme' Mugabe.

Smith signed an 'internal settlement' with Muzorewa and Sithole on 3 March 1978, providing for an interim power-sharing administration to prepare for the election of a new multiracial government of 'Zimbabwe-Rhodesia'. These proposals were rejected by the PF and the guerrillas because they entrenched control of the security forces, judiciary and civil service firmly in white hands. Prime Minister Muzorewa's so-called government never exercised authority over the whole territory of 'Zimbabwe-Rhodesia' and many Africans saw the bishop as a tool of the white regime. Over 7000 were killed during 1979, including some 400 members of the security forces; the country was placed under martial law and PF forces became the effective government in many areas. The new right-wing British Conservative government led by Margaret Thatcher, returned in May 1979, wanted to accept the new constitution, recognize the Smith–Muzorewa government as legitimate, and end sanctions. Under strong pressure from black Commonwealth governments prudence prevailed, however, and a final constitutional conference was held in London's Lancaster House from September to December 1979.

Lord Carrington, the pragmatic new Foreign Secretary who chaired the conference, did not share the readiness of the Tory Right to discount the Commonwealth now that it had become a means by which African states could bring pressure on Britain, and persuaded Mrs Thatcher to insist on a genuine test of African opinion, though privately hoping this would endorse the Muzorewa compromise. Appointing Christopher Soames as governor temporarily resumed Britain's effective as well as legal control over the former colony and, with the support of a Commonwealth monitoring force of 1548 men, he managed at last to implement the precarious ceasefire. The guerilla armies were preserved in their assembly points for integration into the forces of the new state, rather than being disarmed by a white Rhodesian army, and an election was conducted under equitable conditions on 29 February 1980 which largely split along the Shona–Ndebele ethnic divide. Muzorewa was routed; Nkomo's ZAPU won just 20 of the parliamentary seats but, in a shock to the British government, Mugabe's ZANU (PF) party secured a clear majority of 57 out of the 80 African seats (Boyce, 1999). On 18 April 1980 Britain transferred the last remnants of her colonial authority to a coalition government under Robert Mugabe. Between April 1980 and October 1981, 32,000 whites departed. Zimbabwe's remaining citizens began living side by side, with equal rights – although the white minority still retained the land, property and wealth amassed during the Rhodesian era. Twenty years after independence, the invasions of nearly 1,200 white-owned farms by Mugabe's ZANU-PF supporters (some veterans of the independence war), largely to preclude a strong election challenge from a new opposition party, threatened renewed turmoil amid a crumbling economy, soaring inflation and fuel shortages.

Portuguese Angola, Mozambique and Guinea

In 1962 Ronald Segal, the South African editor of a Penguin paperback series on the 'New Africa', predicted that the Portuguese would be driven from Angola, Mozambique and Guinea, just as they had been from Goa – the last vestige of European colonialism in India – by a UN-condoned Indian invasion at the end of 1961, 'only the number of months left to them allows speculation' (Wilson, 1994: 177). Yet it was to take another 13 years, and the 1974 'Revolution of the Flowers' in Lisbon, before Portugal's African territories were finally set free. The Portuguese empire in Africa is also noteworthy because it proved a further exception to the supposition that a European colonial system could not resist the onslaught of militant nationalism. Until the 1974 revolution within Portugal overthrew military ruler General Salazar's successor Marcello Caetano, brought about in large part by the military's dissatisfaction with Lisbon's management of the anticolonial struggle, the Portuguese had made no genuine preparations to terminate colonial rule.

The 'corporative and unitary Republic' or dictatorship of António de Oliveira Salazar, prime minister of Portugal from 1932 to 1968, never intended to promote independence in territories like Angola and Mozambique, seen as Portuguese 'overseas provinces'. Salazar sternly resisted pressure to begin transfer of power to African hands. Portugal, one of the poorest countries in Europe, whose colonial interests were central to its economic existence, hung on grimly to its African possessions until the mid-1970s. The Portuguese people, accustomed to authoritarian rule at home, were unmoved by authoritarianism in the colonies. Salazar consistently played upon feelings of national pride and glorified the achievements of Portuguese imperial rule as an inducement to future greatness. Yet Portuguese Africa was almost completely undeveloped and a financial burden to the metropole. Public works, sugar and other estates, and the few mines, were operated largely by African forced labour.

In the 1930s and 1940s a spate of grandiose colonial legislation from Lisbon gave the impression of great change but merely laid the foundations for future growth. The development of Angola and Mozambique in the 1950s was none the less considerable. As Salazar had earlier suggested: 'The rich, extensive colonial lands, underdeveloped and sparsely populated, are the natural complement for metropolitan agriculture. In addition they will take care of Portugal's excessive population' (Oliver and Atmore, 1977: 272). Surprisingly large numbers of Portuguese peasants with minimal education and few skills migrated to these African possessions: by 1960 there were over 200,000 settlers in Angola, and 90,000 in Mozambique. The African populations were 4,500,000 and 6,200,000 respectively. Europeans controlled agriculture and mining, particularly the Angolan diamond mines. Portugal's African colonies had become white/brown-settler territories, though without self-government as in the Central African Federation of the 1950s.

Portugal's racial policy was, in theory, similar to the French policy of assimilation but citizenship secured few political rights, either in Africa or in Portugal, and in any case was difficult for Africans to obtain. Schools were few, despite boasts about civilizing native peoples, and economic opportunities lacking, so that by 1950 there were only 30,000 assimilados ('civilized' Africans with citizenship) in Angola and 25,000 in Mozambique. The vast majority of the population were indigenas ('natives'), whose main function in the eyes of the Portuguese was to provide slave labour. The 'native' was civilized by instilling into him the Western moral precept that he had no right to live without

175

working. Portugal also benefited from this labour, as the colonies expanded, until about 25 per cent of the national budget was derived from Africa. In 1951 the colonies were theoretically incorporated into Portugal as overseas 'provinces' but the inferior status of the African *indigenas* remained. Until 1966, in terms of preferential markets, over 40 per cent of Angola's imports and a third of Mozambique's were provided by Portugal (Maxwell, 1982).

Armed Struggle in the 1960s

Like the Belgians in the Congo, but with far more determination, the Portuguese refused to heed the course of events in the rest of Africa. In November 1960, a few months after Macmillan's famous 'wind of change' speech in Cape Town, Salazar declared: 'We are not in Africa like so many others. We will continue as always our policy of integration. To this end it is necessary for us to be what we have always been, and we will not change' (Oliver and Atmore, 1977: 273). Not long after, in February 1961, serious rioting occurred in Luanda, and in March a widespread revolt broke out in northern Angola, led from across the border by the Union of Peoples of Angola, later to become the Angolan National Liberation Front (FNLA). This was essentially a rural Bakongo movement; its leader Holden Roberto. Bloody Portuguese reprisals followed this ill-planned rising.

There were similar uprisings in West Africa's Portuguese Guinea late in 1962 led by the African Party for the Independence of Guinea and Cabo Verde (PAIGC) and revolutionary nationalist Amilcar Cabral, probably the most important theorist of African revolution, who captured two thirds of the countryside despite well-armed and substantial Portuguese forces. But the war in Guinea drifted towards stalemate with the Portuguese holding the cities and a number of fortified camps. Another 40,000 Portuguese troops were used to subdue the Angolan rebellion, which received support from neighbouring Zaïre (former

Belgian Congo), as well as from other African states. The initial stages of the Angolan war were over by 1963 but, by the end of the 1960s, even more intensive African resistance had broken out in all three of Portugal's African territories. Both the Angolan and Mozambique nationalist groups were divided by bitter factional rivalries, from which the Portuguese were able to profit.

Strung out along the Indian Ocean coast, Mozambique was the eastern remnant of Portugal's vast territorial claims after stronger European powers had seized those parts of the interior which promised most in the way of mineral riches during the late-nineteenth-century 'scramble for Africa'. The Mozambique Liberation Front (FRELIMO), the main anti-colonial movement since 1962, was based in Tanzania (former Tanganyika) and led by Eduardo Mondlane, the major Portuguese-speaking African nationalist, with Julius Nyerere's backing. Crossing the border from Tanzania, independent since 1961, FRELIMO's initial successes were gained in the Makonde areas of northern Mozambique. At FRELIMO's Second Congress in 1968 a bitter struggle took place between the 'revolutionaries', Marxist young men who had returned from military training in Algeria, and the neo-traditional chiefs, who were accused of 'tribalism' and 'bourgeois tendencies'. The young activists suffered in 1969 from the assassination of Mondlane in Tanzania, probably as a result of internal divisions within FRELIMO.

Former hospital nurse and long-time guerilla fighter Samora Moises Machel became the next leader of FRELIMO but the internal disputes were not so much resolved as shelved, because of his insistence on the overriding importance of the military struggle. From 1970 FRELIMO's military effectiveness drastically improved when it was allowed to operate from bases in neighbouring Zambia (former Northern Rhodesia), attacking the Trans-Zambesi and Beira railways and the Cabora Bassa hydroelectric project. The latter was the most ambitious development ever mounted by a colonial government, intended to attract a million Portuguese immigrants, but also an ideal target for guerilla harassment. FRELIMO failed to establish a base among the Muslim Makua, the largest ethnic group in Mozambique. Portugal had Africanized the armed forces in all its colonies, so that by the end of these guerilla wars perhaps 60 per cent of troops fighting the nationalists were themselves black.

The war in Angola was perhaps the most bitter struggle between Africans and their colonial rulers in modern African history, but here nationalists were more divided. The Popular Movement for the Liberation of Angola (MPLA), despite political, ethnic and personal rivalries, mounted the most consistent military challenge and adopted the most sophisticated revolutionary doctrine for the 'liberation' of, in Frantz Fanon's phrase, the 'wretched of the earth'. Yet they faced divisive rivalry from the FNLA, which still enjoyed the support of Zaïre (former Congo), and after 1966 from the National Union for the Total Independence of Angola (UNITA), a movement of the southern Ovimbundu people, the largest of Angola's ethnic groups, which drew some support from Zambia (former Northern Rhodesia). Leaders of the Angolan guerilla movements knew that final military success would depend on the battle for 'hearts and minds' (Templer's phrase in Malaya), on convincing those peasants whose initial aim was simply to free themselves from Portuguese rule of their possible future within a free, modern, people's state.

In Angola's liberated areas, this often meant confronting deeply-held African beliefs and taboos based on oral culture about the authority of elders, the power of witches and the proper duties of women. It was not a matter, as for party leaders in less violently decolonized empires, of gradually taking over a well-ordered colonial state. The MPLA leader, Agostinho Neto, spoke of 'freeing and modernising our people by a dual revolution – against their traditional structures which can no longer serve them, and against colonial rule' (Davidson, 1975: 279). By the 1970s remarkable progress had been achieved in this heroic enterprise but at the cost of increasingly evident weaknesses, such as reviving the ethnic identity of 'primary tribal nations'. In 1973, although the guerillas had not succeeded in driving out Portugal's well-equipped modern armies, the PAIGC controlled most of Guinea; FRELIMO was the dominant force in Tete province and was beginning to operate in southern Mozambique; and the MPLA could at least claim to be the broadest-based of Angola's three resistance movements.

The Effects of the Portuguese Revolution

Though unable to complete their own liberation, the guerillas eventually produced conditions for the liberation of Portugal itself. Dr Marcello Caetano had succeeded Salazar as prime minister of Portugal in September 1968 after the latter suffered a blood clot to the brain and introduced some devolution of power between metropolitan Portugal and the so-called overseas provinces. The maintenance of large conscript armies, up to 40,000 men in Guinea, over 60,000 each in Angola and Mozambique, placed increasing strains on Portuguese society and its economy. Between 1960 and 1971 military spending rose to 45.9 per cent of total government expenditure, while 7674 soldiers died in nearly 14 years of colonial war, only half of these in action. The conditions in which these campaigns dragged inconclusively on were demoralizing to the Portuguese conscripts and frustrating to their commanders. Thus on 25 April 1974 a conspiracy of middle-ranking army officers seized key points in Lisbon and installed a military junta under General António de Spínola, who had recently returned from the command in Guinea complaining that the army was being frustrated by the lack of any long-term strategy for Portugal's African empire (MacQueen, 1997).

179

This bloodless coup ended almost 50 years of right-wing dictatorship and Spínola hoped to negotiate peace in Africa with the promise of a fairly speedy transfer of power within some continuing federal framework. But the 'Revolution of the Flowers' in Lisbon had destroyed the willingness of the colonial armies to continue fighting and on 27 July Spínola announced that negotiations for an early transfer of power would open immediately, beginning with Guinea. As revolutionary pressure increased, Spínola himself resigned on 30 September 1974, leaving the increasingly left-wing leaders of the Movement of the Armed Forces (MFA) to negotiate the liquidation of Portugal's African empire with nationalist leaders. In June 1975 independence was also promised for Portuguese East Timor in the Indonesian archipelago but in December the Jakarta military regime sent in troops and took control which led to continued guerilla warfare with a frighteningly high civilian casualty rate, demonstrating that former colonial subjects could themselves become vicious oppressors.

In Guinea, where Portugal's economic interests were small and the resistance most united and effective, negotiations with Luiz Cabral, brother and successor of Amilcar (assassinated in 1973) were rapid, and independence as Guinea-Bissau was recognized on 10 September 1974 before Spínola's resignation. Shortly before this, FRELIMO agreed to a ceasefire in Mozambique, to be followed by a transitional government which led the country to eventual independence on 25 June 1975. The victorious guerilla movement, after suppressing a short-lived settler rebellion in Lourenço Marques (Maputo), embarked on the difficult task of creating an authentically African version of Marxist socialism in a particularly hostile international environment. FRELIMO's triumph in Mozambique had also broken the deadlock in the long struggle for power in Southern Rhodesia (Zimbabwe). President Samora Machel not only enforced sanctions against the white-settler regime in Rhodesia, at a considerable cost to the Mozambique economy, but intensified military and other aid to the guerillas of the Popular Front. In return, from the late 1970s the white Rhodesians, and later South African military intelligence, encouraged destabilization through the Mozambican National Resistance (RENAMO), drawn from sections of the population who did not accept FRELIMO's authority, such as former African members of the Portuguese special forces and the Makua people. The increasingly authoritarian Machel died in a plane crash near the South African border in 1986 whose immediate cause is still uncertain, even if the political beneficiaries were self-evident. Civil war between FRELIMO and RENAMO continued until in October 1992 a peace accord was signed in Rome by Joaquim Chissano, who had become the Mozambican president, and RENAMO leader Afonso Dhlakama. This led to UN-supervised elections won by FRELIMO two years later, after which Dhlakama was prevailed upon to become the leader of the opposition.

In Angola, the economic stakes were higher and the opportunities for divide and rule by the new state's enemies that much greater. Spínola's strategy had been to follow the ceasefire by setting up a coalition government, with all three resistance movements represented, which would prepare for independence during a transitional period of two years – his real aim was to avoid possible dominance by the Marxist-inspired MPLA. Since that party was suffering internal splits, and since both UNITA and the FNLA controlled substantial regional power bases, this was not an unrealistic plan. It was frustrated partly by the ineptitude of its patrons in neighbouring African states. President Mobutu of Zaïre's patronage of UNITA and FNLA made them suspect to more radical colleagues; even more damaging to both parties were their anti-communist friends in South Africa and the United States. The CIA, which had long-established links with the FNLA, now regarded Jonas Savimbi's UNITA as a stronger barrier against the MPLA's Marxism. Savimbi himself was imbued with an almost messianic sense that he was destined to rule. By July 1974 the CIA was supplying arms and advice to UNITA, hoping to place Savimbi in a dominant position before Portuguese withdrawal; the Soviet Union, meanwhile, continued its support to the MPLA. Such superpower interference led to justifiable accusations that, as the Vietnam war drew to a close, the Cold War was being fought by proxy in southern Africa (Maxwell, 1982).

During the months which were supposed to prepare for an orderly transfer of power before Angola's planned independence date of 11 November 1975, fighting among the various claimants led to a breakdown of law and order and the flight of many foreigners and their capital. The MPLA, though strong in Luanda, in some eastern areas, and among the Mbundu people, lacked the degree of nation-wide support which made FRELIMO and PAIGC the unavoidable heirs of Portugal in Mozambique and Guinea. In the struggle for power the MPLA came to rely on sympathizers among the Portuguese revolutionaries, particularly the last governor, Admiral Rosa Coutinho, but also on military assistance from the Soviet Union and their allies, notably thousands of Cuban combat troops. This outside military support enabled the MPLA to assume power in Luanda on independence day, while evidence of South African and American support discredited their rivals UNITA in the eyes of other African states as the fighting spread (MacQueen, 1997).

Once the new MPLA government consolidated power, multinational companies like Gulf Oil made the best terms they could with the nominally Marxist regime in order to exploit Angola's resources. Continuing civil war from the late 1970s onwards in Angola would greatly impede attempts to negotiate a decolonization of Namibia (former German South-West Africa) which had been incorporated into South Africa in 1950. Namibia was only decolonized in 1990 after a long guerilla war and intense UN diplomacy. Angola's rival factions are still using arms bought with diamond and oil dollars to fight the longest-running but only remaining serious conflict in southern Africa. Persistent civil war over the last 20 years has cost thousands of innocent lives lost through military shelling and starvation, despite UN-supervised elections (1992), peace missions (1998) and emergency food aid.

South Africa: From White to Majority Rule

It might be argued that post-1945 decolonization is not relevant to South Africa as it has been an independent sovereign state since 1910, when the British, not long after fighting a second and drawn-out war (1899–1902) against the so-called 'Boer' republics, conceded dominion status to a Union of the Cape Colony, Natal, the Orange Free State and the Transvaal. Yet over a million and a quarter Afrikaner descendants of the original seventeenth-century Dutch settlers, to whom power was devolved, retained colonial-style white political supremacy and so the four million black population (exclusive of coloured, Asian and Anglo-South Africans) awaited self-rule. Following the Statute of Westminster in 1931 the British surrendered their last opportunity to protect the rights of South Africa's black subject peoples who now lived within a political system exclusively controlled by a white Afrikaner and English-speaking electorate. There were also three High Commission protectorates, Basutoland (Lesotho), Swaziland and Bechuanaland (Botswana), kept out of the Union by the British but largely dependent on South African mining, manufacturing and farming for employment (Beinart, 1994).

Afrikaner politicians like F.W. de Klerk, who in 1989 displaced an authoritarian P.W. Botha as National Party leader and state president, adopted the classic decolonizing tactic of looking for partners among their opponents. One possible choice was the Inkatha Freedom Party (IFP), a Zulu-based political party led by Chief Mangosuthu

Buthelezi that approved of 'Bantustan' units of segregated administration and was secretly armed and supported by the security services, bringing severe tribal conflict to South Africa as it moved towards constitutional reform. The African National Congress (ANC), a Xhosa and communist-led black nationalist movement, held a long-term commitment to nonracial democracy and a widespread appeal far beyond the IFP's regionally-limited KwaZulu-Natal power base. In 1990 de Klerk ended the 30-year-old ban on the ANC, sanctioned the February release from long-term imprisonment of its effective leader, Nelson Mandela, and gradually dismantled apartheid's racial legislation. The country's first nationwide, democratic election held among 29.1 million blacks, 3.3 million coloureds, one million Asians and five million whites in April 1994 saw an outstanding ANC success, the Afrikaner-dominated National Party cast into minority opposition and de Klerk's installation as vice-president of a majority-rule South Africa with a sanctified Mandela as president (until June 1999). Despite unresolved issues of land ownership, crime and poverty, after three centuries of white domination this election represented a transition from a system of racial exclusion and oppression to a democratic, culturally diverse, multiracial society.

Conclusions

This chapter has focused on the particular problems which European settler occupiers, cultivating a privileged position in those African colonies conducive to white residence, presented to an imperial power faced with indigenous resistance to colonial rule. The bitter and uncompromising history of the Algerian struggle for independence (1954–62) not only illustrates a tragic French failure to decolonize peacefully but also how far settler opinion could exert pressure on metropolitan policy, to a degree unapproached elsewhere in Europe. There was even the fear in 1958 and again in 1961 of a military take-over of the French government to secure *Algérie Française*. The presence of large numbers of white settlers in British East and Central Africa also helps explain a marked difference in decolonization as compared with the less violent, more controlled process in British West Africa. The immediate problem confronting Britain at the end of the Second World War in the former was not African nationalism but the demand of white settlers for greater freedom from metropolitan interference.

In terms of constitutions based on the premise of entrenched racial and ethnic privilege, European powers faced such aspiring 'South Africas' as were presented by the settlers of Southern Rhodesia, Kenya, and even – if the terms for 'assimilation' into France were not right – Algeria. This meant that Britain and France increasingly faced the delicate task of dealing with rival European, Arab and African nationalisms, with the metropolitan power employing its own delaying tactics of 'divide and rule', if less effectively than realized at the time. Competing settler and native nationalisms proved mutually reinforcing and the sheer expense of maintaining metropolitan control rapidly threatened to become prohibitive (Wilson, 1994). Accordingly, withdrawal from settler colonies, often after long-drawn out and inconclusive guerilla wars, was determined as much by public opinion and financial imperatives in the European metropole as by the nationalist resistance of the indigenous peoples.

7

OVERSEAS TERRITORIES AND DOM-TOMS: REMNANTS OF EMPIRE

This chapter opens with a roster of Britain and France's remaining colonial or quasi-colonial responsibilities, mostly islands which are often either too small or too poor to seek independence. If empires have been compared to 'extended families', then these are the 'sickly infants' and 'unmarriageable daughters', consisting of Britain's 13 'overseas territories' (OTs) and France's ten *départements d'outre mer et territoires d'outre mer* ('overseas departments and territories', or DOM-TOMs). In regard to the former, particular reference will be made to war with Argentina over the Falkland Islands (1982) and Britain's departure from Hong Kong (1997). If Britain has shown itself consistently unprepared to concede sovereignty to Argentina over the Falklands, then why did it behave so differently towards China over Hong Kong? France's troubled overseas *territoire* of New Caledonia and, again in the South Pacific, the former Franco-British condominium of the New Hebrides (Vanuatu) also receive extended attention. Despite their dependent status, most (though not all) of the last 'colonies' enjoy a large degree of self-government and considerable economic benefits from their attachment to metropolitan states.

Although the focus here is on French and British dependent territories, Portugal did not withdraw from its oldest colony, Macao, until the end of 1999, while the Atlantic islands of the Azores and Madeira remain 'autonomous regions' with their own legislative assemblies which elect deputies to the Lisbon parliament. Spain remains in two North African enclaves (Ceuta and Melilla) and the Canary Islands. Denmark continues to influence Greenland and the Faeroes, and even the Netherlands continues to hold on to two groups of islands in the Caribbean, among them Curaçao and Saba (see Chapter 5). European powers are not alone: the United States retains 'territories' and 'commonwealths' in the Pacific, Oceania and the Caribbean, notably American Samoa, the Northern Mariana Islands, Guam and Puerto Rico; whilst in the South Pacific, Niue and Tokelau are New Zealand territories and Norfolk Island and the Coral Seas Islands Territory are linked to Australia. Developing nations also have dependent territories, such as Mauritius and Rodrigues, or Chile and Rapanui (Easter Island). Even within some countries, like Australia, particular states have overseas territories, such as Tasmania and Macquarie Island, with distinct governmental arrangements. 'In many respects the permutations of dependence and administrative difference are almost endless' (Aldrich and Connell, 1998: 2).

Britain's Overseas Territories

All that remains of the once-extensive British Empire are a baker's dozen of overseas territories (until 1999 called 'dependent territories') scattered around the world, mostly remote island archipelagos. The Falkland Islands are dealt with separately below which leaves Gibraltar (see Chapter 4), Britain's eight remaining inhabited OTs and several uninhabited islands. The Cayman Islands, three islands in the Caribbean, total area 100 square miles, population 36,000, represent a tax-free, offshore financial centre well-served with banks. Bermuda comprises about 100 small islands in the Atlantic, with a total area of 21 square miles, population 61,000, and has had internal self-government since 1968. Anguilla is a Caribbean island of 35 square miles, population 12,000, a British colony since 1650 whose acrimonious separation from the 'associated state' of St Kitts-Nevis in 1967 led to a British military occupation two years later. After six months British paratroops withdrew in September 1969 but select members of London's Metropolitan Police Force were retained on the island (a source of comic fun in the metropole) until the Anguilla police force was set up in 1972. Formal separation came in 1980, before St Kitts-Nevis became independent in 1983, and Anguilla reverted to the status of a British dependent territory.

In the middle of the south Atlantic, St Helena is a mountainous and largely forgotten island, 700 miles from its nearest neighbour and dependency Ascension, also 1300 miles from dependency Tristan da Cunha. St Helena was seized from the Dutch in 1659 by the British East India Company and the exiled Napoleon Bonaparte died here in 1821. The island relies on fish exports and a yearly £3.2 million subsidy from Britain. Its 5500 native 'Saints', descendants of British settlers and sailors, Chinese coolies, African slaves and Indian labourers, pursued a lengthy campaign for restoration of full British citizenship rights. The Turks and Caicos Islands are 30 islands about 50 miles south east of the Bahamas of which eight are inhabited, population 20,000, they rely on tourism and offshore finance. Part of the colony of the Leeward Islands from 1872 until 1956, only 11 of the 46 British Virgin Islands are inhabited, population 19,000, with self-government in most internal matters and a steady growth in offshore financial services. The 38-square-mile Caribbean island of Montserrat, which became a British colony in 1632, has an active volcano which erupted in June 1997, killing 19 people. Many islanders felt that British financial aid after the disaster was either insufficient to redevelop habitable areas or too slow in arrival, leading Labour's International Development Secretary, Clare Short, to complain injudiciously about 'wanting golden elephants next'. Montserrat's remaining population of 4500 is concentrated in the northern third of the island.

Pitcairn Island is also volcanic, this time in the South Pacific, population just 54 descendants (all Seventh-Day Adventists) of the Bounty mutineers and their Tahitian mistresses. Governed by the British High Commissioner in New Zealand, revenue comes solely from postage stamps. Uninhabited British territories (bar scientists and technicians manning survey stations or military personnel) embrace: British Antarctic Territory, designated in 1962, which includes the South Orkney Islands and South Shetland Islands; South Georgia, a military garrison 800 miles from the Falklands; the South Sandwich Islands, a chain of volcanic islands; plus the islands of the Chagos archipelago or British Indian Ocean Territory, the largest of which, Diego Garcia, is leased from Britain for use as an American aircraft base (the unfortunate native Ilois people were removed in the late 1960s).

The Falkland Islands

Britain had continuously occupied the Falkland Islands, in the remote south Atlantic off South America, since the 1830s but successive Argentinian governments also claimed sovereignty over the islands, despite the islanders' evident preference for retaining their association with the British who were clearly determined to keep control over what was regarded as an important strategic base. After 150 years of continuous occupation, Britain had a strong claim to ownership of the islands under international law. The 1981 Defence White Paper, however, had announced significant cuts in the size of Britain's surface fleet, one consequence of which was the withdrawal in November of the only remaining Royal Navy frigate to have been permanently stationed in Port Stanley. This cost-cutting exercise was clearly viewed in Buenos Aires as an indication of Britain's weakening commitment to maintaining a presence in the islands. With negotiations over possession of the islands deadlocked, General Galtieri's military junta decided to take control of the 'Islas Malvinas' by force of arms, to counter mounting domestic criticism. On 2 April 1982 the advance guard of an invasion force eventually numbering 12,000 took over the military garrison at Port Stanley and soon afterwards repatriated 67 Royal Marines and the British Governor, Rex Hunt, to Britain. The Argentinians appointed a military governor, imposed martial law and announced the 'materialization' of Argentina's 'historic sovereignty' over the islands and their 2000 inhabitants (Gough, 1992).

Galtieri had not anticipated the firm reaction of Margaret Thatcher's Cabinet which immediately began preparations of a task force for repossession of the islands. As an attack on a British colony, the invasion was a direct challenge to British sovereignty which the government could not allow to go unpunished. The Falklands' remoteness from Britain, 8000 miles distant in the storm-set south Atlantic, persuaded most observers that they could not be recovered by military action, none the less Mrs Thatcher was determined to make the attempt. By mid-June 1982, as a result of an outstanding amphibious and military campaign, Britain's professional armed forces had defeated inexperienced Argentinian conscripts, retaken Port Stanley and regained control of the islands. A substantial garrison and naval contingent were permanently stationed in and around the islands thereafter, at considerable expense to the British taxpayer. General Galtieri was court-martialled when democracy returned to Argentina in 1983 and sentenced to 12 years' imprisonment for negligence in starting and

losing a humiliating war. In spite of the scale and determination of the British response to the invasion, 'the Falklands
episode was nothing more than a temporary reversal
of the long process of imperial retreat' (Sanders, 1990:
125).

Since the election of President Carlos Menem's government in Argentina in 1989, there has been a considerable
rapprochement between the two former combatants. In
1990 British diplomatic relations, broken off in 1982,
were restored with Argentina, both sides in effect agreeing
to disagree on sovereignty over the islands. In mid-July
1999 an historic agreement between the two former enemies re-established an air link between Chile, Argentina and
the Falklands (severed by Santiago in March in protest at
the British detention of General Augusto Pinochet) and
allowed all Argentinians, not just relatives visiting war
graves, to visit the disputed islands for the first time since
the war. Neither side gave any ground over the still-
disputed question of sovereignty.

Hong Kong

The rocky and precipitous island of Hong Kong, one of the
hundreds scattered in the Pearl River estuary on China's
south-east coast, had been acquired as a result of the 1839–
42 Anglo-Chinese or Opium War and most of the mainland
colony or New Territories had been leased from China in
1898. From 1941 the Japanese were in occupation of this
appendage to China but with their surrender on 15 August
1945, Hong Kong's prewar Colonial Secretary, Franklin
Gimson (later to become Governor), newly released from
captivity and fearful of a Chinese–American takeover being
planned by Chiang Kai-shek and American General Joe
Stilwell, secured the consent of the Japanese to set up a
new British administration before they could contemplate
handing control over to the Chinese. So effective was this
fait accompli, British flags everywhere replacing Chinese

191

and American ones, that when Admiral Sir Cecil Harcourt sailed into Hong Kong harbour on the morning of 30 August, the colony was effectively being run by former British POWs and internees. Despite the promise of a joint American–Chinese thrust towards the Canton and Hong Kong area, nationalist China lacked the military strength to recapture the colony, thus undermining her legitimate claim and reinforcing the notion that she remained a second rate power (Welsh, 1997).

By the 1990s the international position was reversed and Hong Kong, which had become a major manufacturing, financial and communications centre of nearly six million people whose Gross Domestic Product (GDP) per capita exceeded that of Britain, was now dwarfed by communist China, its giant neighbour with over a fifth of the world's population. Britain had become a third-rank power, in effect, which could do little to prevent Hong Kong's eventual reversion to Chinese rule. In December 1984 Mrs Thatcher had formally agreed to a complete withdrawal from Hong Kong in 1997, before the lease of the New Territories ran out. Whereas Britain could reasonably expect to resist any Argentine threat to the Falklands, it was powerless to resist had the Chinese chosen to take Hong Kong by force. On the other hand, the last British governor, 1992's political appointee Chris Patten, insisted on pressing ahead with political reforms previously delayed (so he claimed) by British mandarins, such as broadening the electoral franchise following the first direct elections to the Legislative Council in 1991.

The Beijing government protested against these timid measures allowing Hong Kong's people to have some voice regarding their future and insisted that the old colonial order be restored – they wished to take over a colony, not an emerging democracy. At midnight on 30 June 1997, Prince Charles and Governor Patten were present at a tearful handover ceremony and communist China regained sovereignty over Hong Kong. Next morning

Chinese People's Liberation Army troops marched through the streets of the new Special Administrative Region. The Legislative Council, elected under Patten's new rules in 1995, was abolished as soon as the British left and replaced by an appointed legislature filled with reliable sycophants.

Nearby Portuguese Macao with its 430,000, mainly Chinese, inhabitants, a tiny territory of 22 square kilometres at the mouth of the Pearl River where Portuguese sailors first landed in 1513, followed Hong Kong in reverting to Chinese sovereignty at midnight on 19 December 1999. This handover signified the end of one of the world's longest-surviving empires. For Portuguese imperialism hung on grimly in Africa until 1975, long after independence in British and French Africa (see Chapter 6). The vast majority of Macao Chinese actively looked forward to returning to the motherland. The main business of Macao remains the provision of gambling casinos (takings account for a quarter of GDP), drugs, prostitution and hotels for citizens of Hong Kong and further afield, all rich pickings for the Chinese Triads.

France's DOM-TOMs

France was left with only ten overseas outposts by the 1980s but these *départements d'outre mer et territoires d'outre mer* (DOM-TOMs), legally part of France, are populated by 1.8 million multi-ethnic French citizens and total 120,000 square kilometres of land, in addition to Terre Adélie, the uninhabited French region of Antarctica. The DOM-TOMs give France a sovereign and internationally recognized presence in the Caribbean, the Indian and Pacific Oceans and Antarctica, and also serve as showcases for French language and culture. A high commissioner represents the French state but there are also elected territorial assemblies and heads of government with relatively broad powers. Residents of DOM-TOMs enjoy full right of abode in France and in other DOM-TOMs. Except for

Antarctica, all the DOM-TOMs elect members to both chambers in the French assembly on the basis of universal suffrage.

Since 1946 the fully-fledged French overseas *départements* (DOMs) with representation in the French parliament and a locally elected assembly have been Martinique and Guadeloupe in the West Indies (see Chapter 5), Guyane (French Guiana) in South America and Réunion in the Indian Ocean. Currency, the legal code, postage stamps, and governing bodies are the same in these *vieilles colonies*, which France first took over in the 1600s, as in the *métropole*. The overseas *territoires* (TOMs), represented by French Polynesia, New Caledonia, and Wallis and Futuna in the South Pacific, have a greater degree of administrative and political autonomy, but France still controls foreign relations, law and order, financial policy and immigration. Nevertheless, the principle of non-assimilation and the possibility for decentralized self-government differentiates the TOMs from the DOMs. Then there are the *collectivités territoriales*, midway between overseas *départements* and *territoires*, of Saint-Pierre-et-Miquelon off the coast of Newfoundland and Mayotte in the Indian Ocean. Lastly, the virtually uninhabited *Terres australes et antarctiques françaises* (TAAF), or French Austral and Antarctic Territories, are administered from Paris.

Saint-Pierre-et-Miquelon, an archipelago settled in the seventeenth century, and Saint-Barthélémy (a tiny island dependency of Guadeloupe) have ethnically European populations, cod-fishing is the commercial resource base. Guyane, used for French convict settlements (like Devil's Island in the Iles du Salut) from 1852 until 1945, has a population of about 150,000, of whom over half are of African descent. Réunion, an island in the Indian Ocean, population 600,000, became increasingly dependent on government transfers and emigration to France with the collapse of sugar production. Mayotte, part of the Comoros archipelago off the east coast of Africa, population 95,000, voted against independence in 1974 and is sustained by perfume essences and spices. The Polynesian islands of Wallis and Futuna (between Fiji and Samoa), population 14,000, have no appreciable exports and rely on French aid and welfare spending. French Polynesia, population 220,000, represents the other scattered French possessions in the South Pacific or five archipelagos of 120 islands (among them Tahiti), organized into a single colony in 1903, that rely on pearl exports, government employment and state investment. The islands were also, from the mid-1960s until 1992, a site for French nuclear testing (Aldrich and Connell, 1992, 1998).

In most of the DOM-TOMs, small if vocal dissident groups called for independence in the 1970s and 1980s and, in Guadeloupe, Réunion and French Polynesia, violent episodes of protest occurred but only in France's overseas *territoire* of New Caledonia did the *indépendantistes* fare well electorally at all levels and in all institutions. In the smaller isolated and exceptionally dependent DOM-TOMs, such as Wallis and Futuna, there has been hardly any discussion of independence, let alone an independence movement. Nearby New Caledonia, however, witnessed a genuine upsurge of Melanesian nationalism in the 1980s and a corresponding French settler reaction. In 1980 itself, the South Pacific islanders of the New Hebrides had managed to secure for themselves an independence so far denied New Caledonia, only to be faced with a secessionist rebellion.

Vanuatu (New Hebrides)

The Melanesian archipelago of 80 South Pacific islands north of New Caledonia which now comprises Vanuatu received the attentions of the British, the Australians and the French. London and Paris finally arranged that the New Hebrides should from 1906 become a Franco-British condominium under joint administration. In a unique arrangement neither nation held outright sovereignty over the islands and so two flags flew, two currencies circulated and the few schools taught in English or French. Native Melanesians remained ineligible for either British or French citizenship and, in international law, were stateless. Political change was hampered because of this awkward (which side of the road to drive on?) and sometimes comic-opera dual government. There were also strong local loyalties on the more than 60 populated islands, divisions over religion and custom, and between the one third who were Francophone and the two thirds Anglophone majority. In 1957 a consultative council was set up, none the less, followed by more wide-ranging reforms in 1975. In succeeding years, Father Walter Lini, an anti-colonial cleric who had taken leave from the Anglican priesthood, led the pro-independence National Party, subsequently to become the Vanua'aku Party (VP) and the country's largest political grouping.

The French Comoros Islands in the Indian Ocean had meanwhile proclaimed independence as an Islamic republic in 1975 and two years later French Somaliland on the horn of Africa became the Republic of Djibouti. Thus encouraged, in 1977 the VP boycotted new elections and set up a provisional government, leaving the largely Francophone *Union des Partis Modérés* to take all the seats in the legislature. The following year, the two parties cooperated to form an autonomous government led by Lini which worked out a plan for the independence of the archipelago. In 1979 Lini became the last chief minister of the New Hebrides and a year later he was the first prime minister of an independent Vanuatu ('Our Land Forever'). The decolonization of the New Hebrides proved, however, to be the catalyst to a strengthening of French resolve to retain control of its remaining Pacific territories and also led to discouragement of nascent independence sentiments elsewhere (Aldrich and Connell, 1992).

When independence arrived on 30 July 1980 the British were eager to leave but French authorities were more

196

reluctant and did nothing to discourage secession movements in the largely French-speaking islands of Espiritu
Santo and Tanna, conscious of both settler interests and
the impact of independence in the New Hebrides on
nearby New Caledonia. Rebellion was led by eccentric
local plantation owner Jimmy Stevens, with the support
of many Francophone residents, Catholics and French
planters. There were attempts to form separate governments, evacuations and the killing of a local representative
in a conflict which quickly became known as the 'coconut
war'. Paris, embarrassed at these developments, recognized
the independence of Vanuatu and sent in a token force
of troops who joined 200 British Royal Marines to
restore order. They soon withdrew and Lini used troops
from Papua New Guinea to finally crush the secessionists
and cement his reputation as a determined leader
whose support mainly came from the English-speaking
community.

In 1981 the new government expelled the French
ambassador and relations between France and Vanuatu
remained stormy, aggravated on the Melanesian side by a
feeling that the French had opposed independence and
fostered divisions by supporting the rebels. The new nation
showed great economic promise with a booming tourism
sector and tax-haven potential but damage from cyclones,
falling commodity prices, uncontrolled government spending and political uncertainty all took their toll. Walter Lini,
widely regarded as the South Pacific's elder statesman after
the two military coups in nearby Fiji in 1987, led the New
Hebrides from confused Franco-British rule into a sometimes turbulent (an unsuccessful coup in 1988) independence as Vanuatu but stepped down as prime minister in
1991. Throughout the chaotic coalition rule of the 1990s
Lini occupied various posts, including deputy prime minister, and as justice minister ordered the mass arrest of the
islands' paramilitary force after a rebellion over unpaid
allowances (he died in February 1999).

New Caledonia

New Caledonia in the south west Pacific (450 km long) was annexed, together with the Loyalty Islands, by a French admiral in 1853 and its population of 197,000 is 34 per cent French and 44 per cent Melanesian. Reserves of nickel represent the greatest natural resource base of all the DOM-TOMs and nickel ore provides almost all of the archipelago's exports, the latter subject to sharp downturns in prices on the international commodities market. As other parts of the South Pacific became independent, especially neighbouring Vanuatu in 1980, and a Socialist government took power in France in 1981, there were renewed Melanesian expectations for self-government. These hopes were not realized and those who supported independence (Kanaks) were angry that no electoral reform was proposed to disenfranchise recent arrivals and enable Melanesians to exercise a majority. In 1984 Kanaks abandoned the struggle for constitutional change and formed a new coalition, the *Front de Libération Nationale Kanake et Socialiste* (FLNKS), that mounted a militant struggle to secure independence, including road blocks, the occupation of gendarmeries and attacks on *Caldoches* or long-term French settlers. This led to a loyalist anti-independence counter-campaign mounted by the *Rassemblement pour la Calédonie dans la République* (RPCR) and similarly violent attacks on Melanesians. The FLNKS briefly held the small town of Thio and declared a provisional government of the Republic of Kanaky with Jean-Marie Tjibaou of the mildly reformist *Union Calédonienne* (UC) as president. Violent loyalist reaction followed: ten Kanaks were killed in an ambush and ten more Kanaks and Europeans lost their lives in various bloody incidents.

Right-wing settler opposition to Kanak militancy grew, the military presence was strengthened, and Kanak militants, without French or urban support, were unable to gain power. Independence in association with France, approved by referendum and with France retaining control of defence and foreign affairs, was rejected by the FLNKS as a 'neocolonial' solution. The French prime minister, Laurent Fabius, devised new proposals which divided New Caledonia into four regions, each with its own council responsible for development planning. Recognition that direct action would not guarantee an independent Kanaky with only minority support led to a more pragmatic willingness to negotiate and to develop a more self-reliant Melanesian society and economy in rural areas. In the elections for the regional councils in September 1985 the FLNKS won three of the four regions, though the RPCR did so well around the capital, Noumea, that it retained control of the Territorial Congress: 38 per cent, mainly on the east coast and in the islands, supported independence and 61 per cent were opposed. The 1986 elections that brought the conservative Jacques Chirac to power in France in uneasy alliance with President Mitterrand were boycotted by the FLNKS, hence the new and extreme conservative *RPCR-Front National* coalition swept New Caledonia by gaining 89 per cent of the vote cast and two representatives in Paris, although the participation rate was only 50 per cent (Aldrich and Connell, 1992).

Chirac's new French conservatism and determination to retain control of the South Pacific was amply demonstrated by the appointment of Bernard Pons as Minister for DOM-TOMs and by Gaston Flosse, newly re-elected President of French Polynesia and an ardent supporter of the French presence in New Caledonia, as Secretary of State for the South Pacific. Pons played down Melanesian demands, encouraged further immigration, dispersed some of the 6000 garrisoned French troops throughout the countryside and emphasized that no movement towards independence, or even greater autonomy, would now be contemplated. Yet in December 1986 the UN General Assembly voted 89 to 24 (with 34 abstentions) in favour of referring New Caledonia to the UN Committee on Decolonization, effectively classifying New Caledonia as a colony not a *territoire*.

The French government took umbrage but went ahead with plans to hold a referendum on independence in September 1987 that the FLNKS Congress had voted to boycott. This resulted in 57 per cent of the electorate voting in favour of remaining with France, though no more than about 20 per cent of Melanesians voted against independence. Chirac declared in Noumea, four days after the referendum: 'You have said yes to France and France is happy and proud to keep you close to its heart' (Aldrich and Connell, 1992: 225). Meanwhile, he appeared determined to intimidate and marginalize the FLNKS by public demonstrations of troop activities in rural areas, rather than by seeking to convince uncommitted Melanesians that their future lay with France.

Two days before both the French presidential elections and the New Caledonian regional elections in April 1988, a commando group of Kanaks made a dawn raid on the gendarmerie at Fayaoue on Ouvea, an outer island, killing four gendarmes and taking 27 hostages who were transported to a coral cave. Kanaks then demanded the withdrawal of the military from the island and a new referendum supervised by the United Nations. As the elections went ahead, violent events took place elsewhere in New Caledonia. Two days before the second round of the presidential elections, with Mitterrand apparently well ahead of Chirac, crack army units stormed the cave, rescued the remaining 23 hostages and killed 19 Kanak militants (three after their capture), including their leader Alphonse Dianou. Two soldiers were also killed. Once again violence had led to the deaths of many more Kanaks than any other ethnic group. The election results suggest that the French electorate on New Caledonia preferred Mitterrand's promise of renewed dialogue with the FLNKS to Chirac's hard-line confrontationist policies. The new Prime Minister, Michel Rocard, held talks in Paris attended by both the FLNKS leader, Jean-Marie Tjibaou, and the RCPR leader, Jacques Lafleur, which led to the signing of the Matignon Accord. This agreement established direct rule from France for a year, divided New Caledonia into three new regions (two of which were to be controlled by *indépendantistes*), established new economic development strategies for the Melanesian areas and proposed a second referendum on independence in 1998 with a new electoral system. Rocard described his proposal as 'decolonisation within the framework of French institutions' (Aldrich and Connell, 1992: 229).

A year after the violent events on Ouvea, at a memorial service for the victims, Tjibaou and his deputy leader were murdered by a dissident member of the FLNKS, angered over the signing of the 1988 Matignon Accord. Nevertheless, the signing of the Accord brought a period of relative peace to New Caledonia, although the independence issue was left in abeyance. Ten years later, on 21 April 1998, after two months of talks, an agreement between the French government, the FLNKS and the anti-independence RPCR was initialled in Noumea which delayed a potentially destabilizing referendum on the issue of independence for a further period of between 15 to 20 years. The new accord allowed for greater autonomy for the indigenous people in the intervening period, agreed to redistribute industry to the Kanak-dominated north of the island and pledged to decentralize further the administration of the territory. On 5 May 1998 French Prime Minister Lionel Jospin attended the signing ceremony, stating that the transitional period should not be seen as a time of 'passive waiting', but rather as a period of 'shared sovereignty' during which both pro- and anti-independence forces should be actively engaged in the implementation of the accord.

Conclusions

Nearly all of Britain's imperial remnants have suffered from years of neglect, loss of British citizenship, a mentality of dependence and a habit of acquiring mostly second-rate

Foreign Office officials to govern them. In 1999 a Labour government white paper promised to restore full citizenship rights to the people of Britain's overseas territories (the Falkland Islands and Gibraltar were excluded since they already enjoyed full British citizenship). This does not become law until 2001 and should affect 150,000 people, most of whom lost their automatic right to a British passport with the Nationality Act of 1981. French DOM-TOMs have long conferred citizenship and are more closely integrated than Britain's dependencies into the political economy of the *métropole*. As formal decolonization apparently draws to a close, micro-states and territories which have a 'special relationship' with a metropolitan power may be better off than those which do not. The remaining British overseas territories can only improve their situation through strengthening their ties with the United Kingdom in the manner that some French 'colonies' became DOM-TOMs (Aldrich and Connell, 1998).

France has been more reluctant than Britain to cast her remaining overseas domains adrift and retains strong ties with her island archipelagos in the West Indies, the Indian Ocean and the South Pacific, whether they have the status of *départements*, *territoires*, or *collectivités territoriales*. Only in New Caledonia has a majority of the indigenous population (itself a demographic minority) overwhelmingly supported an independence movement; elsewhere pro-independence parties are losing support and have not won territorial elections. In the 1980s New Caledonia even invited comparison on a reduced scale with Algeria, particularly as the total of French gendarmes and troops present during the elections of April 1988 reached more than 9000. 'It is an irony of history that the most vigorous independence movement in the South Pacific has not achieved its aim and is unlikely to do so', write the authors of an account of France's overseas frontier, noting that 'throughout the DOM-TOMs, the heyday of the independence movement is over' (Aldrich and Connell, 1992: 250).

8

CONCLUSIONS: EXPLANATIONS REASSESSED

This closing chapter offers a re-evaluation of the various explanatory hypotheses (nationalist, international and metropolitan) put forward in the first chapter to account for the post-Second World War emergence of decolonization as a seemingly irresistible historical force. Close study of the changing basis after 1945 for political cooperation between imperialist rulers and collaborative elites on the 'periphery' may recommend an alternative approach to decolonization (see 'The Role of Collaborative Elites'). Most non-Marxist contemporary historians would agree that imperial dismemberment, like the acquisition of colonial empire, must have been multicausal. The major elements that contributed towards decolonization were interwoven and it is only by investigating them all that we can hope to comprehend the muddled complexity of past events.

The changing attitudes of the old and new indigenous elites towards colonial rule 'in interaction with events in the metropolitan societies and developments in the international system ... determined not only the methods, but also the timing and the eventual outcome of European imperialist control' (Mommsen and Osterhammel, 1986:

340). Only by researching the various strands of the inter-related historical processes of decolonization, starting with a discussion of the specificity of the colonial state, can we hope to understand its real significance as one of the prim-ary historical themes of the post-1945 global landscape. The student's job must be to distinguish, therefore, between the causal triptych of the 'peripheral' experience, the international context and metropolitan policy, and then to reassemble and analyse them as a unified whole. All of the explanations dealt with in the opening chapter are important, despite the caveats lodged below. No one strand alone can begin to portray the process of decolonization for it is the linkages between these political and economic arenas which provide the crucial element.

(1) Nationalist Explanations

Was the revolt of the 'periphery' the key factor in triggering the dissolution of imperial rule? Would international pres-sures and domestic constraints have had much impact *with-out* the disposition to rebel against colonial rule that appeared so widespread in the colonial empires after 1945? Those who make a detailed case study of a particular colony are perhaps over-inclined to see the growth of anti-colonial political organization in the territory itself as the pacemaker in the long march to self-rule and independ-ence. Focusing on the politics of imperial disengagement in a single region or colony can easily lead those sympathetic to the anti-colonial struggle to overlook significant interna-tional and metropolitan influences on withdrawal. The new self-governing elites who took over the reins of power from departed European rulers also tended to exaggerate and mythologize the role of nationalist resistance in order to reinforce their legitimacy as true inheritors of the anti-colonial struggle.

Western historians, brought up in a cultural tradition in which, until recently, the growth of the nation-state held

204

pride of place, were once widely sympathetic to the suggestion that a similar historical process was occurring in the European-ruled colonial empires. Since the 1980s, however, strong arguments have been made against attributing to anti-colonial political movements the strength and cohesion perceived by liberal or Marxist academics in the 1960s. The latter were concerned to celebrate 'nation building' in newly independent states as a primary moving force of history or overly impressed by charismatic Third World leaders like Ahmed Sukarno in Indonesia, Kwame Nkrumah on the Gold Coast and Gamal Abdul Nasser in Egypt. The crude monocausal view that European empires were solely disrupted and overthrown by the nationalisms of their subjects, who were mobilized against colonial rule *en masse* and whose opposition made it unworkable, is now much more difficult for the historian of decolonization to sustain (Darwin, 1991).

Some have grown wary of versions of the colonial past too obviously designed to flatter either the omniscience of European colonial rulers or their immediate nationalist successors. Also, the rise of nationalism is no longer seen as inevitable and sometimes as initiated by the ineptitude of the governing imperial power. Hence Malay nationalism developed slowly under British rule because Malays felt more loyalty to individual states and their sultans rather than to 'Malaya' as a country. It took the British miscalculation during and after the Second World War of trying to create a Malayan Union, imposing a unitary state and giving equal rights to Chinese and Indians, to incite politicization among Malays and in 1946 to inaugurate a Malay nationalist organization (UMNO). Severe repression of embryonic nationalist movements by either white-settler occupiers or their homeland's troops, as in French Madagascar (Malagasy Republic) and New Caledonia, could also backfire and lead to rising popular support for those who laid claim to be resisting colonial oppression.

Colonial nationalists enjoyed the retrospective comfort of a seemingly inevitable victory that was not always so self-assured at the time. Hence in the second Dutch 'police action' or invasion of central Java in December 1948, the republic's provisional capital at Yogyakarta was captured, along with leaders Ahmed Sukarno, Dr Mohammad Hatta and most of the Indonesian cabinet. By the end of that month all the major republican towns of Java and Sumatra were in Dutch hands. Ultimately, diplomatic or international pressure, as much as republican armed resistance, obliged the Dutch to surrender sovereignty (Cribb and Brown, 1995). Outright defeat by the Vietminh at Dien Bien Phu had in 1954 driven the French out of North Vietnam but in the subsequent Algerian war, spectacular new French offensive operations under General Maurice Challe had by mid-1959 secured almost total defeat of the Algerian national liberation army (ALN). Yet three years later independence was attained, owing as much to President de Gaulle's emphasis on safeguarding the *métropole* as it did to nationalist pressure (Clayton, 1994). In East Africa, the Kikuyu-dominated Mau Mau uprising had been all but eradicated by the end of 1956 as a threat to British colonial rule in Kenya, whose negotiated departure did not come until 1963. In Southern Rhodesia, central Africa, the downfall of the Portuguese empire in 1974–1975 and South Africa's cruel withdrawal of support compelled the outcast white republic into submission in December 1979 (and a temporary reversion to the status of a British colony) rather more than the increasingly intensive guerilla warfare waged by Patriotic Front black nationalists (Chamberlain, 1985).

In a further riposte to the simplistic nationalist explanation, a study of the collapse through the 1960s and early 1970s of Portugal's centuries-old Empire in Africa argues that, except in Guinea, the Portuguese military were quite capable of defeating the rebel insurgents. Thus the nationalists posed no crucial threat to the Portuguese presence in

Angola during the entire course of the 13-year-old armed struggle, after 1961 the major centres of European settler population were virtually untouched by the conflict until the struggle's end. If not for the army's loss of morale, the 1974 officers' coup in Lisbon and the setting up of the new Spínola-led republic, Portugal would probably have been able to hold on to its vast African colonies, Angola and Mozambique, except in isolated rebel-held areas, for much longer. Whatever their varied military success during the long-drawn-out colonial wars, therefore, the nationalist movements only proved adept in seizing and deploying the political initiative *after* the Lisbon coup. The extent to which the 'push' from Africa generated by the nationalist wars enhanced the 'pull' exerted by Portugal's opportunities to become more economically involved in Europe – making African colonies less vital to the metropole – is problematic. So unavailing was UNITA's campaign against the colonial forces in Angola, and so preoccupied did Jonas Savimbi become with his conflict with the rival MPLA, that in 1972 UNITA actually sought a truce with the Portuguese that lasted until the beginning of 1974 (MacQueen, 1997).

If we place nationalism within the broader setting of a 'peripheral' explanation, focusing on overseas possessions located away from a metropolitan centre, the force of local colonial pressures after 1945 becomes much more credible. We can see how European colonial administrators stirred up powerful opposition by their post-Second World War policies and alienated their essential allies or 'collaborators' in colonial society (see below). Driven out by fear of tribal and civil wars, from this perspective Europeans backed out, handing over the reins of state power to the only credible nationalist leaders who could succeed them. Hence Viceroy Lord Mountbatten did not 'grant' independence to India and Pakistan on 15 August 1947 because power had already been taken away from the British by rioting mobs, Congress and the Muslim League (see Chapter 4). Where the European withdrawal was too hasty, as from the Belgian

Congo in 1960, tribal and civil-war anarchy followed in any case (see Chapter 5). The British congratulated themselves on a planned and phased abandonment of empire, calmly leaving behind the rudiments of law and parliamentary government, but in many of the new African nations these were rapidly overturned.

Thus the 'peripheral' interpretation of the end of empire recognizes the significance of nationalist movements but places them in a larger context. The growth and influence of nationalism reflected the fact that the basis for cooperation between imperial rulers and colonial ruled had ceased to exist, at least on anything like the old terms. When the European colonialists attempted to exploit their colonies properly, as during the 'second colonial occupation' of Africa in the late 1940s (see Chapter 6), they found that resistance grew rapidly and collaboration declined. Faced with the enormous costs of large-scale overseas coercion to the metropolitan or home governments and the risks of colonial disorder, European imperial powers invariably decided to come to terms with the most prominent anti-colonial nationalist movement of the territory. It only remained to transfer political power as soon as it could be decently arranged and to hope that the successor independent state would hold together and maintain trading relations. In this scenario, domestic and international politics play an essentially subordinate role in a primarily colonial process (Darwin, 1991).

(2) International Explanations

Did changes at the international level serve as the trigger for a whole variety of dramatic shifts that together destroyed the old prewar relationships of imperial rule and colonial subordination? The timing of decisions on colonial self-government or imperial withdrawal suggests that, for the most part, eagerness to adjust to a new international climate served to reinforce or accelerate the end of colonial rule rather than acting as the precipitant cause. It has also been questioned whether the appearance of more powerful states on the post-1945 international scene invariably signals the downfall of comparatively dilapidated multi-ethnic empires of the kind that Britain possessed. There is little evidence to show that resilient European colonial empires simply caved in because of irresistible international pressures from the superpowers or the lesser anti-colonial states. The Dutch, for example, remained indifferent to UN Security Council resolutions condemning their 'police actions' in Java in 1947 and 1948 and only agreed to negotiate with republican nationalists after long overdue American threats to withdraw Marshall Aid from the Netherlands. After 1960, certainly, British governments found the prospect of defending colonial rule against vociferous international criticism tiresome and unrewarding. The Portuguese, though, until 1968 under dictator Salazar, continued to wage savage colonial wars against rebel forces in Angola, Guinea and Mozambique without paying much attention to a hostile world opinion. Only with the ending of the Cold War in 1989 did Afrikaner, anti-communist South Africa experience a real withdrawal of Western investment and, under President de Klerk, recognize that to appease international opinion the state apparatus of apartheid would have to be dismantled.

In addition, over the period 1945–70 the international climate was not as consistently hostile towards the European colonial powers as has sometimes been suggested. America's ailing President Roosevelt was certainly antagonistic towards colonialism as a war leader, particularly the French record in Indochina, but his successors, Truman and Eisenhower, adopted a more accommodating approach. During the late 1940s and 1950s there was little evidence of any American desire to hasten the collapse of European empires or great power pretensions, with the major exceptions of Britain's Palestinian mandate and the 1956 Suez crisis. On the contrary, British politicians felt entitled to claim American support based upon their contribution to the containment of communism in Malaya, while French governments played upon the 'red scare' to secure American arms and funding for the war in Indochina. Following Mao's advent to power in China, colonial powers in South East Asia acted within the anti-communist parameters of the Cold War struggle. American signing of the North Atlantic Treaty in April 1949 also guaranteed protection against Soviet aggression and offered Western European nations much greater security than they had enjoyed in the 1930s. In other words, the postwar anti-colonial front quickly dissolved once Truman's advisers in Washington came to recognize the value of Western European support against the Soviet Union and, after 1949, as a bulwark in South East Asia against Chinese communism.

Moreover, although the British trailed far behind the Russians and Americans in terms of military power, they still remained inhabitants of the world's third great power for 15 years or more after 1945, much stronger than other colonial powers like France, Portugal or Belgium. A large sphere still remained in the 1950s in which Britain maintained its historic military presence, for example in the Mediterranean, the Indian Ocean and the Arab emirates of the Gulf. Arguably, not until the early 1960s, well after the Suez debacle, did Britain's third power status and the advantages it brought begin to fall away sharply. At the Nassau meeting of December 1962 in the Bahamas between 68-year-old Prime Minister Harold Macmillan and a youthful President Jack Kennedy, the British still expected to be treated like a valued ally with third power and independent nuclear status, even if the Polaris missile negotiations revealed the emptiness of this claim (Murray, 2000). In any case, the abandonment of colonial empire was not an inevitable corollary of declining world status, as the case of tiny and ineffectual Portugal indicates. The three-way connection between international politics, imperial policy and the colonial setting has to be more carefully measured.

(3) Metropolitan (Domestic) Explanations

Was there really a slackening of the European 'will to rule' overseas possessions? Did domestic politics and public opinion propel decolonization by persuading politicians that there were no votes to be lost in abandoning colonies? Recently it has been queried whether European public opinion was necessarily anti-imperial in the postwar years. The British Labour government, anguishing in 1946 on how to get out of India, was afraid of adopting any policy which could be represented as a 'scuttle', or as a prelude to the 'liquidation' of the British Empire. The same postwar socialist government supported both Dutch 'sovereignty' over the former NEI and the French return to Indochina, despite the presence of strong nationalist, pro-independence movements in both areas (see Chapter 3). As the Cold War developed, Labour's strategic aims were not primarily geared to the development of a special relationship with America or a place in NATO but rather to the development of a British imperial system which would be equal to and independent of both the United States and the Soviet Union. Preserving paramount influence in the Middle East and the eastern Mediterannean, despite abandonment of formal controls over large parts of Asia, was an essential element of that part of Britain's imperial strategy designed to prevent any further erosion of great power status. The strategy for rebuilding this power and status before 1950 was seen to depend on new links ('the second colonial occupation') between Europe and the colonial empires in Africa (Kent, 1993).

While left-wing intellectuals proclaimed their anti-imperialism, much of British popular culture upheld an imperial world view, 'made up of patriotic, military, and racial ideas only vaguely located in specific imperial

211

contexts, glorifying violence and a sense of national superiority', which secured greater cultural penetration in the
period after the First World War, 'and indeed prolonged
their shelf life until the 1950s' (MacKenzie, 1984: 254, 256).
Neither was there much sign of any protest among the
British public in the latter decade against the deployment
of national servicemen in Malaya or Cyprus, nor against the
costly military effort to defeat Mau Mau in Kenya. British
military commitments east of Suez also continued to
expand after 1960, until the crisis of devaluation in 1967
led Harold Wilson's Labour government to promise withdrawal in a few years' time. As late as the 1980s, the view
that British public opinion was too enlightened to support
imperial adventures overseas received a setback with the
widespread public support for Mrs Thatcher's 1982 war
with Argentina over the invasion of the Falklands (see
Chapter 7).

All this implies that a claim that the climate of European
domestic politics or public opinion after 1945 was unfa-
vourable to the defence of empire needs to be treated
with a certain scepticism. The historical record suggests
that public reaction on imperial and colonial issues was
highly differentiated and unpredictable, for there did not
exist any collective public attitude towards empire and
imperial power. Some colonial possessions excited public
opinion far more than others. Not all those who felt deeply
in the 1950s about the fate of white settlers in Kenya dis-
played the same degree of concern about Britain's influence in Egypt or other parts of the Middle East (Darwin,
1991). Right-wing, communist and socialist parties in the
French national assembly were all initially reluctant to leave
Algeria, supported by the Army and the settlers. Only the
arrival of de Gaulle as premier in 1958 shifted French
policy towards departing from 1962, at the cost of alienating mutinous sections of the military. Yet Frenchmen who
believed Algeria was an integral part of France, and who
supported an eight-year war to resist Arab nationalism,

212

proved indifferent to the fate of neighbouring 'protected states' Tunisia and Morocco which received independence in 1956.

'Empire' was not seen by public opinion, or its European parliamentary representatives, as a single momentous issue, to be fought out between those in favour and those against. Colonies raised a variety of moral and political issues, of which some threatened to produce a fierce public and parliamentary reaction while others raised hardly any interest. Traditional notions of the moral or civilizing basis of colonial rule and post-1945 changes in European public attitudes towards explicitly racial claims to political dominance after the world war against Japan and Nazi Germany, exercised a somewhat unpredictable influence on public opinion, but those politicians anxious to accelerate the pace of constitutional change played upon liberal middle-class guilt feelings over racism and imperialism. British premier Macmillan had an eye on progressive, 'middle voters' in the run up to the 1959 general election, sensitive about Africa at a time of the Hola camp massacre in Kenya and the Devlin 'police state' report on Nyasaland, and this may have contributed to the final decolonization of British East and Central Africa (Ovendale, 1995). The postwar expansion of the welfare state, and middle-class attachment to it, also helped to pave the way for imperial disengagement, as colonies came to seem increasingly redundant and burdensome. Once independence had been granted, the much more competitive international environment of the 1960s was a key economic factor in transforming the end of empire from a merely constitutional process into a real loss of power and influence (Holland, 1985).

The Role of Collaborative Elites

A subsidiary explanatory approach to decolonization which has an increasing following among historians emphasizes not so much the rise of anti-colonial nationalism,

213

international pressures, or the role of domestic politics, as the changing terms of political cooperation or 'collaboration' between the European imperial power and the most powerful vested interests in the subordinate colony. The role of collaborative elites on the 'periphery' in assisting external rulers or in withdrawing their support and backing in favour of nationalists was often crucial during the process of decolonization. Where imperial rule depended upon a ready supply of indigenous collaborators, if the stock ran out Europeans would be forced to reconsider their right to govern. The spread of nationalism might, of course, be one reason for the inability to recruit fresh sets of allies in non-white colonial society (Darwin, 1991).

Equally, the mobilization of mass anti-colonial support could threaten established or collaborating elites, particularly if the nationalists were led by communists or radicals hostile to the property rights and land ownership of chiefs, sultans, headmen and sheikhs. Faced with a resolute colonial government, local elites who both legitimized and acted as conduits for colonial rule, such as Western-educated *évolué* leaders in French West and Equatorial Africa, had to calculate whether support for mass nationalist movements would be worth the risks to their established position within the colonial order. Conversely, where anti-imperialist political parties aspired to take over the whole colonial territory, they had to reckon with powerful regional or tribal leaders often better placed than they to raise a nationalist following and control the grass roots (Low, 1993).

Who then were willing to become 'collaborators' within an externally imposed structure of European colonial rule? The collaborative elite in postwar Kenya were 'traditional' Kikuyu chiefs, Christian converts committed to British modernization programmes, making them a target for the Kikuyu-led Mau Mau, along with others who profited from colonial rule, land shortage and inflation. Those nationalists who threatened the colonial state in British East Africa were often mission-educated clerks and ex-*askaris*, working

214

along party-political lines, along with poor, landless squatters more likely to resort to violence. Hence Kikuyu loyalists supported British efforts to destroy the Mau Mau,
defeated long before there was any prospect of African
independence (Throup, 1985).

There were also collaborative non-elites, such as over a
quarter of a million poor Muslim arabs who enrolled on the
French side during the 1954–62 Algerian war of independence. Local collaborators, known as *harkis*, had little choice
but to emigrate in large numbers to southern France once
independence came in 1962 or suffer the full force of FLN
vengeance. Their subsequent history, like that of many who
served under the British Raj or the Dutch in Indonesia,
makes for sombre reading. Living in poor conditions in
concrete tower blocks on the outskirts of French cities, a
younger generation of *harkis* rioted in Nimes in 1991 and in
a housing estate on the edge of Amiens in 1994. 'We should
be thanked for our contribution to the war 30 years ago.
But [French] people treat us as though we were just scum',
according to one of the latter estate's few residents in work
(*Guardian*, 19 November 1994).

Despite the small size of European occupying forces,
particularly where white settlers were not present because
of disease or poor resources, colonial government was only
seriously threatened once collaborative elites became convinced that foreign rule was slackening in the face of
nationalist, domestic and international pressures. 'Although
satyagraha or violent upheaval never pushed the British into
the Indian Ocean, there accumulated during the 1940s
indisputable evidence of the weakening of the network of
collaboration on which the British had relied for imperial
stability and the routine functioning of their [Indian]
administration' (Brown, 1985: 314). Dutch recovery of the
East Indies after Japanese surrender in 1945 was considerably hampered by the erosion of traditional collaborative
elites. Many *rajas* of the outer islands, village headmen and
leading families, on whom the colonial system had hinged

prior to 1942, were eliminated by nationalist revenge or communal violence (Ricklefs, 1993).

The allegiance of collaborative groups to the colonial power was often unpredictable as decolonization became more widespread. Black politicians drawn from the assimilated Francophile elite of the French possessions in West Africa were prepared in 1958 to accept continued territorial status within a new (French) Community in exchange for special privileges, development funds and access to cultured Paris society. Only a year later, in September 1959, these same *évolué* black rulers withdrew their collaboration and asked President de Gaulle to transfer complete authority to them, as permitted under the new constitution, followed in mid-1960 by total independence for the former colonies of French West and Equatorial Africa (see Chapter 5). In Malaya during the early 1950s, on the other hand, the educated professional and business elite – Chinese, Malayan, and Indian, came out in support of Britain's promise of future independence bestowed from above and against the largely Chinese-communist anti-colonial struggle, as demonstrated in the cross-party alliance led by sultan Tunku Abdul Rahman, the future Malayan prime minister (see Chapter 3).

African collaboration with white rulers became more difficult because colonial governments, in their postwar anxiety to develop colonial economies as rapidly as possible, started to interfere in areas of social and economic life previously left untouched. French West Africa saw unsuccessful and grandiose state development projects to increase the supply of raw materials otherwise needing dollars, notably the notorious *Office du Niger* which by 1961 was costing about a million francs a hectare under cultivation and had produced only 1000 of the projected 300,000 tons of raw cotton (Aldrich, 1996). The aftermath of the Second World War added new grievances to be exploited in British East Africa because of ambitious plans to provide austerity Britain with urgently needed foodstuffs and raw materials. When margarine ran short, for example, the infamous Tanganyika groundnut scheme (1946–51) demonstrated both the depths of greedy exploitation and failure to promote sustainable African 'development'. In those years Britain extracted some £140m from its colonies, putting in only about £40m for colonial development. Local vested interests or chieftains on whose support the British had once relied were challenged and, in some places, colonial rule now appeared much more favourable than before to white settlers, especially in east and central Africa (see Chapter 6).

Preoccupation with agricultural productivity during the so-called 'second colonial occupation' drove colonial governments into policies like terracing against soil erosion using conscripted black labour, or the destruction of diseased cocoa trees, which were easily misinterpreted as an attack on the property and rights of their African subjects. In the post-1945 colonial state, the reluctance of the colonized to cooperate with white rulers whose presence was once taken for granted could also be explained by the atypical involvement of their European rulers in conflicts caused by land hunger, inflation, ethnic antagonisms and religious disputes. Hence the 'nationalisms' which mobilized support in many colonies in the last phases of colonial rule were symptomatic of a much more extensive withdrawal of cooperation, 'the visible part of a great iceberg of resentment and resistance which steadily but inexorably blunted the effectiveness of colonial rule and narrowed its choice of collaborators, eventually to nothing' (Darwin, 1991: 96).

Closing Remarks

Empires are now topics largely of interest to the historian, for they do not exist in the present. The collapse and disappearance of European empires from 1945 onwards changed the nature of the world we live in – no longer was mere possession of a white skin, and the scientific, military and technical knowledge it signified, sufficient to authorize command over others. The legacy of colonial rule has cast a long shadow, however: independence often meant multi-ethnic, fragmented states that were too small to be economically viable, and cut off from the rest of the world. While many former European colonies embarked on self-government with high expectations and a relatively healthy bank balance, not many of these hopes were fulfilled. The record of post-colonial Africa, for example, suggests that, judged by Western standards, the commitment of many new states to democratic values and human rights was precarious and soon nearly all were heavily in debt (Mayall and Payne, 1991).

In East Africa, Kenya under the autocratic Daniel arap Moi, president since 1978, resembles a going concern in the late 1990s but only because many of her neighbours, such as Somalia and the Sudan, are in far worse shape. In former British West Africa, the mechanisms of parliamentary democracy largely failed to take root in Nigeria, Sierra Leone and Ghana, so that, following the military coups of 1966, independence alternated until recently between military government and short-lived attempts to restore civilian rule – setting a pattern for many other ex-colonies (First, 1972). The worst excesses of single-party rule, corruption, civil war and decay have been evident in much of sub-Saharan Africa, where the proxy Cold War struggles of the 1970s coincided with hugely expensive investment projects, collapsing commodity prices and the piling up of unpayable foreign debts. The former Belgian Congo, hastily decolonized in 1960, was ruled by tyrannical but pro-Western General Joseph Mobutu from 1965 until he was overthrown in 1997 by Laurent Kabila, who proved little better than the man he replaced. The Congo's recent civil war has now escalated into a regional conflict. History has few happy endings. Ever since Angola's independence from Portugal in 1975, MPLA government forces have remained locked in a struggle for supremacy with UNITA, hundreds of thousands have died in one of the longest-running civil wars in the post-colonial world.

Yet there are now grounds for optimism in West Africa, despite bloody civil war in Sierra Leone, with the restoration in February 1999 of presidential elections in Nigeria and with Ghana becoming the 'flagship' country in the International Monetary Fund (IMF) and World Bank campaign for African recovery. Furthermore Mozambique, one of the world's poorest countries, is now considered a role model for other African nations stumbling towards democracy and was admitted to the Commonwealth in 1995, even though it was colonized by Portugal. Whether the campaign for African debt relief will improve conditions for the large majority, if not made conditional on responsible use of the funds freed up, remains to be seen. Decolonization may have released millions from the undignified servitude of European colonialism but freedom and independence often brought undemocratic political outcomes and neocolonial economic penalties.

BIBLIOGRAPHY

Titles below are mostly in English for ease of student reference. PRO in the text refers to quotations from Colonial Office or Foreign Office documents consulted in the Public Record Office in London. The invaluable HMSO 'End of Empire' series has so far published printed volumes of documents on the decolonization of British India, Burma, Ceylon, the Gold Coast and Malaya.

Ageron, Charles-Robert, *La Décolonisation Française* (Paris, 1991).
Albertini, Rudolph von, *Decolonization: the Administration and Future of the Colonies, 1919–60* (New York, 1971).
Aldrich, Robert, *Greater France: a History of French Overseas Expansion* (London, 1996).
Aldrich, Robert, and Connell, John, *France's Overseas Frontier: Départements et Territoires D'Outre Mer* (Cambridge, 1992).
Aldrich, Robert, and Connell, John, *The Last Colonies* (Cambridge, 1998).
Allen, Louis, 'Transfer of Power in Burma', *The Journal of Imperial and Commonwealth History*, 13 (1984), pp. 185–94.
Allen, Louis, '"The Escape of Captain Vivian": a Footnote to Burmese Independence', *The Journal of Imperial and Commonwealth History*, 19 (Jan. 1991), pp. 65–9.
Amin, Samir, *Neo-Colonialism in West Africa* (Harmondsworth, 1973).
Anderson, David, 'Policing and Communal Conflict: the Cyprus Emergency, 1954–60', *The Journal of Imperial and Commonwealth History*, 21 (Sept. 1993), pp. 177–207.
Anderson, David M., and Killingray, David (eds), *Policing and Decolonization, 1917–1965* (Manchester, 1992).
Ansprenger, Franz, *The Dissolution of the Colonial Empires* (London, 1989).

220

Bibliography

Balfour-Paul, Glen, *The End of Empire in the Middle East: Britain's Relinquishment of Power in her Last Three Arab Dependencies* (Cambridge, 1991).

Beinart, William, *Twentieth-Century South Africa* (Oxford, 1994).

Bennett, George, and Smith, Alison, 'Kenya: From "White Man's Country" to Kenyatta's State, 1945–1963', David Low and Alison Smith (eds), *History of East Africa*, vol. 3 (Oxford, 1976), pp. 108–55.

Betts, Raymond, *France and Decolonisation, 1900–1960* (London, 1991).

Birmingham, David, *The Decolonization of Africa* (London, 1995).

Boyce, D. George, *Decolonisation and the British Empire, 1775–1997* (Basingstoke, 1999).

Brown, Judith, *Modern India: the Origins of an Asian Democracy* (Oxford, 1985).

Cain, P.J., and Hopkins, A.G., *British Imperialism: Crisis and Deconstruction, 1914–1990* (Harlow, 1993).

Campbell-Johnson, Alan, 'Mountbatten and the Transfer of Power', *History Today*, 47 (Sept. 1997), pp. 34–40.

Carruthers, Susan L., *Winning Hearts and Minds: British Governments, the Media and Colonial Counter-Insurgency, 1944–1960* (Leicester, 1995).

Caute, David, *Under the Skin: the Death of White Rhodesia* (Harmondsworth, 1983).

Chamberlain, Muriel E., *Decolonization: the Fall of the European Empires* (Oxford, 1985, new edn 1999).

Chamberlain, Muriel E., *The Longman Companion to European Decolonisation in the Twentieth Century* (London, 1998).

Charters, David A., *The British Army and Jewish Insurgency in Palestine, 1945–47*, (London, 1989).

Chew, Ernest C.T., and Lee, Edwin (eds), *A History of Singapore* (Oxford, 1996).

Chipman, John, *French Power in Africa* (Oxford, 1989).

Clayton, Anthony, *Counter-Insurgency in Kenya: a Study of Military Operations Against Mau Mau* (Nairobi, 1976).

Clayton, Anthony, *The Wars of French Decolonization* (Harlow, 1994).

Cloake, John, *Templer, Tiger of Malaya: the Life of Field Marshal Sir Gerald Templer* (London, 1985).

Bibliography

Coates, John, *Suppressing Insurgency: an Analysis of the Malayan Emergency, 1948–1954* (Boulder, Col., 1992).

Cohen, Michael J., *Palestine and the Great Powers, 1945–1948* (Princeton, N.J., 1982).

Cohen, Michael J., *Palestine to Israel: From Mandate to Independence* (London, 1988).

Cooper, Frederick, *Decolonization and African Society: the Labour Question in French and British Africa* (Cambridge, 1996).

Cribb, Robert, and Brown, Colin, *Modern Indonesia: a History since 1945* (London, 1995).

Darwin, John, 'British Decolonization since 1945: a Pattern or a Puzzle?', in R.F. Holland and G. Rizvi (eds), *Perspectives on Imperialism and Decolonisation* (London, 1984), pp. 187–209.

Darwin, John, *Britain and Decolonisation: the Retreat from Empire in the Post-War World* (London, 1988).

Darwin, John, *The End of the British Empire* (Oxford, 1991).

Davidson, Basil, *In the Eye of the Storm: Angola's People* (Harmondsworth, 1975, edn).

Diamond, Jared, *Guns, Germs and Steel: a Short History of Everybody for the Last 13,000 Years* (London, 1996).

Duncanson, Dennis J., 'General Gracey and the Viet Minh', *Royal Central Asian [Society] Journal*, 55 (Oct. 1968), pp. 288–97.

Dunn, Peter M., *The First Vietnam War* (London, 1985).

Easton, Stewart C., *The Rise and Fall of Western Colonialism* (New York, 1964).

Edgerton, Robert B., *Mau Mau: an African Crucible* (New York, 1989).

Eliot, T.S., *A Choice of Kipling's Verse* (London, 1963 edn).

Fieldhouse, D.K., *Black Africa, 1945–80: Economic Decolonization and Arrested Development* (London, 1986).

First, Ruth, *The Barrel of a Gun: Political Power in Africa and the Coup d'État* (Harmondsworth, 1972).

Fraser, T.G., *The Middle East, 1914–1979* (London, 1980).

French, Patrick, *Liberty or Death: India's Journey to Independence and Division* (London, 1998 edn).

Furedi, Frank, *The Mau Mau War in Perspective* (London, 1989).

Gardiner, Nile, 'The Colonial Service', in Lawrence James (ed.), *The Daily Telegraph: The British Empire, 1497–1997: 500 Years that Shaped the World* (London, 1997), p. 167.

Bibliography

Gifford, Prosser, and Louis, W.R. (eds), *The Transfer of Power in Africa: Decolonisation, 1940–1960* (Cambridge, Mass., 1982).

Gifford, Prosser, and Louis, W.R. (eds), *Decolonisation and African Independence: the Transfer of Power, 1960–1980* (Cambridge, Mass., 1988).

Girardet, Raoul, *L'Idée coloniale en France* (Paris, 1972).

Gough, B., *The Falkland Islands/Malvinas: the Contest for Empire in the South Atlantic* (London, 1992).

Grimal, Henri, *Decolonization: the British, French, Dutch and Belgian Empires* (London, 1978).

Hargreaves, J.D., *The End of Colonial Rule in West Africa* (London, 1976).

Hargreaves, J.D., *Decolonization in Africa* (London, 1988).

Harper, T.N., *The End of Empire and the Making of Malaya* (Cambridge, 1999).

Henissart, Paul, *Wolves in the City: the Death of French Algeria* (St Albans, 1973, edn).

Hewitt, Vernon, 'Kashmir: the Unanswered Question', *History Today*, 47 (Sept. 1997), pp. 60–4.

Hitchens, Christopher, *Cyprus: Hostage to History* (London, 1984).

Holland, R.F., *European Decolonization, 1918–1981: an Introductory Survey* (London, 1985).

Holland, Robert, *Britain and the Revolt in Cyprus, 1954–1959* (Oxford, 1998).

Hopkins, A.G., 'Back to the Future: From National History to Imperial History', *Past and Present*, 164 (1999), pp. 198–243.

Horne, Alistair, *A Savage War of Peace: Algeria, 1954–62* (London, 1972 ed).

Hutchinson, Martha Crenshaw, *Revolutionary Terrorism: the FLN in Algeria, 1954–1962* (Stanford, Calif., 1978).

Hyam, Ronald, 'The Geopolitical Origins of the Central African Federation: Britain, Rhodesia and South Africa, 1948–1953'. *The Historical Journal*, 30, 1 (1987), pp. 145–72.

Jackson, Robert, *The Malayan Emergency: the Commonwealth's Wars, 1948–1966,* (London, 1991).

James, Lawrence, *The Rise and Fall of the British Empire* (London, 1995 edn).

Jeffrey, Robin (ed.), *Asia: the Winning of Independence* (London, 1981).

Bibliography

Judd, Denis, *Empire: the British Imperial Experience from 1765 to the Present* (London, 1997 edn).

Kahler, Miles, *Decolonization in Britain and France: the Domestic Consequences of International Relations* (Princeton, N.J., 1984).

Kanza, Thomas, *Conflict in the Congo: the Rise and Fall of Lumumba* (Harmondsworth, 1972).

Karnow, Stanley, *Vietnam: a History* (New York, 1991 edn).

Keay, John, *The Last Post: the End of Empire in the Far East* (London, 1997).

Kelly, George M., *Lost Soldiers: the French Army and Empire in Crisis* (Cambridge, Mass., 1963).

Kent, John, *British Imperial Strategy and the Origins of the Cold War, 1944–49* (Leicester, 1993).

Kettle, Michael, *De Gaulle and Algeria, 1940–1960: From Mers-el-Kebir to the Algiers Barracades* (London, 1993).

Kyle, Keith, *Suez* (London, 1991).

Kyle, Keith, *The UN in the Congo* (Coleraine, 1995).

Kyle, Keith, *The Politics of the Independence of Kenya* (Basingstoke, 1999).

Lapping Brian, *End of Empire* (London, 1985).

Louis, William Roger, and Robinson, Ronald, 'The Imperialism of Decolonization', *The Journal of Imperial and Commonwealth History*, 22, 3 (1994), pp. 462–512.

Louis, William Roger, and Stookey, Robert W., *The End of the Palestine Mandate* (Dallas, 1986).

Low, D.A., *Eclipse of Empire* (Cambridge, 1993 edn).

Macdonald, Peter, *Giap: the Victor in Vietnam* (London, 1994 edn).

McIntyre, W. David, *Commonwealth of Nations: Origins and Impact* (London, 1977).

McIntyre, W. David, *British Decolonization, 1946–1997* (London, 1998).

Mackenzie, John M., *Propaganda and Empire: The Manipulation of British Public Opinion, 1880–1960* (Manchester, 1984).

McMahon, Robert J., *Colonialism and Cold War: the United States and the Struggle for Indonesian Independence, 1945–49* (Ithaca, 1981).

MacQueen, Norrie, *The Decolonization of Portuguese Africa: Metropolitan Revolution and the Dissolution of Empire* (London, 1997).

Mamdani, Mahmood, *Citizen and Subject: Contemporary Africa and the Legacy of Late Colonialism* (Kampala, 1996).

Bibliography

Marr, David G., *Vietnam 1945: the Quest for Power* (Berkeley, Calif., 1995).

Martin, Ged, 'The Irish Free State and the Evolution of the Commonwealth, 1921–49', in Ronald Hyam and Ged Martin (eds), *Reappraisals in British Imperial History* (London, 1975), pp. 201–23.

Maxwell, Kenneth, 'Portugal and Africa: the Last Empire', in Prosser Gifford and William Roger Louis (eds), *The Transfer of Power in Africa: Decolonization, 1940–1960* (New Haven, Conn., 1982), pp. 337–85.

Mayall, James, and Payne, Anthony (eds), *The Fallacies of Hope: the Post-Colonial Record of the Commonwealth Third World* (Manchester, 1991).

Mommsen, Wolfgang, and Osterhammel, Jürgen (eds), *Imperialism and After: Continuities and Discontinuities* (London, 1986).

Murray, Donette, *Kennedy, Macmillan and Nuclear Weapons* (London, 2000).

Neillands, Robin, *A Fighting Retreat: the British Empire, 1947–1997* (London, 1996).

Oliver, Roland, and Atmore, Anthony, *Africa since 1800* (Cambridge, 1977 edn).

Ovendale, Ritchie, 'Macmillan and the Wind of Change in Africa, 1957–1960', *The Historical Journal*, 38, 2 (1995), pp. 455–77.

Pandey, B.N., *The Break-up of British India* (London, 1969).

Pearson, Raymond, *The Rise and Fall of the Soviet Empire* (London, 1998).

Porter, A.N., and Stockwell, A.J. (eds), *British Imperial Policy and Decolonization, 1938–1964*, vol. 2 (London, 1987).

Preston, Paul, *Franco: a Biography* (London, 1995 edn).

Ricklefs, M.C., *A History of Modern Indonesia since c.1300* (London, 1993 edn).

Roberts, Andrew, *Eminent Churchillians* (London, 1995 edn).

Rosie, George, *The British in Vietnam* (London, 1970).

Sanders, David, *Losing an Empire, Finding a Role: British Foreign Policy since 1945* (London, 1990).

Sanger, Clyde, *Malcolm MacDonald: Bringing an End to Empire* (Liverpool, 1995).

SarDesai, D.R., *Southeast Asia: Past & Present* (Boulder, Col., 1994 edn).

Short, Anthony, *The Communist Insurrection in Malaya, 1948–1960* (London, 1975).

Smith, R.B., 'Some Contrasts between Burma and Malaya in British Policy towards South-East Asia, 1942–1946', in R.B. Smith and A.J. Stockwell (eds), *British Policy and the Transfer of Power in Asia: Documentary Perspectives* (London, 1988), pp. 30–76.

Springhall, John, '"Disaster in Surabaya": the Death of Brigadier Mallaby during the British Occupation of Java, 1945–46', *The Journal of Imperial and Commonwealth History*, 24 (Sept. 1996), pp. 422–43.

Stockwell, A.J., *British Policy and Malay Politics during the Malayan Union Experiment, 1942–1948* (Kuala Lumpur, 1979).

Stockwell, A.J., 'British Imperial Policy and Decolonization in Malaya, 1942–52', *The Journal of Imperial and Commonwealth History*, 13 (1984), pp. 68–87.

Stockwell, A.J., 'Southeast Asia in War and Peace: the End of European Colonial Empires', in Nicholas Tarling (ed.), *The Cambridge History of South East Asia*, vol. 2 (Cambridge, 1992), pp. 329–85.

Stubbs, Richard, *Counter-Insurgency and the Economic Factor: the Impact of the Korean War Prices Boom on the Malayan Emergency* (Singapore, 1974).

Stubbs, Richard, *Hearts and Minds in Guerilla Warfare: the Malayan Emergency, 1948–1960* (Oxford, 1993 edn).

Tarling, Nicholas, 'Lord Mountbatten and the Return of Civil Government to Burma', *The Journal of Imperial and Commonwealth History*, 11, 2 (Jan. 1983), pp. 197–226.

Tarling, Nicholas, *Britain, Southeast Asia and the Onset of the Cold War, 1945–1950* (Cambridge, 1998).

Thompson, Roger C., *The Pacific Basin since 1945: a History of the Foreign Relations of the Asian, Australasian and American Rim States and the Pacific Islands* (London, 1994).

Throup, David W., 'The Origins of Mau Mau', *African Affairs*, 84, 336 (July 1985), pp. 399–433.

Throup, David W., *Economic and Social Origins of Mau Mau, 1945–1953* (London, 1987).

Throup, David, 'Crime, Politics and the Police in Colonial Kenya, 1939–63', in David M. Anderson and David Killingray (eds), *Policing and Decolonization, 1917–1965* (Manchester, 1992), pp. 127–57.

Bibliography

Turnbull, C. Mary, *A History of Malaysia, Singapore and Brunei* (Sydney, 1989).

Welensky, Sir Roy, *Welensky's 4000 Days: the Life and Death of the Federation of Rhodesia and Nyasaland* (London, 1964).

Welsh, Frank, *A History of Hong Kong* (London, 1997 edn).

Williams, Ann, *Britain and France in the Middle East and North Africa, 1914–1967* (London, 1968).

Williams, Charles, *The Last Great Frenchman: a Life of General de Gaulle* (London, 1995 edn).

Wilson, H.S., *African Decolonization* (London, 1994).

INDEX

228

Index

Index

Index

Index

Index

Index

Index

Index

Index

Index

Index

Index